EARLY CHILDHOOD EDUCATION SERIES

NANCY K. FILE & CHRISTOPHER P. BROWN, EDITORS

ADVISORY BOARD: Jie-Qi Chen, Cristina Gillanders, Jacqueline Jones,
Kristen M. Kemple, Candace R. Kuby, John Nimmo,
Amy Noelle Parks, Michelle Salazar Pérez, Andrew J. Stremmel, Valora Washington

To look for other titles in this series, visit www.tcpress.com

continued

D1452896

Early Childhood Education Series, *continued*

Principals as Early Learning Leaders

Effectively Supporting Our Youngest Learners

Julie Nicholson, Helen Maniates, Serene Yee,
Thomas Williams Jr., Veronica Ufoegbune,
and Raul Erazo-Chavez

TEACHERS COLLEGE PRESS

TEACHERS COLLEGE | COLUMBIA UNIVERSITY

NEW YORK AND LONDON

Published by Teachers College Press,® 1234 Amsterdam Avenue, New York, NY 10027

Copyright © 2022 by Teachers College, Columbia University

Front cover design by Rebecca Lown Design. Front cover images by (clockwise from top left): Jacob Lund / Shutterstock; FatCamera / iStock by Getty Images; skynesher / iStock by Getty Images; Ridofranz / iStock by Getty Images.

Chapter 8 photographs by Maria Allis
Chapter 11 photographs by Heather Richardson

Library of Congress Cataloging-in-Publication Data is available at loc.gov

ISBN 978-0-8077-6617-0 (paper)
ISBN 978-0-8077-6618-7 (hardcover)
ISBN 978-0-8077-7998-9 (ebook)

Printed on acid-free paper
Manufactured in the United States of America

Contents

Introduction

As a direct result of the expansion of preschool programs in public school districts, the majority of public school principals now have responsibility for supervising and evaluating early childhood teachers and classrooms (National Association of Elementary School Principals, 2014). In 2016, the National Association of Elementary School Principals (NAESP), the leading organization for elementary and middle school principals in the United States, conducted a survey of their members and found that among the 550 principals who responded (representing schools located in 49 states or territories and the District of Columbia), 70% reported that they had an early learning program located at their school sites or had responsibility for leading early childhood programs in their communities (Abel et al., 2016). Among the respondents who did not have a preschool program, 78% reported being interested in establishing an early learning program. Only 12% stated that they did not consider early childhood a priority for their school. These trends are creating a sense of urgency across the nation to prepare principals to be effective instructional leaders and supervisors of early childhood teachers (Brown et al., 2014).

Unfortunately, information on child development and early childhood education is not a mandatory component of administrative training programs for principals in most states, nor is it a top priority for professional development for administrators working in public school districts (NAESP, 2014). Nationwide, principals are expressing their interest in learning more about early childhood education so that they can become effective early learning leaders.

> When principals understand what teaching and learning look like in a preschool classroom and the complex role of preschool teachers to continuously guide, scaffold, and direct children's learning through play, they are able to provide ongoing support and constructive feedback and to be effective leaders for their early childhood staff.

This book is written to support principals and others responsible for leading preschool/pre-K programs in learning about the foundations of high-quality early childhood classrooms and programs. The approaches discussed throughout this text are based on neuroscience and developmental science; culturally, linguistically, and trauma-responsive practices; and antiracist/antibias approaches to early education. In reading this book, principals will learn about the pivotal role they can play in improving equity for young children, their families, and the early childhood workforce. They will also discover how they are uniquely positioned to be bridge builders who can support the foundations for high quality to be integrated across ages and grades in early childhood classrooms.

The audience for this book includes anyone responsible for the supervision of early childhood teachers and/or providing instructional leadership for early childhood programs, including the following:

- New and experienced elementary school principals and vice principals
- Educators enrolled in administrative credential programs preparing to be future principals
- District administrators and staff in leadership positions (superintendents, chief academic officers, teacher leaders, etc.)
- Instructional coaches supporting early childhood program staff
- Other district administrators and support personnel with backgrounds outside of early childhood who will increasingly be asked to support and work with early childhood educators
- Multisession inservice and professional development audiences
- University faculty teaching administrative credential courses
- Leaders working in educational nonprofits
- Site supervisors and directors leading early childhood agencies and programs

> To be effective instructional leaders who can help advance teacher practice, elementary school principals, who are increasingly responsible for overseeing pre-K classrooms, must understand how young children learn. (Lieberman, 2019, p. 2)

We include descriptions of contemporary theories, emerging issues, and the most current research and evidence-informed practices in the field of early childhood. Each chapter includes authentic examples and sample conversations that support readers to see the application of the ideas in an early learning context. Additionally, practical actionable strategies are introduced that provide principals with suggestions for immediate implementation at their schools. Reflection and discussion questions are woven throughout the book. These prompts can be used for individual reflection or to guide group discussions at staff meetings or in other professional learning contexts with principals and district administrators. Each chapter ends with key takeaways.

ORGANIZATION OF THE BOOK

Chapter 1, "The Urgent Need for Principals to Become Early Learning Leaders," opens with a rationale for the book. Next, the foundations of high-quality early childhood classrooms are introduced, including the field's increased focus on equity. The chapter ends with an overview of the demographics and unique aspects of the early childhood workforce.

Chapter 2, "What Principals Need to Know About How Young Children Develop and Learn," begins with an overview of brain development in early childhood. Next, we discuss principles of child development and learning, including the integrated nature of young children's learning process. Popular theories and approaches that inform early childhood pedagogy are introduced.

Chapter 3, "Understanding Identity and Inclusion in Early Childhood," opens by discussing the importance of supporting young children's healthy racial and gender identity development. This is followed by a section on bilingual and multilingual development in early childhood. The final section focuses on young children with disabilities and developmental delays and the importance of creating inclusive environments.

Chapter 4, "Understanding Toxic Stress and Trauma in Early Childhood," begins with an overview of healthy versus unhealthy stress, followed by a discussion of adverse childhood experiences and trauma in young children. Next, neuroplasticity is introduced, as well as the importance of creating trauma-responsive environments in preschool.

Chapter 5, "Understanding Curriculum in Early Childhood," begins by discussing the process of curriculum planning in early childhood education (ECE), and two example curriculum plans are provided. Several approaches to curriculum in early childhood are introduced. We end by discussing why standardized and scripted curriculum are not recommended for early childhood.

Chapter 6, "Instruction in the Early Childhood Classroom," describes the importance of individualizing instruction for young children and the range of learning formats early childhood teachers provide in preschool classrooms. We then discuss play as a primary context for teaching and learning with young children and the different types of play-based learning principals should see in early learning settings.

Chapter 7, "Creating a Caring Community of Learners," opens with an overview of the Social Emotional Foundations for Early Learning (SEFEL) Pyramid Model and the important emphasis on social–emotional learning in preschool classrooms. We introduce several strategies that are commonly used in early childhood classrooms to support children to develop social-emotional competence. The chapter closes by describing the urgent need to disrupt exclusionary discipline practices in preschool classrooms.

Chapter 8, "A Closer Look at Powerful Learning in Early Childhood Classrooms," invites principals into micromoments within an early childhood learning environment to see examples of developmentally responsive curriculum and instruction in action. Through brief vignettes and authentic photos, readers are guided to see what play-based learning and the integrated approach to learning with young children looks like in high-quality, play-based preschool programs.

Chapter 9, "Assessment in Early Childhood," describes characteristics of effective assessment environments and practices with young children. We define authentic curriculum-embedded assessment and direct decontextualized assessments and outline the benefits and drawbacks of each format. Concerns with one-time "snapshot" assessments and standardized testing in early childhood are addressed. This chapter ends by describing the role of parents and families in the assessment process with young children.

The book includes several resources (books, videos, websites) that principals will find helpful in learning more about early childhood. The appendices include a guide for conducting effective early learning walk-through observations and a district model for providing professional development for principals to learn about high-quality early childhood education.

CHAPTER 1

The Urgent Need for Principals to Become Early Learning Leaders

The first 8 years of life, starting in the prenatal period and extending through 3rd grade, are a critical period that can influence children's development, academic achievement, and well-being over the course of their lifetimes (Center on the Developing Child, n.d.; Institute of Medicine & National Research Council, 2015). It is now well recognized that 90% of children's brain development occurs by the age of 5 years (Casey et al., 2005; Halfon et al., 2001), and investments in high-quality early learning programs result in the most significant return, unparalleled by interventions at any other period in a child's educational trajectory (see Figure 1.1; Heckman & Masterov, 2007; Heckman, et al., 2010).

Dr. James Heckman is a Nobel Prize–winning economist who examines the relationship between children's participation in high-quality early childhood programs and later returns on investment to society or "lifecycle benefits." Dr. Heckman's research shows that children who participate in high-quality birth-to-5 programs have better outcomes in indicators of health, quality of life, participation in crime, labor, income, IQ, and school achievement. Further, mothers whose children are enrolled in high-quality early learning programs have increased labor income as a result of subsidized child care. The return on investment for 1 year of quality early childhood education is as much as 13%, more significant than investment at any other period across the life span, a finding represented in the Heckman curve shown in Figure 1.1 (Heckman & Masterov, 2007).

Increased understanding about the importance of the early childhood years has led to efforts across the nation to more formally link early childhood with primary school. System-reform advocates believe that creating "sturdy bridges" between early learning programs and elementary schools (Institute of Medicine & National Research Council, 2015; Riley-Ayers & Costanza, 2014) is a promising way to address our nation's persistent gaps in opportunity and achievement (Kauerz & Coffman, 2013; U.S. Department of Education, 2016). These efforts have increased interest in supporting the transition between preschool and kindergarten, expanding the presence of preschool within public school districts, and aligning and coordinating high-quality preschool with primary school education in what

Figure 1.1. Investing in the Early Years—The Heckman Curve

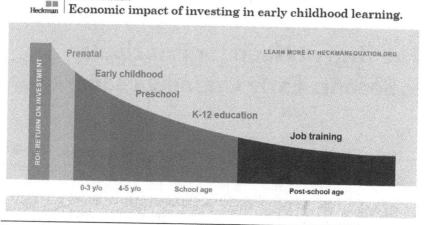

Source: https://heckmanequation.org/resource/the-heckman-curve/

is often described as P–3 or pre-K–3 initiatives (Institute of Medicine & National Research Council, 2015; Kauerz et al., 2021).

Linking preschool and elementary school is a complex and challenging endeavor. There are significant differences between the fields of early childhood education and public schooling; these include distinct histories and purposes, different funding streams, separate regulatory policies and governance structures, and significantly divergent workforce preparation requirements and workplace conditions (Kagan & Kauerz, 2012). Effectively joining preschool with elementary school requires that elementary principals and staff learn how to adapt public school practices to integrate principles of child development and early childhood pedagogy.

> Images of children; understandings about how children learn and construct knowledge; discussions of the role of teachers, families, and the environment in children's education; and beliefs about how to assess children's skills, knowledge, and capacities often differ between the fields of early childhood and public education (Halpern, 2013).

FOUNDATIONS OF HIGH-QUALITY EARLY CHILDHOOD CLASSROOMS

High-quality early childhood programs emphasize:

- The development of strong relationships with teachers and caregivers

- Curriculum and instruction that are informed by individual developmental variation among children and an understanding of each child's interests, strengths, vulnerabilities, and needs
- A focus on social and emotional health
- The integration of play as a foundational pedagogy
- The development of strong partnerships between teachers and families
- Assessment that involves the child's family and frequently a multidisciplinary team of professionals and relies on the use of observations and multiple forms of documentation on multiple occasions over time

To be effective, early learning leaders and principals need to learn about:

- What is unique in the process of supporting preschool-aged children's learning and development
- The theories, approaches, and evidence base that inform the field of early childhood
- The foundations of developmentally, linguistically, and culturally responsive curriculum, instruction, and assessment practices with preschool children
- The distinct role of families in early learning programs
- Issues of equity/inequity that emerge in preschool and teaching practices used to disrupt bias and cycles of oppression with young children

Despite the reality that a growing number of principals currently have responsibility for leading early childhood classrooms and supervising early childhood teachers, there is significant concern that they are not being prepared adequately to effectively execute these new responsibilities (Brown et al., 2014; Loewenberg, 2015; National Association of Elementary School Principals [NAESP], 2014). Unfortunately, information on child development and early childhood education is not a mandatory component of administrative training programs for principals in most states nor is it a top priority for professional development for administrators working in public school districts (NAESP, 2014). A 50-state review revealed that only nine states explicitly require principal preparation programs to offer coursework in early learning and/or child development, and state principal preparation policies do not adequately address the role of principals as early learning leaders (Lieberman, 2017).

> A review of principal licensure standards across 50 states found that only nine states explicitly require principals to have coursework in early learning and/or child development (Lieberman, 2017).

THE NEED FOR PRINCIPALS TO BE EFFECTIVE
EARLY LEARNING LEADERS

Given the increasing number of principals who are responsible for overseeing early childhood programs and classrooms—and the significant impact principals have on children's learning and achievement in school—it is essential that they gain the skills and knowledge needed to become effective and equitable early learning leaders. Research underscores that principals have a significant impact on the quality of teachers' instruction, the overall quality of the learning environment, and student outcomes at their school sites (Lieberman, 2017; Liebowitz & Porter, 2019). After teachers, principals and school leaders are "the most significant in-school factor impacting student achievement" (Lieberman, 2017, p. 5).

Principals responsible for leading preschool programs, in addition to elementary grades, at their sites often find themselves navigating the tension between very different philosophies about how to support students' learning. On the one hand, preschool programs generally follow a developmental approach, where adults support children's emerging abilities by providing opportunities for active exploration across cognitive, social, physical, and emotional domains. When students begin kindergarten, however, educators are faced with meeting academic standards in the subject areas that are outcome-oriented and may not reflect either normative child development or the needs of individual students. There is pressure to get an early start on academics so that students don't come up short later. And there are legitimate concerns that the youngest and/or most underserved children may not be prepared for the demands of an increasingly academic kindergarten curriculum. However, there are opportunity costs in using precious preschool years to prepare for later academics rather than optimize the possibilities of a more experiential and child-centered environment.

Early childhood educators most likely would bristle at the notion that they are "preparing" rather than nurturing children. This is a perennial tension described by educator Lillian Katz in 1973 as "education for the afterlife" (p. 396). But high-quality preschool environments do create the conditions for later academic success. The twist is that they do not do this by mimicking elementary teaching practices but by play-based, relational practices that foster healthy human development. Principals are well positioned to push back against the unhealthy pressure for preschool to implement developmentally inappropriate curricula.

SIX COMPETENCIES FOR EFFECTIVE INSTRUCTIONAL
LEADERSHIP IN EARLY CHILDHOOD

The National Association of Elementary School Principals (NAESP; 2014), the leading organization for elementary and middle school principals in the United States, has outlined six competencies that define "what principals should know and be able to do as effective leaders of pre-K–3 learning communities" (p. 7). NAESP recommends that principals working as early learning leaders:

- Embrace the pre-K–3 early learning continuum.
- Ensure developmentally appropriate teaching.
- Provide personalized and blended learning environments.
- Use multiple measures to guide student learning and growth.
- Build professional capacity across the learning community (e.g., building knowledge about what is age and developmentally appropriate across the pre-K–3 continuum).
- Make their schools hubs for pre-K–3 learning for families and the community (Kauerz et al., 2021).

Despite emphasizing the urgency and importance of principals becoming effective early childhood leaders and creating these competencies and encouraging their widespread use, NAESP concedes that "little attention is being paid to leadership development in Pre-K–3" (NAESP, 2014, p. 4). These competencies represent important goals. However, knowledge of these competencies and investment in training and professional learning opportunities for principals and other school administrators and leaders focused on instructional leadership in early childhood is not widespread. Work needs to be done at a preservice level in principal licensure programs as well as with in-service principals leading schools to raise awareness about the critical role they have as instructional leaders for education in the early childhood years.

INCREASED FOCUS ON EQUITY IN EARLY CHILDHOOD

All children have the right to equitable learning opportunities that help them achieve their full potential as engaged learners and valued members of society. Thus, all early childhood educators have a professional obligation to advance equity. (National Association for the Education of Young Children, 2019, p. 1)

Attention to issues of equity is becoming more urgent across the field of early childhood. There is wide disparity in childhood outcomes, leading to calls for:

- Required training on the history of race, racism, oppression, privilege, and White supremacy and the neurobiology of stress and trauma
- Training, ongoing coaching, and professional development on antiracism pedagogy and antibias approaches

- Culturally and linguistically responsive and equity-centered curriculum and pedagogy
- Trauma-responsive, healing-centered practices for early childhood leaders and teachers

The National Association for the Education of Young Children's (NAEYC) (2011) Code of Ethical Conduct states:

> Above all, we shall not harm children. We shall not participate in practices that are emotionally damaging, physically harmful, disrespectful, degrading, dangerous, exploitative, or intimidating to children. This principle has precedence over all others in this Code. (p. 3)

Building on this Code of Ethical Conduct and Statement of Commitment, NAEYC (2019) recently published a position statement on equity created in collaboration with a wide range of early childhood educators across the nation. The statement includes specific recommendations for different stakeholder groups—educators, administrators, individuals who facilitate educator preparation and professional development and public policymakers. NAEYC outlines several recommendations for principals and other school leaders responsible for overseeing early childhood settings and improving equity outcomes for children, families, and the early learning staff they supervise.

The Children's Equity Project (CEP) is another important stakeholder group influencing the growing focus on equity in the field of early childhood. CEP is a collaborative comprised of researchers and advocates at several universities and organizations across the United States working through research, policy, and practice to close opportunity gaps and dismantle systemic racism in early learning settings. CEP's work addresses a range of equity issues in the early years and the early grades. The CEP publication *14 Priorities to Dismantle Systemic Racism in Early Care and Education* (Meek et al., 2020) is widely influencing early childhood reform initiatives across the country. Table 1.1 describes a sample of the CEP priorities for dismantling systemic racism in early childhood and their implications for principals.

REFLECTION AND DISCUSSION QUESTION

- Reviewing CEP's equity priorities, what can you identify as strengths of your program/school? Where are there gaps that need greater focus and attention?

Table 1.1. CEP Equity Priorities and Their Implications for Principals

Equity Priority for Early Care and Education (ECE)	Suggestions for Principals
Disseminate public funds equitably. "Realizing racial equity requires equitable funding that considers historical and current marginalization—including on the basis of race, resource gaps in communities, and disparities in outcomes" (Meek et al., 2020, p. 5).	Understand the history of chronically underfunding early childhood programs. Conduct an equity audit with this in mind to examine whether the budget at your school site is sufficient to resource a quality preschool program.
Address workforce equity. "White teachers are more likely to be hired in school-sponsored ECE programs, which provide higher pay and benefits. Teachers of color are overrepresented in aide/assistant teacher roles compared to white teachers, who are overrepresented in lead teacher roles" (Meek et al., 2020, p. 8).	Conduct an equity audit of preschool staff and compensation at your school site. Strive to hire and sustain Black, Indigenous, and People of Color (BIPOC) in lead teacher and supervisory roles in preschool and support parity in compensation with the elementary school teachers at your school.
Embed equity in workforce preparation and development. "Equity is missing or an inadequate component in early childhood educators' preparation and professional development opportunities. Anyone working in the ECE system should have comprehensive and sustained training on the history of race and racism, implicit bias and its manifestations in decision making, culturally responsive and sustaining practices and pedagogy, dual language learning, inclusive best practices, and building positive relationships with diverse families, among others" (Meek et al., 2020, p. 9).	Prioritize funding for all ECE staff to have professional development that includes a focus on equity and specifically structural racism and antiracist, antibias teaching practices. Ensure that preschool staff have access to the training during the school day or that they are compensated for participating after hours.
Explicitly include equity in the definition of quality. "Explicitly include equity in the definition of quality" (Meek et al., 2020, p. 10).	Understand that tools developed to rate quality in early childhood classrooms have often left out indicators that explicitly address equity. Ensure that observation and evaluations of teachers and their classroom practices include metrics of equity.

(Continued)

Table 1.1. (continued)

Equity Priority for Early Care and Education (ECE)	Suggestions for Principals
Ensure high-quality curriculum and pedagogy are accessible and culturally responsive. "The content of widely used pedagogies and curricula in early childhood rarely (if at all) addresses equity" (Meek et al., 2020, p. 11).	Know that all standardized or "off the shelf" curricula must be adapted so that teachers can bring in culturally and linguistically responsive materials and activities to ensure that content is meaningful to the children and families being served.
Eliminate harsh discipline. "Harsh discipline—including expulsion, suspension, corporal punishment, seclusion, and inappropriate restraint—reduces valuable learning time and has devastating effects on children's feelings of safety and belonging, social and emotional development, family relationships, and school engagement. It is essential that the ECE system prohibit these harmful practices, attend to and address racial disparities in these and other forms of harsh discipline, and prioritize workforce preparation and development that is trauma-informed, explicitly anti-racist, and developmentally appropriate" (Meek et al., 2020, p. 13).	Build awareness of the problem of harsh discipline in early childhood and how it looks different in preschools than in older grades. Analyze discipline data in preschool, disaggregating it by race, disability, gender, and language. Create explicit policies and procedures to eliminate suspension and expulsions in preschool. Provide teachers with support including professional development on this topic (see Chapter 7 for a discussion of this topic).
Address equity in early intervention and special education access, identification and inclusion. "Children of color are generally underrepresented in early intervention and preschool special education services which is concerning given the importance and effectiveness of early intervention services. Half of all preschoolers receiving special education services receive them in settings segregated from their peers without disabilities. Further, racial/ethnic disparities exist in the types of disabilities children are identified with, with Black children being more likely to be identified under categories that require a greater degree of subjectivity in the diagnostic process" (Meek et al., 2020, p. 14).	Have developmental screening available for all preschool children with the knowledge that children of color are often underrepresented in early intervention services. Strive to disrupt this pattern at your school site. Create inclusive early learning programs that include and support children with special needs and disabilities. Ensure that staff have sufficient professional development and supports/resources to create inclusive preschool environments that set a trajectory for children to transition to inclusive K–12 education.

Equity Priority for Early Care and Education (ECE)	Suggestions for Principals
Implement a data-driven continuous quality improvement (CQI) cycle. "All ECE programs should engage in a CQI process that centers equity by using disaggregated data to inform practice and policy change in order to reduce opportunity gaps and disparities in children's outcomes. Access to data is also key to improving opportunities for Tribal Nations where Tribal consultation must be honored in the process" (Meek et al., 2020, p. 15).	Create time and space for preschool teachers to participate in a CQI process. This includes having regular opportunities to reflect and talk with their colleagues about their practice and to have access to disaggregated data that will help them discover the strengths, gaps, biases, and areas in need of improvement in their curriculum and instruction. Preschool teachers should have a voice in selecting the data to be examined (as they will look different from data in older grades). CQI should not become a high-stakes and sanctioning process but, instead, it should incentivize teachers to continually learn and improve their practice.
Expand family leadership and engagement efforts. "ECE has a history of challenges meeting the needs of families, especially families of color, linguistically diverse families, immigrant families, and families with children with disabilities. A central focus of building more equitable ECE must be more meaningful family engagement and partnerships" (Meek et al., 2020, p. 16).	Work in partnership with preschool teachers to ensure that family engagement is an important element of the preschool program. Raise awareness in self and others about the shift in the field of early childhood away from parent involvement toward family engagement, where the goal is building genuine partnerships and acknowledging the wide range of different ways families support their young children's learning and development (see Nicholson et al., 2021, for an overview).
Equitably expand access to dual language immersion approaches for DLLs. "Dual language learners (DLLs) make up about one third of all young children under age 8, the most of whom speak Spanish at home. Research demonstrates that bilingualism/multilingualism is associated with cognitive advantages early in life and economic benefits later in life. Although bilingual learning models are expanding, there is more representation of affluent, white, native English speakers than children who bring the gift of bilingualism from the home; an inequity that must be addressed across the ECE system" (Meek et al., 2020, p. 18).	Work with preschool teachers and staff to ensure that your preschool program supports bilingual and multilingual children and that speaking more than one language is recognized as an asset (see discussion of this topic in Chapter 3). Ensure that young emergent bilingual/multilingual children and families have access to bilingual programs and that enrollment is not overrepresented by White native English speakers.

Adapted from Meek et al. (2020) with permission.

THE EARLY CHILDHOOD WORKFORCE

Despite the critical and profoundly important impact early childhood programs have on young children's positive life outcomes, working in early childhood is among the lowest paid professions in the country. In fact, joining the early childhood workforce has been described as a "pathway to poverty" that poses a risk to early educators' health and well-being with consequences that extend to the educators' families and the children they serve (McLean et al., 2021). Early childhood educators have not been recognized as belonging to a profession with a unique set of skills and expertise (Institute of Medicine & National Research Council, 2015).

Key Facts About the Early Childhood Workforce

- Early childhood educators are primarily women, almost 40% of whom are women of color (Whitebook et al., 2018; McLean et al., 2019).
- A high percentage of families of early childhood educators rely on public income support and health care programs (e.g., Federal Earned Income Tax Credit [EITC]; Medicaid and the Children's Health Insurance Program [CHIP]; Supplemental Nutrition Assistance Program [SNAP], and Temporary Assistance for Needy Families [TANF]). These programs target the lowest-earning households in the United States. Half (53%) of child-care worker families and 43% of preschool and kindergarten teacher families rely on these subsidies, percentages that are much higher than those among elementary and middle school teachers (21%) and/or the overall U.S. workforce (21%) (McLean et al., 2019; Whitebook et al., 2016, 2018).
- Compounding the absence of a living wage, it is common for early educators to lack access to health and dental insurance and retirement benefits. Many have little or no paid time off, including sick leave, vacation time, or family leave (McLean et al., 2019).
- Early childhood educators rarely have access to the types of supports that are routinely provided in most other occupations, including paid time during work hours to complete responsibilities associated with their job expectations (e.g., conducting observations, completing documentation and assessments, planning for curriculum and instruction, taking breaks, meeting and reflecting with supervisors and colleagues, completing paperwork). It is common for early educators to complete these responsibilities during their own unpaid time (evenings and weekends) or while simultaneously supervising children (McLean et al., 2019).
- Early educators have few if any opportunities to engage in professional learning opportunities and/or provide input and participate in decisionmaking regarding the policies and practices

that directly impact them at the workplace (Whitebook et al., 2016).

- In addition to lack of support, early childhood educators are offered inadequate incentives/rewards for increasing their education, professional learning, and experience (e.g., Whitebook et al., 2016).

The impact of low wages combined with the poor working conditions early childhood educators experience has an impact on their well-being. Research documents high levels of economic worry, including concerns about how to pay monthly bills, afford housing, pay for routine health care costs, and feed their families (McLean et al., 2019; Center for the Study of Child Care Employment, n.d.).

Early Educator Wages Are Not Livable Wages in Most States

The Center for the Study of Child Care Employment (CSCCE) at the University of California, Berkeley conducts research on the early childhood workforce that tracks compensation and workplace conditions for early educators across the United States. The 2020 Early Childhood Workforce Index (McLean et al., 2021) compares median hourly wages for child-care workers, preschool teachers in school and community settings, and kindergarten/elementary school teachers. The Index has shown that preschool teachers working in school settings have higher hourly wages in comparison to early childhood staff working in other settings; however, in the majority of districts across the country their compensation is significantly less than kindergarten and elementary school teachers working in the same buildings.

> **EARLY EDUCATORS FACE A PAY PENALTY FOR WORKING WITH CHILDREN 0–5**
>
> Even when early educators hold a bachelor's degree, there is a pay penalty for working with children from birth to age five, compared to working with school-age children in the K–8 system, in all states. (McLean et al., 2021, p. 57)

Isolation and Inequitable Treatment

There is a long history of preschool/pre-K teachers feeling isolated and being treated inequitably in elementary schools. Here are some of the many examples:

- Staff meetings are often not accessible to them, as there is not funding available to hire substitutes so that these teachers can step out of the classroom without impacting adult-to-child ratios (required by licensing standards). Even when funding does exist, many districts struggle to keep a list of substitute teachers who are skilled and/or interested in working in preschool classrooms.

- The content discussed in staff meetings and professional development is most often not inclusive of preschool classrooms. Therefore, even when preschool teachers are able to participate in these meetings, their voices and contributions are rarely included in a meaningful way.

- Preschool teachers' work is often disparaged, and their professionalism (knowledge and skills) is not recognized. This is reflected in comments in which they are referred to as "babysitters," and their work is described in ways that obscure the complexity of early childhood pedagogy (e.g., colleagues who imply that teaching in preschool is easy, fun, or just play; "it must be so fun to play all day").

PRINCIPALS AS BRIDGE BUILDERS

Early childhood programs can be isolated from the elementary school program at their site for many understandable reasons. The location of these classrooms or differences in their daily schedule mean that preschool and elementary teachers may not routinely cross paths. Further, although they have earned certificates and/or degrees in the field, other school personnel may see preschool teachers and child-care providers as less educated or less prepared than credentialed teachers. Their expertise with young children may not be appreciated by those who discount the role of early childhood education in students' trajectories. Also, if the preschool children at a site are not slated to feed into the school's K–5 program, some staff may feel that they are not "their" students. Principals as bridge builders can break through these uninformed perspectives.

In their book *Transforming Sanchez School: Shared Leadership, Equity, and Evidence* (2019), Isola and Cummins describe a school environment of reciprocal relationships that "emphasize the notion of interdependence involving teamwork and learning from one another while respecting and understanding the distinct responsibilities . . . of staff, parents, and students (p. 111). They attribute much of the success of their model to the inclusion of the preschool teachers, teacher assistants, and parents of the preschool on their site. Every schoolwide activity and opportunity for collaboration was extended to include the early childhood program. Over time, this blurred the lines between pre-K and K–5, and inclusion became part of the school culture. Specific strategies drawn from their experience touch on integrating preschool students, teachers, and families into the life of the school, such as:

- Planning a seamless transition for students between preschool and kindergarten, including sharing child observation and assessments, parent visits and orientation, regular visits of preschool students to kindergarten, and co-teaching lessons

- Including preschool teachers in grade-level collaboration meetings to analyze schoolwide data and plan aligned curriculum pre-K–5
- Providing preschool teachers with the same preparation periods as elementary counterparts by scheduling "specials" during the school day (art, music, dance, technology, gardening)
- Involving preschool families in the school's parent–teacher organization, including in leadership roles
- Organizing schoolwide projects that involve all ages and grades, such as renovating the playground, planting a garden, creating murals and sculpture gardens, and workshops by artists, musicians, and educators

At Sanchez Elementary School, these strategies had widespread and lasting impact. Preschool parents continued to offer leadership in the parent–teacher organization throughout their child's time at the school. The perspective of preschool teachers in analyzing achievement data added depth and richness of a developmental perspective and helped K–5 teachers wind back to foundational skills that students needed. Being acknowledged by having a voice and having preparation periods professionalized teacher assistants, who went on to earn other certification and credentials. And the mural, gardens, playground, and sculpture garden continue to beautify the whole community.

REFLECTION AND DISCUSSION QUESTIONS

Principals establish conditions for quality. . . . For leaders to know whether teachers are providing appropriate instruction to their students and to best support both teacher and child development, they must understand how young children learn. Principals need preparation and professional development to build the knowledge and competencies outlined in [the] Transforming the Workforce [report]. They also need sufficient time, resources and supports to effectively run their programs and provide high-quality learning environments for young children. (Lieberman, 2017, p. 5)

- After reading the quote, reflect on the knowledge and competencies you possess and your next steps for further development. What support do you need to effectively lead high-quality learning environments for young children?

KEY TAKEAWAYS FOR PRINCIPALS

- The first 8 years of life, starting in the prenatal period and extending through 3rd grade, are a critical period that can influence children's development, academic achievement, and well-being over the course of their lifetimes.
- The number of principals who have responsibility for leading early childhood classrooms and supervising early childhood teachers is increasing. Yet information on child development and early childhood education is not a mandatory component of administrative training programs for principals in most states, nor is it a top priority for professional development for administrators working in public school districts.
- Principals have a significant impact on the quality of teachers' instruction, the overall quality of the learning environment, and student outcomes at their school sites. To be effective, early learning leaders and principals need to learn about what is unique in the process of supporting preschool-aged children's learning and development.

CHAPTER 2

What Principals Need to Know About How Young Children Develop and Learn

There are many facets of early development and learning that are crucial for elementary principals to know and understand if they are to lead a school with classrooms of young children. In contrast to the discrete subject areas of formal schooling, teaching and learning in early childhood classrooms are integrated across domains and expressed through play. To guide their work, preschool teachers draw on traditional theories as well as reconceptualist scholarship that recognizes the range of individual, sociocultural, and political–historical factors that influence development and learning.

BRAIN DEVELOPMENT IN THE EARLY CHILDHOOD YEARS

The first 5 years of a child's life is a time of rapid brain development, reinforcing why the early childhood years are so critical. *One million new neural connections are being built every second.* The human brain exhibits dramatic development during the preschool years and roughly quadruples in weight before the age of 6 (Dobbing & Sands, 1973), at which time it has acquired approximately 90% of its adult volume (Courchesne et al., 2000; Iwasaki et al., 1997; Kennedy et al., 2002; Lenroot & Giedd, 2006; Paus et al., 2001). Synaptic growth—during which neurons are connected to other neurons—is influenced by the environments and experiences children have—both supportive and harmful.

Healthy brain development is the result of children's opportunities to experience consistent, caring, and responsive relationships and opportunities to play, explore, discover, and interact in an environment where they feel safe and experience a sense of belonging. Healthy brain development and synaptic growth can easily be derailed if children experience inconsistent or harsh caregiving or teaching, if they lack opportunities for engagement and stimulation, or if they experience toxic stress and trauma or live in environments that repeatedly leave them feeling unsafe and unsupported.

Early Childhood Teachers Have Important Influences on Children's Brain Development

Young children's brains develop in response to the relationships and experiences they have. The pruning process is one of the key reasons why early childhood environments are so essential to children's early brain development. Nicholson, Perez, and Kurtz (2019) explain:

> During the pruning process, synaptic connections that are used in a child's brain are strengthened and those that are not used are eliminated. As children develop relationships and have experiences, the neural connections that have the most 'usage'—the neurons that fire most often in the child's brain—will be strengthened and maintained and those that are used least often will be 'pruned away' making room for new neural growth to take place. This is often referred to as 'Use It or Lose It.' (Perry et al., 1995, p. 3)

This is why the quality of early interactions and experiences can have such significant and long-term effects for children. If, for example, a child does not have caring-attuned relationships (see Chapter 5 for information on attunement) with adults in their earliest years, the neural pathways that support emotional regulation can be significantly impaired. Additionally, if a child is not exposed to expanded vocabulary or provided with many opportunities to actively explore their environment, the healthy neural networks they need for future schooling may be lost, instead of developed and strengthened through the pruning process.

Early childhood educators are brain builders. They are in a position to create environments and learning opportunities for young children that support their healthy development including the neurobiological wiring of their brains (Wolfe, 2007). The necessary processes for healthy brain development, and for learning and development more generally, are dependent on children's experiences with the world around them. Early childhood education programs are foundations to ensure that these experiences are rich and responsive to their needs. See Figure 2.1 for a description of the different parts of children's brains that develop and their key functions.

Figure 2.1. Brain Development in Early Childhood

The Brain Stem and Midbrain—"Primitive, Survival Brain"

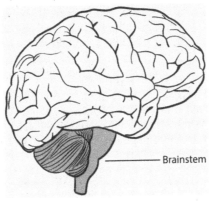

——— Brainstem

The brain stem and midbrain, described as our primitive brain, are the first parts of the brain to develop in utero and the first part of the brain to be fully developed in a young child. The brain stem and midbrain are responsible for regulating our autonomic functions (e.g., breathing, sleeping, and blood pressure).

Sometimes referred to as the brain's alarm center, our primitive brain is continually scanning our environment (e.g., inside our bodies and externally) for potential threats/dangers (Asking, am I safe?). If danger is detected, our primitive brain quickly mobilizes a survival fight, flight, or freeze response. With a trauma history, this part can be rewired to be on constant alert.

Suriya, sitting at the lunch table, sees another child take the last tortilla. She dives across the table and hits him and grabs his tortilla. Food insecurity is a trauma trigger for Suriya and activates her hindbrain into a "fight" response.

The Limbic Brain—"Emotional or Mammalian Brain"

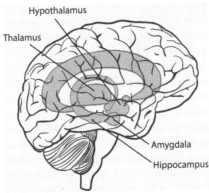

Hypothalamus

Thalamus

Amygdala

Hippocampus

The limbic brain generates our feelings and their emotional intensity and is responsible for our desire for attachment and connection and the human need to belong. Children are born with an experience-dependent limbic system and need

(Continued)

Figure 2.1. *(continued)*

many repeated positive relational interactions to support the development of a healthy limbic system (Conkbayir, 2017; Twardosz, 2012).

The *amygdala*, the alarm center of our brain, is located within the limbic brain and is responsible for the activation of fear. The amygdala is fully developed at birth, and this is why it has such a strong influence on young children's behavior. The amygdala triggers the brain's alarm system, sending stress chemicals through children's bodies to mobilize and to protect them from real or perceived danger (e.g., when a child's heart beats intensely during a thunderstorm). The amygdala is what leads children and adults to feel frightened when they perceive that they do not have agency or control in their environment, when a past trauma memory is triggered, when their emotions are intense, or when they experience too much uncertainty and stress.

> *Peter walks up to a group of children playing in the sandbox and tries to step in to add a block to the tower they are building. The children look at Peter and yell, "No, go away." Peter's emotional buttons are pushed (limbic brain) and he knocks over their tower and runs away (hindbrain "fight" reaction).*

The Cortex and Frontal Lobes—"Executive or Thinking Brain"

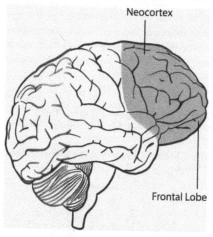

The cortex is the part of the brain responsible for higher-level functions, including abstract thinking, problem solving, logical thinking and rational thought, reflective capacities, and perspective taking. The frontal lobes (part of the prefrontal cortex) are the part of the brain responsible for people's ability to engage in complex cognitive processes and the executive function skills. The neocortex is not fully developed until young adulthood. *Executive function and self-regulation* skills support children to focus their attention, remember instructions, think through challenging problems, and regulate their behavior. Together they provide a foundation for children to develop emotional resiliency.

The Center on the Developing Child (n.d.) reinforces the critical role of early childhood experiences and environments in children's development of self-regulation and executive function capacities:

Figure 2.1. (continued)

Children aren't born with these skills—they are born with the potential to develop them.

Some children may need more support than others to develop these skills. In other situations, if children do not get what they need from their relationships with adults and the conditions in their environments—or (worse) if those influences are sources of toxic stress—their skill development can be seriously delayed or impaired. Adverse environments resulting from neglect, abuse, and/or violence may expose children to toxic stress, which can disrupt brain architecture and impair the development of executive function.

Leana was playing outside at recess when she heard a very loud sound from the engine of a car driving by. This sound triggered a traumatic reminder of a recent shooting in her neighborhood and activated her body's fight, flight, or freeze survival response. Leana covered her ears and started to scream loudly. Leana's teacher came running over and asked, "What's wrong, Leana?" but Leana could not speak, as the neural pathways to her frontal lobe/cortex were less accessible as her brain perceived that she was in danger. Recognizing her stress response behaviors, Leana's teacher stayed close to her and reinforced that she was safe—that the teacher would take care of her and she would stay near Leana until she felt better. She encouraged Leana to take deep breaths with her to calm her activated nervous system. Once Leana no longer sensed she was in danger, she was able to talk with her teacher about what happened and how she felt.

Children's Brains Develop in a Hierarchical Process

Children's brains develop sequentially from the "bottom up" (Perry et al., 1995) starting with the brain stem and midbrain. The limbic system and the cortex are the last parts of the brain to fully develop. Because children's brains grow in a sequential manner, if one "layer" of their brain does not grow properly or is impaired during development (e.g., lower brain stem), subsequent sections of the brain will also not develop properly. This is why early exposure to trauma can disrupt every aspect of a child's brain development. Preschool teachers see these impacts when children exposed to trauma enter preschool classrooms with developmental delays and disabilities, and difficulty paying attention, developing relationships, and regulating their bodies.

PRINCIPLES OF CHILD DEVELOPMENT AND LEARNING

High-quality early childhood classrooms are strongly influenced by the science and application of research in how young children learn and develop. Contemporary discussions of the application of developmental science in the field of early childhood discredit the idea of a universal developmental trajectory for healthy growth and development. Instead, as discussed throughout this chapter, it is now widely recognized that young children's development and learning are significantly influenced by a range of individual, sociocultural, and political–historical factors.

DEVELOPMENT AND LEARNING ARE TWO DISTINCT CONCEPTS

Development generally refers to physical, cognitive, or psychological changes from conception onward. These changes can be observed in different areas, or domains, of growth: physical and motor development, cognitive development, language development, and social–emotional development. *Learning* refers to the process of observing, having experiences, or being instructed in a process that results in new ideas and responses to the world. (California Department of Education [CDE], 2021a, p. 26)

Children's development and learning are dynamic processes that are influenced by multiple factors. Children's development and their learning trajectories and pathways vary significantly in response to:

- *Individual factors.* Temperament, interests, abilities, and individual experiences such as exposure to trauma and/or availability of support systems and social categories of identity
- *Sociocultural factors.* Family and societal cultural beliefs and practices, geographical location and community resources, philosophy of the early childhood program/school, and demographics and priorities of the community
- *Political–historical factors.* Access to resources and opportunities, systems of power, cultural and/or historical trauma, significant political events, including wars that cause migration, drought that leads to famine and malnutrition, community violence, and health-related epidemics

The position statement of the National Association for the Education of Young Children (NAEYC, 2019), titled *Advancing Equity in Early Childhood Education,* outlined the following principles of child development and young children's learning. These principles reflect decades of empirical research and the endorsement of hundreds of professional organizations across the United States serving young children and families:

- Early childhood (birth through age 8) is a uniquely valuable and vulnerable time in the human life cycle.
- Each individual—child, family member, and early educator—is unique.
- Each individual belongs to multiple social and cultural groups.

- Learning is a social process profoundly shaped by culture, social interactions, and language.
- Language and communication are essential to the learning process.
- Families are the primary context for children's development and learning.
- Learning, emotions, and memory are inextricably interconnected in brain processing networks.
- Toxic stress and anxiety can undermine development and learning.
- Children's learning is facilitated when teaching practices, curricula, and learning environments build on children's strengths and are developmentally, culturally, and linguistically appropriate for each child.
- Reflective practice is required to achieve equitable learning opportunities (NAEYC, 2019, p. 13).

These principles reflect the foundational knowledge in child development and early childhood education that are discussed throughout this book. Understanding the research and rationale informing each of these principles will support school leaders to better understand what high-quality teaching looks like in preschool classrooms so that they can provide effective support, coaching, and feedback to their early childhood staff.

YOUNG CHILDREN LEARN IN AN INTEGRATED MANNER

Teaching and learning with children in elementary, middle and high school are often organized by subject area. Domains such as mathematics, science, history/social studies, the arts, and language are taught as separate subjects. In contrast to this domain-specific approach, *teaching and learning in early childhood are integrated.* In early childhood classrooms, adults observe children building skills and constructing knowledge in a manner that integrates many developmental domains (cognitive, social, emotional, and physical), subject areas (i.e., mathematical and scientific thinking concepts, language and literacy, etc.), and dispositions for learning, including innovation, problem solving, persistence, risk taking, looking at things from multiple perspectives, and creativity (CDE, 2016).

The following vignette highlights an example of the integrated nature of learning for a 4-year-old girl playing outside in an outdoor classroom:

Maya is playing in a water table that contains a pitcher, a funnel, measuring cups, and small rocks in various sizes. She carefully arranges the rocks in order of size and says, "This is the baby, this is the sister, and this is the mommy. They're going swimming." Picking up the funnel, she positions it over the measuring cups and begins to fill the cups. When one overflows, she dumps it out and begins again. "That's too much," she says to herself.

After observing for a few minutes, the teacher asks Maya to tell him what she is working on. "I'm making soup for the baby," she explains. "He was sick but now he's swimming." The teacher asks what kind of soup she is making. "Vegetable soup, so he can get better," she replies." The teacher suggests they write down the recipe and pretends to hold a piece of paper and a pencil asking, "What should I write down?" "Carrots and beans and rice," Maya answers as the teacher pretends to write down the recipe. "Carrots, beans and rice, is that right?" "Yes!" Maya answers pointing to the imaginary recipe.

This vignette reflects the integrated nature of learning through play for preschool-aged children. We would not observe Maya's play and say that what she was learning was limited to mathematical thinking, oral language, literacy development, or strengthening her fine motor skills. Instead, early childhood teachers would see the integrated nature of Maya's learning that crosses several domains and developmental skills:

- Filling containers → fine motor skills
- Sequencing, volume → mathematical thinking
- Story narrative → oral language
- Understands that speech can be written down and read back → literacy and symbolic representation
- Deep engagement and high level of sustained attention as well as enjoyment of the activity → cognitive and social emotional skills

---

REFLECTION AND DISCUSSION QUESTIONS

- Think how your school is organized. In what ways does the curriculum in the preschool classroom reflect the concept of the integrated approach to learning in early childhood?
- Do you have a specific observation you have made of a preschool-aged child who had an integrated approach to learning? Can you describe the multiple pathways this child took to learn about their interest?

THEORIES AND PERSPECTIVES ON CHILDREN'S DEVELOPMENT AND LEARNING

There are many theoretical and philosophical perspectives that have influenced research and descriptions of child development and how children learn in the early years. Increasingly, scholars and practitioners are acknowledging that many traditional theories and theorists who are pillars in the field of early childhood have centered on White middle-class Eurocentric norms and perspectives that do not represent the diverse children in early learning programs.

The following theories and approaches we discuss here were selected based on two main criteria: (a) historically significant theories that continue to hold relevance in contemporary thinking and scholarship (constructivism, Vygotskian sociocultural theory) and (b) theories and perspectives that aim to address the limitations of traditional perspectives by acknowledging the growing diversity of young children and families and the inequitable contexts that influence children's learning, development, opportunities, and access to high-quality early childhood experiences (Reconceptualist).

Constructivism

Descriptions of high-quality early childhood education draw significantly from the theory and concepts associated with constructivism. Constructivist education is inspired by Jean Piaget's (1965) research on children's cognitive development. Piaget named his theory "constructivism," as he believed that children construct knowledge through active exploration with their environment, a process that leads to the development of more sophisticated mental structures (DeVries et al., 2002).

Key Concepts from Piaget's Theory of Constructivism

- As children actively engage and explore in their environment, they construct schemas (e.g., images, concepts, etc.) in their minds (Piaget, 1962).
- For Piaget, development and learning can't be rushed beyond what is age-appropriate. Constructivist approaches focus on providing children with opportunities to engage and explore with the environments in ways that are developmentally appropriate.
- The most important driver of learning for Piaget is the concept of *equilibrium* or "the mechanism at play in any transformational growth process" (Fosnot & Perry, 2005, p. 16). As children encounter new objects, new environments, and new experiences and engage with or act upon them, they experience disequilibrium. Disequilibrium represents a tension between what they know already (current schemas and mental structures) and new information, experiences, or concepts (that often challenge their current schemas and mental structures). The child can respond to this disequilibrium by: (a) incorporating new knowledge into their existing mental structures (*assimilation*) through repetition and experience, or (b) changing their existing mental structures to incorporate new knowledge (*accommodation*).
  It is the pressure in the mind to stay in equilibrium and resolve this tension or what he termed *cognitive dissonance* that drives children's learning (Piaget, 1962). Specifically, it is the child's

interactions in the environment and the constant pressure to remain in equilibrium that propels the child to develop more sophisticated mental structures (Waite-Stupiansky, 1997).

A young child with a schema for dog, encounters a horse for the first time. The horse has some characteristics that align with the child's concept for dog (tail, four legs) but others that do not match (height, the way it moves, sounds it makes). This creates disequilibrium for the child. Pressure to re-solve this tension and return to equilibrium is the driver that leads the child to accommodate to this new information in the environment and develop a new mental structure or schema for "horse."

Implications of Constructivism for Early Childhood Education

- Young children are active agents in their own learning, and learning is the result of children's active engagement with their environment.

Note: Active learning does not always require that children are physi-cally active, although this will be the case quite frequently in preschool. Active learning also involves mental activity, as the child is inspired to ask questions, experiment, postulate theories, try out new ideas, make discover-ies, and change existing ideas (Waite-Stupiansky, 1997).

- Learning is not understood to be a passive process and children are not expected to learn from rote memorization or by listening passively to adults sharing information with them.
- High-quality teaching in the early childhood classroom involves arranging the environment, designing a curriculum, and using pedagogical strategies to support children to be active constructors of skills, knowledge, and morality. Additionally, teachers are co-constructors who are learners along with the children.
- Teachers arrange the environment to allow children to have significant blocks of time for play and engagement with stimulating materials and activities that inspire active exploration, experimentation, and discovery. They ensure children have many opportunities to interact with peers and to have adults provoke and extend their mental schema through authentic questioning (questions that seek to learn about children's perspectives and mental schemas, not questions to which teachers know the answers).

Teachers in constructivist classrooms ask authentic questions that aim to understand a child's thinking and perspective. Teachers ask themselves, 'Do I already know the answer to this question?' If so, they think of alternative ways to ask so there is more than one right answer. This creates a culture of joint problem-solving and teachers and children co-constructing knowledge together. (Waite-Stupiansky, 1997)

- Knowledge is constructed by interacting with objects and materials firsthand. This suggests that children need to have many opportunities to explore a wide variety of materials and objects in the environment and to learn about topics that are relevant in their daily lives (versus abstractions with which they have no firsthand experience).

  For example, children won't learn about a garden just by reading about gardens in a book. Children learn about gardens by digging in the dirt, planting and watering seeds, and observing as the seedlings grow in a class or school garden. For constructivists, it is the firsthand experience of actively working with materials in their environment that supports children's cognitive growth and learning. Additionally, constructivist teachers emphasize topics that are meaningful and relevant to children's lives. Children living in the desert would not have a curriculum about snow, but instead, they might study desert animals, as the personal connection to the topic would support children's engagement and, therefore, their cognitive development and learning.

- Play is essential to children's development. Piaget concluded that play—especially play with peers—was the most important driver of children's learning and development.

- Constructivist classrooms are not quiet, nor are they chaotic. There is a healthy noise level that reflects children's movement around the classroom, their conversation with peers and adults, and the sounds of their exploration, experimentation, and problem solving.

- Materials are chosen to support exploration, experimentation, prediction, hypothesizing, and testing of ideas. Open-ended materials and "loose parts" (Daly & Beloglovsky, 2014) are frequently used (e.g., blocks, balls, and ramps).

At Red Pine School, preschool classrooms have been organized in line with constructivist tenets, understanding that children this age are active learners. The indoor and outdoor spaces are organized in ways that offer children multiple opportunities for exploration, thinking, and experimentation. For instance, Teacher Kalika has divided the classroom into different sections for children to play/learn in, including a block construction section that includes recycled materials such as PVC tubes and marbles, a water/science section with pipettes and bottles of different shapes and height, a quiet space for books and resting, and a dress-up and pretend play corner. In addition, three small tables are often ready with paper and other art supplies for children to use as they see fit. In the outdoor space, the school has set up a sandbox with shovels, buckets, and plastic animals, and children use often sticks and branches from the nearby trees. With this set up in place, preschool students have plenty of time, space, and opportunity to experiment and explore. Teachers support this learning by engaging in conversations with children and supporting them in problem solving when they have questions.

Lev Vygotsky: The Zone of Proximal Development

Russian psychologist Lev Vygotsky's cognitive developmental theory offers early childhood educators significant guidance in the teaching and learning process with young children.

According to Vygotsky's (1978) sociocultural theory, cognitive development is primarily a social and cultural phenomenon (Berk & Winsler, 1995). Specifically, a child's social and cultural experiences strongly influence how they think and interpret their world. To Vygotsky, social interaction and language are two of the most important factors that stimulate children's cognitive development. *Vygotsky viewed education as the force behind development.*

Vygotsky stated that all higher mental functions initially develop through children's social interaction and collaborative activity. It is through collaboration and interaction with teachers, family members, and peers and through play, that children construct new cognitive skills and abilities that eventually become their own internalized mental processes (Wertsch, 1985; 1991). For Vygotsky, play and social interaction are the critical experiences that fuel young learners as they grapple with new concepts.

Key Concepts in Vygotsky's Theory

The zone of proximal development (ZPD). Vygotsky described learning as existing in a "zone of proximal development" that sits between what an individual already knows and can do and what they can do with support from a more capable "other" (Vygotsky, 1978). The assistance of a more capable peer or adult provides a "scaffold" that supports the learner to enact a skill or behavior that is at the edge of their current level of development. The scaffold or support will help a child attain a skill, strengthen understanding, and increase independence (Wood & Middleton, 1975; Wood et al., 1976). The scaffolding metaphor communicates the idea of a support system that is sensitively tuned and responsive to individual children's needs. A major goal of scaffolding is to engage children in tasks and experiences that keep them within their ZPDs. Teachers create ZPDs for children by:

- Structuring the environment and the curriculum so that the demands on the child are at an appropriately challenging level

(slightly above their current level of independent functioning but not too far above as to become frustrating to the child)
- Constantly adjusting the environment and level of support provided to the child to align with their dynamic learning process

Imaginary play. Vygotsky (1978) described children's imaginary play as a driver of learning and higher mental functions and a leading factor in children's development:

> Play creates a zone of proximal development in the child. In play, the child always behaves beyond his average age, above his daily behavior; in play it is as though he were a head taller than himself. As in the focus of a magnifying glass, play contains all developmental tendencies in a condensed form and is itself a major source of development. (Vygotsky, 1978, p. 102)

Young children are capable of more mature and sophisticated thinking and behavior when they are engaged in a pretend play context. In pretend play, children are stretched to imagine worlds and communicate them to others to keep the play going. They use language to try out ideas externally that will later be internalized into thought. A child who finds it challenging to pay attention during circle time or who struggles to wait in line for lunch is likely more capable of displaying self-regulation when hiding from the dinosaurs at recess or pretending to be a sleeping bear in a pretend play scenario in the dramatic play corner.

Vygotsky describes play as a primary lever of children's development because:

- *Pretend play supports children's ability to manage their own behavior and emotions.* Vygotsky believed that play supports children to learn skills in self-restraint because as they engage in imaginary play, children are learning to follow rules. For example, if a child is pretending to be a dog, that child will be reminded by their peers to follow the rules of "dog behavior." Similarly, a child who is pretending to be a doctor will conform to the rules of doctor talk and behavior. By following rules in imaginary play, children are learning emotional and behavioral self-regulation (e.g., how to control their impulses), as they must continuously act in accordance with the rules of the make-believe context. Play also supports children to manage their "unrealizable desires." When children want something that they cannot have immediately or at all (e.g., when a child asks to go to the park and the parent says "no"), they can invert reality and make their wish come true within the context of a pretend play frame.
- *Pretend play allows a child's thinking to go beyond concrete experience, creating a foundation for abstract thinking and*

symbolizing. When children are engaged in imaginary play, they are responding to internal ideas that are only in their mind, or to the meaning of a situation, instead of being limited by the objects and experiences in the real world. A child can perceive one thing right in front of them (e.g., a blanket) but using their imagination, respond differently to this object. For example, a child can pretend that the blanket represents a sleeping baby because the child is not limited to the perceptual features of the blanket and can imagine the idea of "baby" in pretend play with the blanket. The ability to separate meaning from objects becomes a foundation for later abstract and complex imaginative and innovative thinking (Berk & Winsler, 1995).

Anika is engrossed playing wizards with her two best friends. They run around the playground "shooting" magic spells at each other. Suddenly, one of the friends says, "Oh, I found a magic rock to make potions with," and they all sit pretending to grind the rock and add water. When they are done, their teacher gives them little jars with blank label stickers so that they can save their potions. Anika, who has been very reticent to practice letters or writing, takes a pencil and writes on her label, "P-O-SH-O-N" proudly adding the drawing of a star at the end.

In this example, we see how Anika's ability to engage in symbolic thinking—imagining that the rocks are representing the ingredients of a magic potion—becomes the foundation of literacy (different combinations of lines and sounds represent letters and sounds, which when combined have meanings that help us communicate ideas in writing).

How Play Supports Young Children's Development of Symbolic Thinking

When children use an object to represent another object (e.g., a wooden block for a camera), they are developing important cognitive foundations that will support abstract and symbolic thinking throughout their lives. The wooden block becomes a pivot for separating the meaning of the word *camera* from a real camera. It takes children a long time to learn to symbolize, where they create words, phrases, and thoughts to represent real people and objects. They practice and master this skill through play.

At the earliest stages of symbolic thinking, the pivots children use typically look exactly like or very similar to the objects they symbolize—for example, using a toy phone in play to represent a real phone or using a plastic plate instead of a real plate.

As children develop their symbolic capabilities, often as toddlers, they begin using pivots in more abstract and flexible ways. As with the previous example, a child uses a wooden block to represent a camera one day and the following day uses the same block to be a hairbrush in a pretend game of "getting ready for preschool."

Next, typically in preschool, children learn to symbolize without the support of pivots from the real world. A child might say to a classmate, "Fire! Fire! I'm calling the fire department!" as she pretends to hold her hand in shape of phone and make the phone call. At this stage in their development of symbolizing, children have the ability to hold the meaning for the word "phone" in their minds as a thought without needing to see/perceive the actual tangible object in front of them (e.g., a phone in her hand). It is this type of pretend play—when children can mentally symbolize ideas, people, objects, and experiences in their imagination—that prepares children for later abstract thinking (e.g., mathematical and scientific thinking and formulas) and the use of symbols for artistic expression and literacy (e.g., using different combinations of lines on a page to represent letters and words in a book or the staff, clefs, and notes in sheet music).

The next time you are observing children's imaginary play, recognize that you are seeing the foundations that lead to children's future ability to learn algebra, geometry, and chemistry and to write music, invent choreography, or design innovative solutions to society's most complex problems.

REFLECTION AND DISCUSSION QUESTIONS

- Before reading the previous section, how comfortable were you when entering a classroom where children were talking, moving around, and actively engaging with materials to experiment, explore, and discover? If the answer is "uncomfortable," how does your understanding of how young children learn differ from a constructivist approach?
- How can you support preschool teachers to create an environment that reflects the foundations of constructivism?
- How are your teachers encouraging imaginary play that supports children's development of symbolic and abstract thinking?

Reconceptualist Approaches in Early Childhood Education

The Reconceptualist movement in early childhood education was begun in the 1980s by scholars in many countries who wanted to expand beyond the dominant theories and practices in the field that privileged developmental psychology and Western norms of child development (Berman & Abawi, 2019). Reconceptualists argue:

> Dominant narratives about early childhood and educating young children have been conceptualized through Western norms of childhood development that

are standardized, colourblind, ahistorical, apolitical, and, supposedly, neutral. These norms of development, based mostly on research with white, middle-class, able-bodied, English-speaking children, have vastly informed ECEC curriculum and pedagogy, and promote narrow ideas of children and childhood. (Berman & Abawi, 2019, p. 166)

To counter these narrow views, Reconceptualists draw from disciplines outside psychology (e.g., anthropology, sociology, leadership, gender studies, ethnic studies, and more) and theories beyond the traditional canon in early childhood, including many critical theories (Critical Race Theory, Feminist Theory, Poststructuralism, Queer Theory, Postcolonialism, Posthumanism, New Materialism) (Berman & Abawi, 2019). Reconceptualist scholars problematize how Whiteness operates as a norm throughout early childhood education to privilege White bodies and experiences while marginalizing other perspectives and identities (Escayg et al., 2017).

Critical Race Theory in Early Childhood

By using critical theories to frame and guide their work, Reconceptualists have shed new light on our understandings of young children and early childhood education. An example of this is how Reconceptualists use Critical Race Theory (CRT) to show how the field's conventional beliefs about young children "not seeing race" are quickly discredited when adults take time to carefully listen to, and observe, preschool children.

CRT examines and makes visible the pervasive impact of systemic racism and racial inequalities in society (Ladson-Billings & Tate, 1995). CRT begins with assertions that racism is endemic in American society and that experiential knowledge of BIPOC children and adults is essential for understanding racism and other forms of oppression in society (Crenshaw, 2011; Delgado & Stafancic, 2017). There are several ways that CRT research has informed educational research and practices. CRT has brought visibility to the many ways that educators participate in and perpetuate racial inequality in their work including:

- *Deficit-thinking* (Valencia, 2010) in working with BIPOC children communicates messages that they are lacking and deficient. This approach often places the onus on children, their families, and their cultures for perceived faults (i.e., low grades, lack of English language skills, etc.) instead of questioning the institutional and societal structures and practices that are at the center of the problem (i.e., biased and narrow tests, Eurocentric and biased curricula, etc.).

A preschool teacher is concerned that a recently immigrated child never speaks in class and seems not to follow instructions for activities. She suggests to the parent that they might consider having the child referred for testing. The parent responds that the child is very verbal at home and relates everything in detail that happened at preschool each day on the way home from the program.

- *Acts of racial microaggressions* (Kohli & Solórzano, 2012) are defined as "brief and commonplace daily verbal, behavioral, or environmental indignities, whether intentional or unintentional, that communicate hostile, derogatory, or negative . . . slights and insults" (Sue et al., 2007, p. 271) toward children of color and their parents and families.

Asking questions such as, "Where are you from?" or saying, "You don't look . . . ," or mispronouncing the names of students, even after they've been corrected.

- *Teachers' positions of color-blind racism.* Their refusal to acknowledge the impact of structural racism in society and blaming children and families for children's educational outcomes instead of acknowledging the uneven playing field and histories of oppression that impact opportunities and access to education (Bonilla-Silva, 2013).

"People are people. I don't see race. I only see one race, the human race. Children are young and innocent. They don't notice race."

The only depictions of BIPOC children and families in a classroom are commercial posters of people around the world in folkloric dress.

- *Internalized racism.* Resulting from the daily impact of racism on one's identity and belief system leading BIPOC individuals to reinforce White superiority by privileging the beliefs, values, cultural routines, and practices of the dominant culture while positioning their own heritage and cultural communities as inferior.

Reconceptualists conduct research and promote policies and practices that aim to disrupt inequities that impact young children and their families.

Key Concepts from Reconceptualist Scholarship

- Early childhood as a field has historically denied and continues to deny that young children notice and construct meaning for concepts such as race, racism, and racial identity (Van Ausdale & Feagin, 2001). Early childhood environments are assumed to be "neutral" spaces, and many early childhood teachers do not perceive racism to be an issue in their classrooms (Berman et al., 2017; Berman & Abawi, 2019); therefore, the majority of early childhood educators are not formally prepared to work with children who are racially different than themselves.

- Reconceptualists acknowledge that young children are continually engaged in meaning-making processes in which they construct understandings of race, their own and others' racial identities, beliefs about difference, and awareness of power relationships in a society that privileges Whiteness (Berman et al., 2017; Escayg et al., 2017). And young children are capable of negotiating relationships in ways that can lead them to have positive ideas about race and difference (Boutte et al., 2011; Copenhaver-Johnson, 2006; MacNaughton & Davis, 2009; Pacini-Ketchabaw & Berikoff, 2008).

- Reconceptualists advocate the importance of all educators learning about systemic racism and bias and how racism and prejudice are present and reproduced in all early learning environments (e.g., through children's relationships, talk, play, and daily interactions). Addressing racism, they reinforce, requires that educators have explicit training and support to learn how to work with children who are different than themselves (the majority of teachers are White) as well to learn antiracist and antibias teaching strategies.

- Reconceptualists believe that adults and children need to learn about race, racism, and antiracist/antibias practices and that there are developmentally responsive ways to discuss these topics with children. They emphasize that all children, but especially White children, need to have accurate information about the presence of racism in our society and from the earliest ages and to be introduced to strength/asset-based narratives of racially diverse people, as together these experiences can become a foundation for developing antiracist White identities (Iruka et al., 2020).

REFLECTION AND DISCUSSION QUESTIONS

- How does your early childhood program represent BIPOC children and families in books, stories, and play materials? Are representations mostly historical, or is there a balance of contemporary people experiencing the joys of everyday life?
- Reflect on the ways that "neutrality" can disadvantage students of color in the classroom.

KEY TAKEAWAYS FOR PRINCIPALS

- Principals are well positioned to become powerful advocates for young preschool children and their families and to ensure that schools are ready for all children when they arrive at preschool.
- Learning about the importance of the early childhood years, including the rapid pace of brain development, highlights why investing in high-quality preschool is essential, as preschool creates the foundation for a child's future learning in elementary school and beyond.
- Knowing the research describing how young children learn, and how learning in the early years looks similar to and different from that of older children, is critical for principals. With this information, principals can create schools that are developmentally supportive of preschool children, with environments where children can feel safe and where the outside stressors they experience can be buffered with consistent and caring adults.
- Having familiarity with the different theories and perspectives that inform early childhood pedagogy allows principals to talk with preschool teachers using language and concepts that are familiar to them from early childhood professional training and coursework.

CHAPTER 3

Understanding Identity and Inclusion in Early Childhood

Children develop as whole human beings, and many social categories of identity—for example, race, ethnicity, socioeconomic class, citizenship, religion, primary language, ability/disability, and other factors—influence a child's developing sense of who they are and how they fit into the world around them. This chapter looks at four social categories that have a significant influence on learning and development in early childhood: young children's racial identity development, gender identity development, bilingualism and/or multilingual development, and development with disabilities or delays. Though each of these are discussed separately, as with adults, children's membership in different social categories is intersectional (Crenshaw, 1991), impacting their identity formation, experiences of privilege and/or marginalization, developmental trajectories, and learning experiences in integrated and cumulative ways.

YOUNG CHILDREN'S RACIAL IDENTITY DEVELOPMENT

Little kids don't know about that stuff. They don't understand . . . [there is an] insistence that racism is impossible for young children—they simply do not understand and cannot engage in such ugliness. (Van Ausdale & Feagin, 2001, p. 197)

Early childhood education has this hidden side. It is presented as a 'raceless' field. . . . A substantial part of the socializing piece of early childhood education is to speak objectively to what all children need, such as 'All children need care and relationships.' But nobody would say what it means to be understood culturally and what impact race and racism have on the field of early education. (Bunche-Smith, 2020, p. 151)

Early childhood education as a field has historically denied young children's awareness and understanding of race. One of the key theorists and researchers in child development, Jean Piaget (1962, 1965), described children as naïve and cognitively immature; ideas that led many people in early childhood education to believe that young children were unable to notice and understand complex social constructs like race and the impact of inequitable power relations in society as seen with racism. For many years, child development textbooks and early childhood practices have assumed early childhood to be, as Bunche-Smith described, a "race-less" field. Yet, for decades, scholars and educators have been pushing back on these assumptions and documenting that children's racial awareness, racial self-identification, and participation in the exploration and reproduction of privilege and prejudice develop from birth and are significantly displayed in their talk and behavior in preschool (MacNaughton & Davis, 2009; Ramsey, 2015; Van Ausdale & Feagin, 2001).

Young children's racial identity development is based in an understanding that learning about race and their racial identity is both a social and a cognitive process for young children. Specifically, developing a racial identity requires children's cognitive capacities and their awareness of the social categories of identity—understanding their own social identity groups (ingroups) and the relationships between their own social identity groups and other groups of which they are not members (out groups) (MacNaughton, 2005, p. 27).

Children's racial identity development is understood to be dynamic and influenced by the social contexts in which they live, learn, and construct their racialized lives. Additionally, MacNaughton (2005) explains:

> Children's understanding of racial and other aspects of their identity are limited or made possible through the language, ideas, and meaning systems to which they are exposed. This reinforces why it is so important for teachers to be mindful and intentionally affirm their students' racial identities through conversations, teaching, and the curriculum implemented. (p. 31)

Young Children's Awareness of Race and Racism

> Children are neither naive nor color-blind; race and ethnic relationships are important aspects of their social world. . . . The perception that children are naive is a construction of white adults. (Van Ausdale & Feagin, 2001, pp. 190–191)

Young children are interested in and aware of the physical characteristics referred to in society as "race," especially eye shape, skin color, and hair (Derman-Sparks et al., 2020). Empirical studies document:

- Infants and toddlers are aware of skin color (Katz & Kofkin, 1997).
- Most preschoolers can easily identify and label people by racial group (MacNaughton & Davis, 2009; Ramsey & Meyers, 1990; Ramsey, 2015).

- Though it is common for young children to think that skin colors can be changed (e.g., by the sun, paint, dye), preschoolers are capable of understanding that people are born with the physical characteristics associated with race and they are permanent (Hirschfield, 1995, 2008; Ramsey, 2015).
- Children's development of racial awareness is strongly influenced by their opportunities to have contact and interactions with people from diverse racial groups (Lam et al., 2011; Ramsey, 1991; Ramsey & Myers, 1990; Ramsey, 2015).

Young Children and Prejudice

- Preschool children begin to reproduce stereotypes of different racial groups they see in the world around them (Ramsey, 1991, 2015; Van Ausdale & Feagin, 2001).
- By 3 years of age, White preschool children already show a preference for their own race and have negative racial attitudes toward other racial groups (Iruka et al., 2020; Raabe & Beelmann, 2011). The majority of children in preschool and kindergarten express preferences for certain racial groups over others (MacNaughton & Davis, 2009).
- Children of color, especially Black children, show a pro-White bias throughout the early childhood years. This changes in early elementary grades for some Black children, who begin to report more "pro-Black attitudes" (Iruka et al., 2020, pp. 93–94).
- Young children are continually learning messages from their families, communities, and society about issues of color, race, power, and White superiority, and these ideas enter their language and play in preschool settings (Van Ausdale & Feagin, 2001).
- Early childhood teachers are often unaware that young children can express racial bias (Mednick & Ramsey, 2008; Van Ausdale & Feagin, 2001).

REFLECTION AND DISCUSSION QUESTIONS

- How are racial identities positively reflected in the images around your school (bulletin boards, library materials, displays, commercial decorations, etc.)?
- Is children's racial identity development a part of early childhood staff discussions at your school? If not, why do you think that might be?
- Is there something teachers are already doing that is affirming the racial identities of the students? If yes, what is it and how does it produce the desired effect? If not, then what is one way for teachers

to affirm the racial identities of their young students (e.g., incorporate stories representative of the racial diversity in classrooms and use shared-book reading time to discuss with students the racial identities of the characters)?

> Racism surrounds us, permeates our ideas and conversations, focuses our relationships with one another, shapes our practices, and drives much in our personal, social and political lives. There are few social forces so strong. Children are neither immune to it nor unaware of its power. (Van Ausdale &Feagin, 2001, pp. 197–198)

- After reading the quote, reflect on the following question: What are the consequences of regarding early childhood education outside the context of the social forces of racism?

Paul Westmoreland, author of *Racism in a Black White Binary* (2014) states:

> Only Blacks and Whites count in race discourse in America. Other groups are either assimilated into Blacks or Whites or silenced altogether; as Perea (1997) writes, 'the paradigm dictates that all other racial identities and groups in the United States are best understood through the Black/White binary program' (p. 1220). This paradigm has severe consequences for understanding racism. In brief, it presents the idea that racism only occurs against Blacks by whites and that Anti-Black racism is the best way to understand racism in general. (p. 3)

- Reflect on this quote and consider how discussions about race in your school setting do/do not reflect the complexity of racial relations in America and young children's lives. How can you support teachers to develop their comfort and confidence in speaking about race and racism in ways that go beyond the Black/White binary?

YOUNG CHILDREN'S GENDER IDENTITY DEVELOPMENT

Information about gender and children's gender identity development that reflect accurate accounts of human diversity are being increasingly acknowledged in early childhood. And long-held assumptions about the way gender is discussed in traditional child development theories and early childhood pedagogy are being challenged. It is important that early childhood educators speak about gender with young children, families, and colleagues using accurate language and terms that reflect the reality of human lives and current research on gender. Young children are just beginning to learn about gender, so it is especially important that early childhood teachers know how to create classroom environments that support all children's gender health.

> Gender health results from providing children with the opportunity to live in the gender that feels most real or comfortable for them without being rejected, criticized, ostracized, or restricted from living their authentic gender selves (Hidalgo et al., 2013; Keo-Meier & Ehrensaft, 2018; Pastel et al., 2019). It is the responsibility of all early childhood professionals to support the gender health of all children in their care by being attuned to them and giving them respect and agency.

Gender Vocabulary

Language helps children to learn about themselves as they develop their identities. One of the first steps early childhood teachers can take to support the gender health of all children is to learn some shared vocabulary. This vocabulary can support children to feel a sense of safety and belonging and to help them develop positive gender identities. In contrast, if children don't see themselves in the words and ideas that are used to describe gender, they may make up words to reflect their identities or wonder how they fit in the world without words to describe their experiences (Steele & Nicholson, 2019). This can begin a process of self-doubt and the development of shame, which can have lifelong negative consequences.

Pastel et al. (2019) suggest several terms and definitions that will support educators to discuss gender accurately and openly with children, families, and colleagues:

Gender. Gender is a social system for categorizing people on the basis of many things, including body parts and processes, behaviors, expressions, and more.

Gender Binary. This is the dominant belief that there are only two genders—male and female—and that a child's gender is decided by anatomy and physiology. The gender binary is assumed to determine many aspects of their lives, including children's personal interests and preferences, behavior, roles, and capabilities. The gender binary fails to account for the wide diversity of human experience. Despite its shortcomings, the gender binary is often reinforced in early childhood classrooms; for example, asking students line up by gender (boys' line/girls' line), form teams or groups by gender, call on one gender to respond in unison or be dismissed ("girls, what letter is this?", "boys are excused for lunch").

Anatomy (structure of body parts) and *physiology* (functions and relationship of body parts). In a binary gender system, children are assigned one of two categories (male or female) based on their external genitalia at birth or from an ultrasound before birth. Yet, biology is more varied than two categories suggest. Many children are born with a range of genetic variations beyond the most common presentations of male/female (XY/XX), including intersex children whose anatomy and physiology at birth do not fall easily into either binary category owing to ambiguous genitalia, chromosomal variations, hormone levels or sensitivities, or other factors (http://www.isna.org/faq/frequency).

Legal designation at birth (sometimes referred to as "sex assigned at birth"). Children's legal designations are the gender assignments they are given at birth (based on their anatomy and physiology) that are codified by the laws where they are born. For example, Blake was born intersex but the doctors made the decision—legally codified by the birth certificate—that Blake was a male.

Gender identity. A child's deeply held sense of self related to gender. A child's gender identity is informed by many factors—for example, their culture, family, relationships, and so on—but it is determined internally by an individual. That means that only the child knows their gender identity. Some children's gender identity is aligned with their original legal designation (see section on Cisgender) while other children develop a gender identity that differs from their legal designation at birth (see section on Transgender/Trans). Children's gender identity may stay the same throughout their life span (fixed) or change in different contexts or over time (fluid).

Diane Ehrensaft (2016), the director of mental health at the University of California San Francisco's Child and Adolescent Gender Clinic, explains that when it comes to young children's gender identity, *"It is not for us to say, but for the children to tell."*

What does she mean? Adults cannot know what is inside a child's heart and mind and what they know to be true about their authentic gender identity. Only children can tell us what their true gender identities are. What adults can do is create inclusive and welcoming environments where children feel safe enough to share what they know to be true about their authentic gender identities.

Gender expression. The different ways that children communicate about their gender to others. This includes their choice of clothing and hairstyle. Also included in gender expression are the tone, pitch, intonation, and volume of children's voice, their behavior and mannerisms, the activities they engage in, and the way they move through the world.

Gender attribution. When someone assumes a child's gender based on the child's gender expression (e.g., clothing, hairstyle, voice, behavior) and the visible aspects of their anatomy and physiology (e.g., height, body shape). Cultural norms and beliefs strongly influence gender attribution.

> Some children internalize feelings of anger, sadness or shame when adults make gender attributions that do not match their gender identity. This is why it is essential that adults become conscious of their assumptions and intentionally strive to create early childhood environments that allow children to have agency to identify their own gender (Pastel et al., 2019).

> Ori is 5 years old and it is clear to their family that gender binaries do not apply to them. Throughout their life, Ori has switched pronouns and their own name, seemingly trying to find what felt right without settling on any. Recently Ori's aunt gave them a children's book talking about nonbinary gender identities and expressions and Ori has taken to it with a passion, showing it to everyone in their class and asking people to use "they/them" pronouns when talking about them.

Cisgender. Individuals whose gender identity is the same as their legal designation at birth. A majority of the population can be described as cisgender men and women. In most societies, cisgender experiences are considered *normal* while everyone else is seen as *other* and often disordered. Learning and using the word *cisgender* highlights this power dynamic and begins to disrupt the societal norms that marginalize individuals who do not identify as cisgender.

Transgender/Trans. Individuals whose gender identity is different in any way from their legal gender designation at birth. *Transgender* and *trans* are used here as terms that include individuals who identify outside the male/female gender binary, including people who identify as both male and female, as neither, or as another gender. It is important to note that not all individuals who fall under the trans umbrella as it is defined here actually identify as trans or transgender.

> Since he was 4 years old, Lu has identified as male despite his birth certificate's "female" label. His parents first thought of this as children's play but the intensity of his emotions around preferring to be referred to with "he/him" pronouns and around gender expression (the way he chooses to dress, avoiding at all cost skirts or other clothing usually associated with girls) has made them realize how important respecting this identity is for Lu.

Pronouns. Pronouns are ubiquitous within our written and oral communication. Typically, pronouns reinforce a gender binary (he/him and she/her); however, this may be problematic for young transgender or gender-expansive children. Using the pronoun(s) with which a child identifies communicates a critical message of respect and validation: "I acknowledge and respect your authentic gender identity and welcome you being your authentic gender self" (Pastel et al., 2019, p. 43). For this reason, using accurate pronouns is an important choice teachers can make to create a gender inclusive environment that supports children's gender health. Adults cannot determine what pronouns are most authentic to a child just by looking at them. However, if they create a culture in which children are asked and invited to name their pronouns, and adults model this practice, they reinforce messages of safety and inclusion to children and ensure they can be their authentic selves when they are at school. Young children may explore the use of different pronouns in their play, art, or in conversations with their peers and teachers.

Young children might use different pronouns as they explore their gender identities:

- I want to be called "she."
- I want to be called "she" and "he."
- Today I'm a boy, so I want to be "he."
- I don't want to be called "he" anymore. Can I be called "she" again?
- I like to be called "they."
- I just want to be called "Alex."

Gender expansive(ness). Gender expansive (also described as gender creative) (Ehrensaft, 2016) is a term used to describe individuals who are exploring, expressing, and identifying their genders in ways that challenge the limitations of the gender binary.

Table 3.1 summarizes all these aspects of gender.

Talking About Gender Accurately in Preschool

Throughout the early childhood years, children are developing awareness about gender and their own gender identity development. Children are learning how gender is understood in their families, communities, and in the world around them. The ideas they learn in their first 5 years will influence their understanding of gender throughout their lives, including their own identity development. Unfortunately, dominant views of gender development in traditional child development courses and early childhood textbooks are still commonly based in inaccurate assumptions and beliefs and can have harmful consequences for all children.

Table 3.1. Gender: Putting It All Together

I identify as. . . .	Gender identity. What I feel like inside. What I know my authentic gender to be.
	Boy, girl, transgender, agender, boy/girl, in-betweener, sometimes boy/sometimes girl, neither boy nor girl . . .
Please call me	Pronouns: She/her, he/him, they/them, ze/hir, . . . etc.
My body has	Anatomy and physiology
	Penis, vulva, etc.
When I was born, people thought I was	Legal Designation at birth: Female, male, third designation (in some locales)
Now people look at me and see	Gender attribution
And I want them to see	Gender identity + expression
My favorite toys, games, clothing, hairstyles are	Gender expression
My other identities and experiences are	Intersectionality
	Religion, race, socioeconomic status, ability/disability status, etc.

From *Supporting Gender Diversity in Early Childhood Classrooms: A Practical Guide*, by E. Pastel et al., 2019, Kingsley Press. Copyright 2019 © Authors. Reproduced with permission of the Licensor through PLSclear.

Many transgender and gender-expansive adults report that they were aware of authentic gender identities as young as 2–3 years of age (Pyne, 2014). As toddlers and preschoolers, they knew that their authentic gender (gender identity) was *not* aligned with the gender assigned to them at birth. They also knew that they had to hide their authentic gender self from their families, teachers, peers, and communities as young as the age of 2 (Steele & Nicholson, 2019). When children feel that they have to hide who they are from their caregivers, this begins a cycle of shame and self-doubt that can lead to lifelong negative consequences.

SHIFTING FROM A BINARY TO A MULTIFACETED GENDER DIVERSITY PARADIGM

By supporting the gender health of all children, educators represent the full range of human experience and reinforce that gender is a diverse concept:

- Gender is more complex than represented by the gender binary. It is dynamic and intersectional.
- Anatomy and physiology do not determine a person's gender.
- A person's legal designation does not always align with their gender identity. Many governments are beginning to allow people to change their legally designated gender to reflect their gender identity.

- Gender identity is determined internally by each individual, including children, and just as we support children to have agency over other aspects of their lives, we need to support and trust them to have agency to tell us about their gender identity.

Source: Derman-Sparks et al. (2020), Keo-Meier & Ehrensaft (2018), Pastel et al. (2019), Steele & Nicholson (2019).

How Young Children Communicate About Their Gender

Children have many ways of communicating how they make sense of the world around them. By listening carefully and observing children, early childhood teachers will learn from them what ideas they are grappling with and how they are constructing meaning about the cultural and social norms and values in their families and communities. Additionally, teachers can learn what concerns children have and what they find interesting, puzzling, or frightening and the questions they have and the forms of support they need and desire. If teachers take time to observe and listen to children, they will see that children are continually communicating ideas that reflect their thoughts and feelings about gender in a variety of ways:

- *Through their affect and verbal and nonverbal interactions* (their language, stories, gestures).

A child states "there are all boys at this table" and another child stops chatting and acts withdrawn.

- *In their play* (the pretend play themes, who they include/exclude in their play, the play materials they use). Many gender-expansive children explore gender through pretending—playing characters and roles that are not the gender they are assigned at birth—often playing the animal in a scene with other children (which can be genderless, less gendered, or any gender).

Quinn joins some children who are pretending to be a family and announces, "I want to be the sister!" Jen tells Quinn, "You can't be the sister. You're a boy!" Quinn looks hurt for a moment, but then perks back up and says, "Fine, then I'm a puppy. A puppy named Lila!"

Inclusion and exclusion in games is one clear way children start reproducing societal understandings of gender as binary. For instance, a girl choosing only other girls to play "home/house" and reproducing traditional feminine tasks such as caring for babies or cooking without allowing boys to do so.

Mara and Eva are playing in the loft area of their classroom pretending to take care of their babies when David tries to join with his own doll. Mara turns her back looking at Eva and says, "No David, we take care of the babies. You sit and fix the TV."

- *Through their participation in the expressive arts* (painting, drawing, movement/dance, music/singing, writing, theater/acting/ pretending)

Supporting Young Children's Gender Health

Families, educators, and other significant adults in young children's lives have no control over children's gender identities. Yet they can have extensive influence over children's health and social–emotional well-being by communicating messages of respect and affirmation or shame and rejection. Gender health is best supported when children are in environments that commit to a gender-expansive and affirmative approach (Keo-Meier & Ehrensaft, 2018) based on the following beliefs:

- *Gender is understood to be a complex integration of biology, development and socialization, culture, and context.* Gender identities and gender expressions are diverse and vary across individuals and cultures and can be static or dynamic over a person's life span.
- *No child's gender identity or gender expression should be associated with pathology or deficit* (wrong, "sick," needing to be "fixed").
- *Attempting to pressure a child to live as a gender with which they do not identify does harm.* Children's gender health is supported when they can live in the genders that feel most real and/or comfortable for them and by giving them the freedom to express gender without experiencing restriction, criticism, or ostracism. All children, and especially gender-expansive children, have better mental health when adults support them in expressing their authentic gender identities.
- *All children benefit from early learning environments that celebrate and normalize difference* through information, images, and relationships that highlight human diversity, including gender diversity. Gender-expansive children need to experience the same level of respect, acceptance, representation, safety, and belonging as children whose behavior does not challenge gender norms.

Figure 3.1. Use the Acronym STAR to Support Gender Health

The STAR Tool reinforces four important ways that educators can support children's gender health on a daily basis in their schools and classrooms.

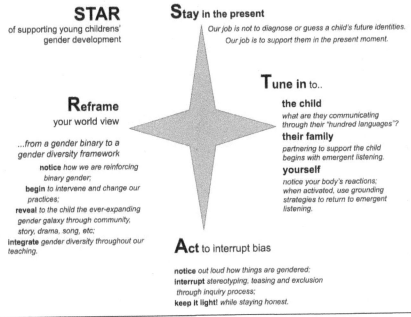

STAR of supporting young childrens' gender development

Stay in the present
Our job is not to diagnose or guess a child's future identities.
Our job is to support them in the present moment.

Tune in to..
the child
what are they communicating through their "hundred languages"?
their family
partnering to support the child begins with emergent listening.
yourself
notice your body's reactions; when activated, use grounding strategies to return to emergent listening.

Reframe your world view
...from a gender binary to a gender diversity framework
notice *how we are reinforcing binary gender;*
begin *to intervene and change our practices;*
reveal *to the child the ever-expanding gender galaxy through community, story, drama, song, etc;*
integrate *gender diversity throughout our teaching.*

Act to interrupt bias
notice *out loud how things are gendered;*
interrupt *stereotyping, teasing and exclusion through inquiry process;*
keep it light! *while staying honest.*

http://bit.ly/STARofsupportingyoungchildrensgenderdevelopment (Gender Justice in Early Childhood, 2019)

- *Young children need advocates who will challenge their own binary thinking while striving to support the gender health of all children* by having policies and practices that recognize *all* gender identities and expressions in the children and families they serve and interrupt and respond to gender bias in the classroom.

See Figure 3.1 to learn about the acronym STAR to support young children's gender health.

REFLECTION AND DISCUSSION QUESTIONS

- Take a moment to observe the subtle ways that gender binaries are communicated in routines in the preschool classroom. How could these be revised to be more inclusive of all children's gender identities?
- Many adults avoid talking about gender identity, have strong beliefs about gender binaries, and/or have grown up in environments with strict binary and gender stereotypes. How could you broach this topic with your staff and support them to learn the key concepts and vocabulary to create a gender inclusive environment for all children, families, and teachers?

BILINGUAL AND MULTILINGUAL DEVELOPMENT IN THE EARLY YEARS

The number of children entering early childhood programs who speak languages other than dominant American English at home is increasing (Castro, 2014; Espinosa, 2015). Unfortunately, deficit views and misunderstandings about what it means to be bilingual/multilingual prevail in the field, often causing harm (e.g., loss of the first language) and missing the opportunity to support children's learning using all the tools and skills they possess. This reality reinforces the urgency for principals and early childhood educators to learn about the latest research on bilingualism and multilingualism with young children.

Current terms being used by scholars and practitioners to describe young children learning and speaking more than one language include:

- *Emergent Bilinguals, Emergent Bilingual Learner, Emergent Multilingual Learner.* These terms acknowledge that young children's home language practices are assets that support them to become bilingual/multilingual (García et al., 2008; Kleyn & Stern, 2018).
- *Emergent Bilingualism and Emergent Biliteracy.* Gort and Pontier (2012) offer the terms *emergent bilingualism* and *emergent biliteracy* as a developmental perspective of young children's bilingualism.

Reflecting on her students' facility in two languages, teacher Deb realizes that using the term *English language learner* does not acknowledge the fluid process of language learning or the dual-language skills of the emergent bilinguals in her class.

Disrupting Deficit Perspectives

These terms represent a critical shift in how bilingualism and multilingualism are described in education. Historically, BIPOC children and children from immigrant, asylee, or refugee families whose home language is other than dominant American English have been perceived through a deficit lens (e.g., as a problem to be solved or as lacking skills). They have been described with language (Limited English Proficient, English as a Second Language, English language learners) that fails to acknowledge the assets afforded by their home languages and suggests that they are disadvantaged, deficient, and behind their monolingual English-speaking peers (Souto-Manning et al., 2019). It is now widely understood that the linguistic resources that young emergent bilingual and multilingual learners have are significant benefits that support and enhance their learning and development.

The Shift to a Holistic Asset-Based Approach

Previous research and professional practice were based in a *monolingual perspective* when describing how young children learn more than one language. A monolingual perspective of young children's language development considers children's learning of different languages as separate processes and only acknowledges individuals as bilingual if they have equal abilities in each language (Souto-Manning et al., 2019). This monolingual perspective is now being replaced with descriptions of *dynamic bilingualism* (García & Wei, 2014), *holistic bilingualism* (Hopewell & Escamilla, 2015), and *translanguaging* (García et al., 2012; Gort & Sembiante, 2015) to acknowledge:

- Young bilingual/multilingual children's language development is a complex, dynamic, and interrelated process (languages do not develop independently), reflecting a significant individual variation versus a universal linear trajectory (García & Wei, 2014; Souto-Manning et al., 2019).
- Children use what they know in one language to make sense of and learn about another language, a process described as *holistic bilingualism* (Hopewell & Escamilla, 2015; Souto-Manning et al., 2019).
- Young bilinguals/multilinguals use all of their linguistic resources in dynamic, flexible, and creative ways—described as *translanguaging*—when they are communicating with others and making sense of and constructing meaning of the world (García et al., 2012; Souto-Manning et al., 2019).

Young emergent bilinguals/multilinguals do not generally switch from one language to another when learning and communicating with others. Instead, they draw upon their full range of linguistic capabilities (mixing languages) and adapt their language use as required in different sociocultural contexts (Souto-Manning et al., 2019). The following vignette illustrates the idea of translanguaging in a situation where a child is confidently using his language repertoire and communication skills drawing from English and Spanish to talk to both his father and his teacher, a confidence promoted by a supportive and multilingual context:

As Max comes into the classroom with his dad, teacher Irene hears him excitedly saying, "... iremos luego a la swimming pool y le daremos a mama una sorpresa, verdad?!" [we'll go to the swimming pool later and we will surprise mama, right?]. Max's dad, laughing, says: "Pues claro! Crees que le va a gustar?" [For sure! Do you think she'll like it?]. Max notices teacher Irene paying attention and with a big smile says to both his father and his teacher: "She's going to be like 'woooow,' encantada!" mimicking a face of delight.

Research Findings: Emergent Bilingual and Multilingual Development

Souto-Manning and colleagues (2019) completed a comprehensive review of the literature on the language practices of emergent bilinguals/multilinguals in early childhood settings. They outline several key findings that have important implications for principals' supervision of early childhood classrooms:

- Children's language learning does not follow a predictable sequence. There are many individual variations (Genishi & Dyson, 2009; Souto-Manning & Yoon, 2018).
- Young emergent bilinguals/multilinguals use language in flexible and dynamic ways (Arreguín-Anderson et al., 2018; Souto-Manning & Martell, 2016).
- Becoming bilingual/multilingual as a young child can positively influence a child's brain development and functioning and increase brain plasticity (Espinosa, 2015).
- Learning more than one language in early childhood does not cause confusion for young children, nor does it negatively impact their language development. To the contrary, children in bilingual preschool classrooms have been shown to increase their vocabulary in both languages at a level that outpaces children enrolled in monolingual preschool classrooms (Simon-Cereijido & Gutiérrez-Clellen, 2014).
- Play-based learning and interactive experiences support bilingual/multilingual young learners' language development (Arreguín-Anderson et al., 2018).

What will principals see in early learning classrooms that optimally support the language development of emerging bilinguals/multilinguals?

- Teachers are building on young children's "mixing" of languages—their translanguaging practices—as this expands and deepens their language learning in both/all languages.
- Children's bilingualism/multilingualism is understood to be a valuable resource that enhances their own and their classmates' learning. And teachers believe and reinforce the message that emergent bilingual/multilingual children's language abilities and language practices are assets for children and families, the classroom/school, communities, and society.

The home languages of the children in Ding's preschool classroom include Spanish, English, and Vietnamese. Ding's home language is Vietnamese, and she speaks English fluently. Ding knows that one child's family owns a food truck. She has invited the family to park the truck outside the center one morning to share food items with the children and show them steps the family takes in preparing and selling food. Ding plans vocabulary activities based on food prices and menus from each child's culture. She chooses related books in all three languages and prepares materials for the children to use in creating a food truck in the dramatic play area.

REFLECTION AND DISCUSSION QUESTIONS

- How does your preschool program build on the language resources that young children bring to school?
- How does your preschool program encourage families to continue to develop their students' fluency in their home language? Reflect on the way you, your staff, and the preschool teachers talk about children who are emergent bilinguals/multilinguals. Think of the labels used to describe them and consider in what ways these labels reflect a strengths-based or a deficit view of bilingual/multilingual children's skill sets.

YOUNG CHILDREN WITH DISABILITIES AND DEVELOPMENTAL DELAYS

Many children enter preschool programs with disabilities that have not yet been diagnosed. In fact, it is early childhood teachers who often first bring attention about a developmental delay, learning difference, or potential health concern to the family and recommend possible referral for additional assessment and evaluation. A foundation of high-quality early childhood education is to use a strengths-based approach in work with all young children and families. This means that early childhood teachers acknowledge that *all* children have strengths and capacities and *all* families have important assets and funds of knowledge that should be identified and emphasized. It is through acknowledging these strengths and communicating that we see the whole child, with all of their complexity and individuality, that early educators build trust with parents and families. There is no person, child or adult, who wants to be defined by one social category of their identity (e.g., race, gender, income, ability), and nobody wants to be defined by a deficit. Therefore, from teachers' first interaction with every family, including families of children at risk for or diagnosed with disabilities, it is important to:

- *See the child as a child first.* The essential responsibility we have as early childhood professionals is to get to know every child as a unique individual and to acknowledge that every child can learn. Children should never be described or defined by their formal disability category. Children with disabilities and developmental delays and their families need teachers to believe in their promise and capacity for growth the same way they would with typically developing children—for example, to have high and realistic expectations for their learning and growth.
- *Individualize teaching strategies to meet children where they are and to support all children to feel a sense of belonging in the classroom.* This is exactly what is needed to optimally support young children with disabilities to thrive in the classrooms. In this way, supporting young children with disabilities and developmental delays begins by reinforcing exactly what early childhood teachers already do for all children.

KEY TERMS USED IN EARLY CHILDHOOD SPECIAL EDUCATION

- *Assistive technology (AT):* any item, piece of equipment, software program, or product system that is used to increase, maintain, or improve the functional capabilities of children with disabilities. Assistive technology helps with speaking, seeing, hearing, learning, walking, and many other functions. Different disabilities require different assistive technologies (wheelchairs, walkers, braces, educational software, pencil holders, communication boards).

- *Developmental delay:* a significant lag in a child's achievement of developmental milestones in one or more areas of development (cognitive, language, motor, social-emotional).

- *Disability:* a physical or mental condition—such as hearing loss, cerebral palsy, autism, or Down syndrome—that affects the way the body works or develops and that significantly limits a person's abilities in one or more major life activities, including walking, standing, seeing, hearing, speaking, and learning (Americans with Disabilities Act [ADA] of 1990 [Public Law 101-336]).

- *Inclusion:* the practice of educating children with disabilities in the same classroom as their same-age peers who do not have disabilities. Inclusion is part of the philosophy that people are more alike than they are different, that differences make classrooms and experiences richer, and that everyone—children with and without disabilities, families, educators, and communities—benefits when children are educated together.

Note: Mainstreaming is not the same as inclusion. Mainstreaming describes a child with a disability participating in a program with her peers for just part of the day or for specific activities where she can participate without the teacher making any changes to the activity. Inclusion is the philosophy that children can engage in activities with their peers even if those activities need to be adapted or modified in some way for children to be successful.

- *Individualized Education Program (IEP):* a written plan for a child between the ages of 3 and 21 that outlines the child's learning goals and the services to be provided to meet his educational needs.

- *Individuals with Disabilities Education Act (IDEA) of 2004 (Public Law 108-446):* the law that governs how states and agencies provide early intervention and special education services to children and young adults.

- *Interdisciplinary (or multidisciplinary) team:* a team of professionals who evaluate a child to determine whether a delay or disability exists and whether she qualifies for services.

- *Least restrictive environment (LRE):* the educational setting that allows a child—to the maximum extent possible—to be educated with same-age peers who do not have disabilities.

- *Referral:* a formal request that is often made by families, physicians, or teachers to begin the special education evaluation process.

- *Sensory processing issues:* difficulty handling and responding to sensory input.

Source: Brillante (2017).

INCLUSIVE ENVIRONMENTS IN EARLY CHILDHOOD EDUCATION

Inclusion is the practice of educating young children with disabilities in the same classroom or early learning environment as their same-age peers who do not have disabilities. An inclusive model allows children of all abilities to learn together. Inclusive programs should have the same characteristics as all high-quality early learning programs, where early childhood teachers create an environment that is responsive to the individual needs of each child and family. All children thrive in contexts with consistent and caring adults who design developmentally, culturally, and linguistically responsive practices that reflect children's interests and provide them with routines and activities that are both interesting and challenging and individualized for each child.

INDIVIDUALS WITH DISABILITIES EDUCATION ACT (IDEA)

Under the federal IDEA Act, states and local school systems are required to provide a free and appropriate public education (FAPE), including special education and related services (e.g., transportation or other services, such as speech, hearing, mental health, occupational/physical therapy, counseling/mental health or health services that support a child with a disability to benefit from education) to all eligible children and their families.

IDEA Part B: The federal requirement and funding allocation in IDEA for services for school-aged children with disabilities (ages 3–21 years). As required by IDEA, written plans are developed for children with disabilities and developmental delays to identify goals for the child and the services needed to meet the goals:

Individual Education Plan (IEP) is a plan or a program written in accordance with the law for any child 3–21 years with a disability who qualifies for Part B IDEA funding and services. Similar to Individualized Family Service Plans (IFSPs), IEPs are developed in collaboration with the family and a multidisciplinary team that includes the early childhood teacher and a school administrator. An IEP describes the child's current level of development, strengths, interests and needs/areas that require support, goals for the child's development and learning (including criteria, procedures and timelines used to evaluate progress), and the specific curriculum, instruction, environmental adaptations, resources, and support services needed to meet the goals.

IEPs are legal contracts developed with an agency—most frequently with a public school district or social services agency.

Creating Inclusive Play Environments

Young children with disabilities are often prevented from participating in play-based learning experiences that are essential for healthy development, friendship formation, and overall well-being (Brown & Vaughan, 2009). There are many reasons for this, including educators' fear that children will experience social exclusion and rejection by peers or because of the educators' lack of knowledge and understanding of how to support inclusive play. In order for inclusive approaches to realize their promise, it is essential that early childhood teachers learn how to create inclusive play environments (see CDE, 2021a for helpful suggestions). To do so, teachers will need district administrators to invest in specialized training so that they can learn how to provide effective guidance and support for young children with disabilities when they are interacting and playing with their typically developing peers. Through training and support, early childhood teachers can also learn techniques in which the children themselves can become effective play guides, supporting their peers with disabilities to be successfully included in classroom activities (Wolfberg, 2009).

Inclusive early childhood play environments should incorporate the following practices:

Access. All children have access to a diverse range of learning opportunities and experiences that build from their individual and group interests, strengths, and needs.

> Teacher Maria packs a wagon to pull out to the school playground. It's filled with books, manipulatives, and games. She spreads the materials out on a picnic table. A variety of children are drawn to the materials on the table, some as a respite from running and climbing, others who prefer quiet activities. "Let's play Candyland again!" Leticia says to her friend Luz. She pushes Luz's wheelchair over the picnic table and sets up the game.

Participation. Teachers create learning contexts that support all children to feel a sense of safety, belonging, agency, and engagement. They support all children to fully participate in a range of classroom learning contexts and experiences that enhance their learning and growth. They intentionally plan, implement, and modify playful learning experiences in ways that meet each child's individual needs, including scaffolding the level of guidance and support offered, modifying materials to support accessibility, and modeling and reinforcing positive and inclusive messages that all children can learn and play together.

> In the classroom, Kevin is quite active in exploring his environment, often moving quickly between activities. In addition, he runs within the open spaces in an attempt to engage his friends in a game of chase. To deter running, the teachers rearranged the furniture to create smaller, defined spaces and to limit straight aisles that allowed for running. To help Kevin sustain his attention at an activity, the teacher becomes a part of the activity by positioning herself in front of the entrance/exit to the play area to serve as a natural barrier. She has his preferred toys, joins his play, imitates his actions, and models language. After several minutes, Kevin approaches the teacher and says, "I want to paint." The teacher models, "Ms. Tucker, I want to paint" and moves to allow him access to the paint table.

Supports. Teachers have the resources and forms of support they need to design and implement supportive play environments and play experiences for every child in their classroom.

> Teachers notice that Jordan finds sand and water play very calming. They ask his parents if they have noticed this at home. They confirm that after he

has an emotional outburst, they often let him play in the kitchen sink to calm down. The teaching team adopts this strategy and keeps the water table available to Jordan throughout the day.

Benefits of Inclusive Programs

There are many benefits of inclusive early childhood programs for students who are or who are not at risk for or diagnosed with disabilities. Some of the major benefits for each group as well as for teachers and other are as follows.

Benefits for young children at risk for or diagnosed with disabilities and their families. When young children who are at risk for or are officially diagnosed with disabilities have the necessary level of support and guidance to participate in inclusive classrooms, studies document that they have an increased level of social interaction with peers (Buysse & Bailey, 1993), more complex play with toys and materials (Bailey & Winton, 1987), and an increased sense of belonging in the culture and ecosystem of the school/ program.

Learning that a young child might or does have a disability can be a very challenging and emotionally complex experience for families and can increase feelings of isolation and stress without sufficient social support and resources. However, families whose children are at risk for or are officially diagnosed with a disability can experience a sense of community and belonging at a critical time when they are participating in an inclusive early learning environment. Not only can they see how their children are developing in comparison to other children—which can help in the process of learning to accept the news about their child's developmental status—but being included within the larger community can also increase the networks they have available to connect to resources and support.

Benefits for young children without disabilities and their families. When young children who are developing typically have opportunities to learn alongside peers with disabilities, they learn from the earliest ages to see human diversity as natural and normal. Having opportunities to develop relationships with children who have a wide range of abilities can support typically developing children to have more respectful and accepting attitudes and more empathy toward people who are different from them.

Parents and families learn positive and affirming messages about human diversity and differences in children's developmental trajectories by seeing firsthand examples within their children's inclusive classrooms. Developing relationships with the parents and family members of children with disabilities can increase their understanding and empathy regarding the unique stressors and inequities within the educational system faced by these families and the different ways that families of typically developing children can be allies in the process of working for change to bring about more equitable educational experiences for children of varying abilities.

Benefits for early childhood teachers and other professionals. Teaching or working within inclusive settings can help all early childhood professionals develop more positive attitudes toward diversity, developmental differences, and the value of inclusive educational environments. As the essence of high-quality early learning environments is meeting each child's unique and individualized learning needs and interests, early childhood teachers often discover that when they have appropriate training, support, and resources, inclusive education is a natural extension of what they already value and do on a daily basis.

When inclusion is implemented successfully, it involves a team approach, with educators and families working in collaboration with specialists, including school and district employees as well as individuals from various community agencies. Examples include speech–language pathologists, inclusion specialists, behavioral specialists, occupational/physical therapists, mental health practitioners, and early childhood special educators, all of whom have specialized knowledge that may be useful in working to meet the requirements of children with specific disabilities and learning needs. Working as a team to meet the specific developmental needs of a child in a manner that acknowledges how the child is developing within the context of a family and community is an important element of an authentic inclusive approach to early education.

Adequate Training, Support, and Resources Are Essential

Effective inclusion is not about physically placing young children with disabilities in early learning spaces without creating the supports and conditions for their ability to learn, grow, and thrive. Early childhood teachers' and administrators' fears of the unknown is one of the most significant obstacles preventing schools from serving more children with disabilities. In order for inclusion to work, it is essential that the necessary teacher training, ongoing professional support, and resources are in place. Specifically:

Training and ongoing professional learning support. Many early childhood teachers receive very little education and/or training on young children with disabilities. To be effective, early childhood teachers of inclusive classrooms need training on necessary topics (e.g., disabilities in early childhood, how to develop curricula and arrange environments to support young children with a range of disabilities, working with cross-disciplinary support teams and families to support young children with disabilities, legal requirements, etc.). The reverse is also true: Early childhood special education teachers and specialized therapists are trained to provide services in specialized settings where they work with children one-on-one or in small groups. As such, they will need training in how to provide their services within the natural setting of the early childhood classroom or in how they can provide consultation to the early childhood teacher about supporting a young child to meet developmental and early intervention goals within the regular classroom.

Many research studies document that training alone will not change teachers' practice. Instead, it is the combination of training and ongoing professional learning that is necessary to change practice. To effectively apply the concepts, practices, and laws in their classrooms, teachers will need opportunities for dialogue, reflection, and sense-making with colleagues over time in such formats as coaching, communities of practice, or reflective book groups.

Resources. A lack of resources—for example, funding, transportation, training, support specialists, and so on—is a significant obstacle that prevents many children from participating in quality inclusive preschool programs. The lack of funding impacts the number of programs and spaces available to families and the amount of support that specialized staff can provide to children in inclusive programs. For example, transportation is often provided to families if they opt in to special education/early intervention programs but not inclusion programs. Additionally, early interventionists and specialized therapists have such high volume of caseloads that they may have little time or availability to support children in inclusive programs. Given how beneficial inclusion is for all children and families, it is important that funding and resources be allocated accordingly. As stated previously, just physically placing children in inclusive classrooms is not effective and can be harmful if their developmental and learning needs are not addressed as a result of the lack of available resources.

> The bottom line regarding inclusion is that it's necessary, it doesn't have to be expensive, it benefits ALL children and ALL educators when done well, it's incredibly incremental, and it's success is mostly dependent on the mindsets of the adults in the program, so a robust professional development and support plan will need to be created and maintained if we expect to see sustained change over time. The data regarding student success for children coming out of our early childhood inclusive preschool and into elementary schools shows that they are scoring similar to or above their district and county peers in all academic areas. It's been beneficial for us to have this data to support our anecdotal measurements of our success in inclusive practices.—Heather Richardson, Director of Early Childhood Education, Eureka City Schools

REFLECTION AND DISCUSSION QUESTIONS

- Challenge yourself and your staff to reflect on how you perceive and talk about children with disabilities. Do you focus on the child first or the disability first? Do you acknowledge the child's strengths, interests, and preferences apart from their disability?
- Review the segments of your early childhood program's schedule with the teaching team. Are there any points in the day when children with specific disabilities cannot participate fully? Brainstorm how to make your day as inclusive as possible.
- What professional development opportunities are needed to support your preschool staff to ensure that your program is inclusive of all children and welcoming of families?

KEY TAKEAWAYS FOR PRINCIPALS

- Children's racial awareness, racial self-identification, and participation in the exploration and reproduction of privilege and prejudice develop from birth and are significantly displayed in their talk and behavior in preschool. It is essential that principals and teachers work together to affirm the racial identities of all young children.
- Principals and early childhood professionals have shared responsibility to support the gender health of all children in their care by being attuned to them and giving them respect and agency. Principals can ensure that everyone in the school knows the vocabulary that promotes positive gender identity and that the school environment is welcoming by acknowledging and respecting gender diversity.
- The number of children entering early childhood programs who speak languages other than dominant American English at home is increasing. Principals can ensure that preschool programs are building on the language resources that young emergent bilingual/multilingual children bring to school, encourage families to continue to develop their children's fluency in their home language, and communicate that speaking more than one language is a valuable asset.
- Many children enter preschool programs with disabilities that have not yet been diagnosed. Early childhood teachers are often the first to bring attention to families about a child's developmental delay, learning difference, or potential health concern and to recommend a referral for additional assessment and evaluation. An increasing number of early childhood programs are practicing inclusion, in which young children with disabilities are educated with the same level of quality in the same classroom or early learning environment as their same-age peers who do not have disabilities.

CHAPTER 4

Understanding Toxic Stress and Trauma in Early Childhood

Just over one-third (35%) of children ages 0–5 in the United States have experienced at least one type of serious trauma. (Bethell et al., 2017)

Early childhood teachers are increasingly serving young children and families impacted by many types of toxic stress and trauma. Research documents that a majority of children in the United States have been exposed to trauma and that the prevalence of trauma is highest for children in their early childhood years (Briggs-Gowan et al., 2010; Shahinfar et al., 2000). Whether racism, poverty, homelessness, deportation, natural disasters and climate-related events, school shootings and community violence, child maltreatment or neglect, domestic abuse, the global health pandemic, or other forms of adversity, a significant percentage of the young children and families entering early childhood classrooms are experiencing overwhelming levels of stress and trauma.

The early childhood workforce is also especially vulnerable to the negative impacts of unhealthy levels of stress and traumatic experiences as a result of their poverty, isolation in the classroom, and limited accessibility to adequate health and mental health services. Further, they are at risk for secondary traumatic stress or vicarious trauma as a result of working with a growing number of children and adults impacted by trauma. Given these realities, there is an urgent need for principals to understand how toxic stress and trauma impact children and adults—their thinking, behavior, capacity to build relationships and learn, as well as their experiences in school. Principals are well positioned to create trauma-sensitive school environments that buffer stress, prevent further harm, and create conditions of safety, belonging, and engagement that not only build resilience but also support healing.

The need for principals to comprehensively integrate trauma-sensitive practices internally and externally (e.g., across policies, practices, protocols, procedures, forms, accountability systems, partnerships, and professional development) is more important than ever and will only increase over the next decade. Initial data suggest that the COVID pandemic has had a significant and negative impact on children's social emotional well-being and has led to an increase in childhood adverse experiences (Bryant et al., 2020). For example, emergency department visits for children ages 5–11 increased 24% in 2020 over the previous year, as did reported rates of loneliness, stress, anger, and anxiety (Leeb et al., 2020). Additionally, over 40,000 children lost a parent as a result of COVID (and these numbers continue to increase), putting them at increased risk for consequences such as traumatic grief, depression, negative educational outcomes, unintentional death, and suicide over their lifetimes (Kidman et al., 2021). Further, children and families—especially low-income and BIPOC—have endured a cascade of additional adversities as a result of the pandemic, including employment loss, food and housing insecurity, learning loss from program/school closures, and lack of access to technology/broadband and child care among other factors.

These data are cause for concern, as children of all ages are absorbing significant levels of stress from their families and communities at a critical and very vulnerable time for their developing brains and bodies. Given the current levels of adversity that children, families, and the early childhood workforce are facing across the United States, the need for trauma-responsive practices "should not be perceived as just another thing that will come and go" (Thomas et al., 2019, p. 445), but instead as a foundational aspect of effective and equitable leadership practice (Nicholson et al., 2021).

HEALTHY VERSUS UNHEALTHY STRESS

Developing a healthy stress-response system is important for all children. This happens when children are exposed to manageable levels of stress that do not overwhelm them. Developmentally appropriate stressors are valuable for children, as they create opportunities for children to develop coping skills and a sense that they are able to manage life's challenges; these provide foundations for building resilience as they mature. The Center for the Developing Child at Harvard University (https://developingchild.harvard.edu/science/key-concepts/toxic-stress/) suggests that we think of stress along a continuum from positive to tolerable to toxic (see Table 4.1).

ADVERSE CHILDHOOD EXPERIENCES (ACES)

Discussion of trauma and trauma-informed practices increased across the United States in response to the Adverse Childhood Experiences, or ACEs, research study. The ACEs study was sponsored and conducted by Kaiser Permanente and the Centers for Disease Control and Prevention from 1995 through 1997 and examined whether trauma in early childhood would predict adult health outcomes. Over 17,000 members of Kaiser Permanent participated in the original ACEs study. More current research on ACEs recognizes the impact of societal conditions, such as racism, immigration, or refugee status, on toxic stress (see Table 4.2).

Table 4.1. A Continuum of Stress

Positive	Tolerable	Toxic
Positive stress responses are manageable for children. When children experience them, they may have a slight increase in heart rate and a mild activation of their stress hormones. Children learn how to manage daily stressors when they are in an environment with supportive adults who can buffer the impact of a stressful experience.	*Tolerable stress* occurs when children are faced with a more significant, persistent or long-term threat. Their brain activates a survival fight, flight, or freeze stress response, which leads to the release of stress chemicals throughout the body. This experience and stress response could become traumatic and lead to negative impacts for the child's brain and body if there is no support system in place. What makes this stressor tolerable is when the activation of the stress-response system is limited in time (versus ongoing) and the child has at least one responsive relationship with an adult who can reduce their stress and help them to cope and manage through the adverse experience. With this type of support, the child is more likely to recover without any long-term negative impacts.	*Toxic or traumatic stress* occurs when a child endures frequent, severe, and/or long-term exposure to adversity without a strong support system—at least one consistent caring adult to help them feel safe and to cope. Toxic stress creates a cycle in which a child's stress-response system is continually activated. This leads to a release of stress chemicals over a long period of time, which can damage children's developing and vulnerable brains and bodies. Children who do not have relational supports to help them cope with a sustained level of toxic stress are more likely to have poorly developed and damaged stress-response systems and impaired brain development that can last throughout their lifetimes.

Positive	Tolerable	Toxic
Examples of Positive Stress	**Examples of Tolerable Stress**	**Examples of Toxic Stress**
A teacher offering an encouraging word when a child is learning to climb up a play structure ("You are working so hard to climb up that tall play structure by yourself").	A child experiences loss of a pet or family member.	Physical or sexual abuse.
	A child's family and community is impacted by a natural disaster (earthquake, flood, hurricane, tornado).	Physical or emotional neglect.
Holding a child's hand and guiding them to a table with playdough on their first day of school.	A child is involved in a car accident or a fall that leads to an injury or undergoes an invasive medical procedure.	Extreme poverty.
Holding a child's hand while a shot is being administered. Bringing a favorite toy to hold on to for comfort.	In all these experiences, the child has support from a consistent caregiver who buffers their stress (by reinforcing messages that they are not alone and that the adult will help them process what happened and return to safety) and helping them to cope with their strong emotions and worries.	Repeated exposure to violence. In these examples, children often experience multiple stressors at the same time. Further, their experiences of stress are long-term, severe (high levels of intensity), and not buffered sufficiently to reduce or prevent negative impacts on their developing brains and bodies.

Table 4.2. Sources of Adversity in Original ACEs Study and Expanded List in Current Research

The original ACEs study looked for the prevalence of seven adverse childhood experiences, asking whether a child ever had exposure to: • Physical abuse. • Sexual abuse. • Emotional abuse. • Household substance abuse. • Household mental illness. • Domestic violence (mother treated violently). • Incarcerated household member (criminal behavior in household). Three additional factors were added in later research: • Parental separation or divorce. • Physical neglect. • Emotional neglect.	Current research often expands the traditional list of 10 ACEs to include additional types of adversity. For example: • Racism. • Witnessing violence outside the home. • Bullying. • Losing a parent to deportation. • Living in an unsafe neighborhood. • Involvement with the foster care system. • Experiencing homelessness. • Living in a war zone. • Being an immigrant. • Witnessing a sibling, father, other caregiver, or extended family member being abused. • Involvement with the criminal justice system. • Attending a school that enforces a zero-tolerance discipline policy.

Key Findings of the Original ACEs Study

- 63% of those who participated reported at least one ACE and 20% of the participants had three or more ACEs (www.cdc.gov/violenceprevention/acestudy/).
- The greater the number of ACEs an individual has in childhood, the more at risk they are to have negative impacts on brain development, which puts them at risk for cognitive, social, and emotional delays in childhood. As shown in Figure 4.1, these delays are associated with an increased risk that as youth they will engage in risky behaviors in adolescence, which predicts increased risk for cognitive, social, physical, and mental health problems in adulthood and premature death (Felliti & Anda, 2010; Felliti et al., 1998; Koplan & Chard, 2014).
- Adverse experiences in childhood place an individual at increased risk for a range of negative outcomes in adulthood, including chronic obstructive pulmonary disease, ischemic heart disease, liver disease, depression, illicit drug use, alcoholism and alcohol abuse, smoking, intimate partner violence, sexually transmitted diseases, obesity, suicide attempts, unintended pregnancies, and fetal death (Felliti & Anda, 2010; Felliti et al., 1998).

Figure 4.1. Negative Outcomes Associated With ACEs

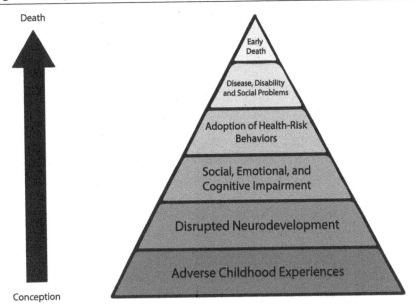

Mechanisms by Which Adverse Childhood Experiences Influence
Health and Well-Being Throughout the Lifespan

Based on the Centers for Disease Control and Prevention ACE Pyramid (https://www
.cdc.gov/violenceprevention/aces/about.html)

Are ACEs the Same as Trauma?

Despite the terms *ACEs* and *trauma* being used by many people inter-
changeably, they are not equivalent terms. ACEs refers to a specific subset
of adverse experiences in early childhood defined by the original ACEs study
and expanded in subsequent years. Unfortunately, young children experience threat and adversity in a wide range of contexts, conditions, and events
that negatively impact their healthy development and well-being. BIPOC
and poor children have disproportionate exposure to, and experiences with,
early adversity.

Though research documents strong associations between early adversity
and negative consequences for learning, development, and life outcomes,
not all adversity and ACEs result in trauma for young children. Young
children who do not have strong attachments with caring adults are most
at risk for the short- and long-term impacts of ACEs. Empirical research

consistently documents that consistent, supportive, responsive relationships with caring adults can reduce or even prevent the negative impacts of ACEs and traumatic stress for young children.

RECENT RESEARCH ON PREVALENCE OF ACES FOR CHILDREN AGES 1–17 IN THE UNITED STATES

An analysis of the *2016 National Survey of Children's Health* (NSCH) examined the prevalence of one or more ACEs among children from birth through age 17, as reported by a parent or guardian. Key findings include:

- 45% of children in the United States have experienced at least one ACE.
- The most common ACEs reported in all states are economic hardship and divorce or separation from a parent or guardian.
- Nationally, the number of children at very high risk—children who have experienced three or more ACEs—is one in 10. And these rates are even higher for children living in Arizona, Arkansas, Montana, New Mexico, and Ohio, where one in seven have experienced three or more ACEs.
- Across the United States, the prevalence of ACEs is lowest among Asian non-Hispanic children, and in most geographic regions, it is highest among Black non-Hispanic children. Specifically, the national percentages of children with one ACE are 61% for Black non-Hispanic, 51% for Hispanic, 40% for White non-Hispanic, and 23% for Asian non-Hispanic (Bethell et al., 2017).

It is essential to note that these data were collected long before the current health pandemic, and emerging data document that there has been a significant increase in ACEs for children across the United States resulting from the negative consequences of COVID (Bryant et al., 2020).

The ACEs study and research on ACEs has increased our national awareness of the prevalence and impact of adverse experiences in the lives of children in every state and city across the nation. Information on ACEs has led to the development of a range of trauma-informed interventions primarily within the fields of child welfare to screen for child maltreatment. Recently, California's new surgeon general, Dr. Nadine Burke Harris, has led an effort to create a system for health providers to screen young children for ACEs and to provide early intervention for children exposed to trauma. We recommend that you view Dr. Burke Harris's TED Talk on ACEs in early childhood (listed on the Resource page).

EARLY EXPERIENCES WITH ADVERSITY DO NOT DETERMINE A CHILD'S FUTURE

Even the most harmful experiences can be prevented from causing enduring harm if a strong support system is available to the child. Caring, attuned, responsive relationships are the most important factor to buffer stress and to prevent children's early adverse experiences from becoming traumatic. As Bruce Perry explains, *"Just as a traumatic experience can alter a life in an instant, so too can a therapeutic encounter. The more we can provide each other these moments of simple, human connection—even a brief nod or a moment of eye contact—the more we'll be able to heal those who have suffered traumatic experience"* (Perry & Szalavitz, 2017, pp. 308–309). Principals and early childhood teachers have daily opportunities, through the power of caring relationships in a trauma-responsive environment, to create therapeutic encounters with children that support their resilience and healing.

REFLECTION AND DISCUSSION QUESTIONS

- What are the common ACE factors that the children and families in your community face? What resilience factors (buffers to stress) are available to children, families, and staff in your programs?

DEFINING TRAUMA

Trauma has been defined in a variety of ways by different scholars, clinicians, and agencies. The following definition is often used to define trauma for children and adults:

> Individual trauma results from an event, series of events, or set of circumstances that is experienced by an individual as physically or emotionally harmful, and that has lasting adverse effects on the individual's functioning and mental, physical, social, emotional, or spiritual well-being. (Substance Abuse and Mental Health Services Administration; SAMHSA, 2014, p. 7)

We include an additional definition identifying what trauma means for young children:

> A traumatic event is a frightening, dangerous, or violent event that poses a threat to a child's life or bodily integrity. Witnessing a traumatic event that threatens life or physical security of a loved one can also be traumatic. This is particularly important for young children as their sense of safety depends on the

perceived safety of their attachment figures. Traumatic experiences can initiate strong emotions and physical reactions that can persist long after the event. Children may feel terror, helplessness, or fear, as well as physiological reactions such as heart pounding, vomiting, or loss of bowel or bladder control. Children who experience an inability to protect themselves or who lacked protection from others to avoid the consequences of the traumatic experience may also feel overwhelmed by the intensity of physical and emotional responses. (National Traumatic Stress Network, n.d.)

Trauma impacts children and their families across all racial, ethnic, income and education levels, family constellations, geographic locations, and community groups. However, Black, Indigenous, and People of Color (BIPOC) children are inequitably impacted by trauma and disproportionately represented in the child welfare system, foster care placements, and national statistics on child maltreatment.

ADULTS CANNOT DECIDE WHETHER AN EXPERIENCE OR EVENT IS TRAUMATIC FOR A CHILD

The experience of trauma is subjective. Whether a specific stressor is perceived by an adult to be intense or not, adults cannot conclude whether a child experienced it as traumatic. This is because, *"trauma is not in the event itself; rather, trauma resides in the nervous system"* (Levine & Kline, 2007, p. 4, italics in original). An event becomes traumatic for a young child when it overwhelms the nervous system's ability to cope with stress, leaving the child feeling unsafe, frightened, vulnerable, and out of control. Traumatic experiences, whether real or perceived, lead children to feel significant levels of *helplessness, powerlessness, and intense fear*—experiences they perceive to be life-threatening to themselves or others.

- Trauma is not an event but the impact of an event or experience on a child's nervous system.
- Trauma is subjective.
- Trauma is associated with fear/terror, perceived loss of control, and helplessness.

Types of Trauma Impacting Young Children and Families

Given the wide range of contexts, experiences, and events that can be potentially traumatic for children and adults, scholars and clinicians often group trauma into different categories. It is common for people to have cumulative traumatic experiences that fall into and cross over these different categories:

Acute trauma. Acute trauma is defined as single traumatic events that are limited in time (don't persist over long periods). Examples of acute trauma include loss (divorce, death, separation, being lost in mall/neighborhood, losing possessions with disasters/foreclosure/theft), accidents and falls, near drowning or suffocation, natural disasters (fires, earthquakes, floods, tornados), witnessing violence firsthand (school shooting, war/displacement) or on TV/videos or videogames, sexual assault, painful and/or invasive medical or surgical procedures, fetal distress and birth complications, poisoning, life-threatening illness or high fevers, animal attacks (dog or snake bite), or environmental stressors (exposure to extreme temperatures, sudden loud noises with arguments, loud thunderstorm, etc.) (Nicholson et al., 2019).

Complex trauma. Complex trauma is defined as the experience of multiple traumatic events that endure over a period of time. Children who experience complex trauma face significant, prolonged, and unpredictable stressors in their lives without adequate and buffering support from adult caregivers. Children who have experienced complex trauma have experienced multiple interpersonal traumatic events from a very young age (e.g., early loss and lack of consistent caregivers, placement in foster care system, sexual abuse, significant neglect, domestic violence). Complex trauma has significant and enduring effects on every aspect of a child's development, functioning, and capability to learn. Complex trauma has a cumulative effect, with each traumatic experience deepening the child's sense of fear, sense of being overwhelmed, vulnerability, and felt lack of safety.

NEGLECT IS THE MOST COMMON FORM OF MALTREATMENT FOR YOUNG CHILDREN

Childhood neglect is defined as "a type of maltreatment that refers to the failure by the caregiver to provide needed, age-appropriate care although financially able to do so or offered financial or other means to do so" (USACF, 2016, p. 106). Despite the fact that neglect is often the most difficult type of trauma to identify, it can be particularly threatening for young children, as they are dependent on their adult caregivers for support, safety, and survival. Neglect is often experienced with other forms of maltreatment and is frequently the result of significant stressors experienced by adult caregivers and/or families (e.g., extreme and persistent poverty and parental substance abuse).

Historical/cultural trauma. Historical and cultural forms of trauma are multigenerational and intergenerational and represent a collective and cumulative emotional wounding that persists in an unresolved state and leads to a pervasive sense of hopelessness that can be passed across generations. Examples of historical and cultural trauma include slavery, racism, prejudice, discrimination, poverty, health disparities that persist in many ethnic minority communities, removal from one's homeland, massacres, genocides or ethnocides, cultural, racial, and immigrant oppression, and forced placement.

When children's brains and bodies perceive that they are in danger or threatened, their stress-response systems will be activated in what is commonly described as a fight, flight, or freeze survival response (see Table 3.3; Perry et al., 1995; Schore, 2003; Stein & Kendall, 2004). *This is an involuntary survival response that happens automatically and is not under the child's control.* When children are frightened and their brains perceive something internally (e.g., thirst, hunger, fever, cold, etc.) or externally (someone they don't know entering the room, loud noise, etc.) as dangerous or threatening, the following will happen automatically:

- The lower parts of their brains are activated and trigger the release of stress hormones, which results in a range of physiological responses (e.g., increased heartbeat, dilation of pupils, redirection of blood flow to organs) that increase the child's chance of survival in conditions of danger.

Jeremiah is lying down during naptime. Outside an ambulance drives by with its siren on. This is a trauma reminder for Jeremiah and activates his stress-response system. He jumps up from his cot and runs to hide under a table. His whole body is shaking and he is hiding his face under his jacket saying, "No, no, no!"

- The more sophisticated parts of the brain (e.g., cortex, forebrain) have reduced functioning in order to prioritize the body's survival response. This means that children will have less access to the parts of their brains that support them to problem solve, focus their attention, regulate their emotions and behavior, or verbalize their experience. The parts of children's brains that they need to access to in order to learn are shut off or greatly reduced in functioning.

A child grabs Martha's toy in the sandbox, and Martha immediately starts to yell and hits the child in response. The teacher approaches and asks Martha to apologize to her classmate and to use her words. Martha runs away crying and shaking, unable to follow these instructions or use her words.

Because of the subjective nature of trauma, it doesn't matter if the triggering event is not what others would perceive as a "real danger." If the child perceives a threat, their brains will automatically trigger this survival response. *Once a child's stress-response system has been activated, the only way to help them regain full access to their cortex is to support them to calm their stress-response system.* How? By reducing their perceptions of threat and danger in the environment and helping them to feel a sense of safety and calm. Table 4.3 describes behaviors educators may see when preschool-aged children's fight, flight, or freeze survival-response system has been activated.

It is beyond the purview of this chapter to provide a comprehensive discussion of how teachers and administrators can determine the difference between developmentally responsive behaviors and stress-related trauma behaviors in young children (see Nicholson et al., 2019 for additional

Table 4.3. Fight, Flight, or Freeze Survival Response Behaviors

A young child's FIGHT response could look like . . .	A young child's FLIGHT response could look like . . .	A young child's FREEZE response could look like . . .
• Cursing • Biting • Kicking • Screaming and yelling • Talking back • Destroying property • Throwing objects • Hitting or hurting self/others • Tantrums	• Running away from teachers • Running out of the classroom or building • Hiding from others • Covering face, eyes or ears • Avoiding an activity • Redirecting attention elsewhere • Refusing to listen to adult directions	• Shutting down, withdrawing • Daydreaming • Appearing sleepy • Blank look on face • Repetitive movements or perseverating on something like picking at skin over and over • Head banging, rocking • Regressive behaviors such as sucking thumb • Falling asleep outside of nap time • Inability to vocalize • Unresponsive to comments, requests, questions, or name being called
Walking in a preschool classroom, you might see:		
A child disrupting other children's play by knocking over a block structure, taking a toy that another child is actively playing with, or destroying their own work by tearing up a finished product.	A child hiding under a table or behind furniture and refusing to respond or come out, running out of the classroom, or covering their face with the hood of their jacket.	A child sitting with others but not being responsive to social interaction, looking at others with a blank or spacey and dazed expression, refusing to move during transitions, or not responding to their name when called.

Note: This list includes many behaviors that are developmentally appropriate for young children and seeing a child display them does not mean the child has experienced trauma. From *Trauma-Informed Practices for Early Childhood Educators: Relationship-Based Approaches that Support Healing and Build Resilience in Young Children*, by J. Nicholson, L. Perez, J. Kurtz, 2019, Routledge. Copyright © 2019 Taylor and Francis Group. Reproduced with permission of The Licensor through PLSclear.

information). The following points are essential for principals and early childhood teachers to know:

- Creating trauma-sensitive schools and classrooms is essential for children impacted by trauma so that they have support to calm their stress-response systems throughout the day.
- Trauma-responsive environments will not cause harm to children who do not have histories of trauma. To the contrary, trauma-sensitive strategies can benefit all children's learning and development in early learning programs.

The Impact of Trauma on Children's Development and Learning

Trauma can impact every aspect of a young child's development and ability to learn (Craig, 2016; Osofsky et al., 2017; Statman-Weil, 2018). It is important to recognize that just as every child is a unique individual, the way children react and the behavior they display in response to trauma varies dramatically. It is not uncommon for different children who experience a similar event (e.g., house fire, divorce, or a natural disaster) to respond to it very differently. When observing children in early learning classrooms, it is helpful to know the various ways that trauma might impact young children's development and learning and experiences in the classroom. For example:

Perceiving the world as a dangerous and threatening place. Young children with histories of trauma—whose stress-response systems are repeatedly activated—come to perceive the world as a continuous stream of threats and dangers. The constant release of stress chemicals on their vulnerable developing brains and bodies can impact their brain development in significant ways. They often perceive situations to be personally threatening when they are not. A loud noise might trigger a whole-body startle response, a group of children laughing together about a game they are playing might be perceived by the child to be people laughing at them, or an unfamiliar adult entering the room to check on a broken sink could easily be perceived as someone threatening and dangerous.

> A stranger delivering a package enters a classroom to drop off a bouquet of flowers for a teacher. One child in the classroom reacts adversely by running over to the teacher and clinging on to her leg as if she is in danger.

The more frequently a child's stress-response system is activated, the more difficult it may be to calm their nervous systems and guide them back to a state of calm. Their brains can become sensitized and easily trigger into a survival response even with very minor stressors. This can often look like an outsized behavioral response that is surprising, confusing, and possibly scary for someone observing as a child appears to go from calm to intensely distraught in a split second—for example, a child hearing a dog bark and starting to scream at the top of her lungs and hyperventilate (Perry et al., 1995).

Impacts on children's language development. Children with histories of trauma may find it challenging to learn how to connect their internal thoughts and feelings to words. When their stress-response systems are activated, they will be less able to use language and verbalize their feelings and needs because of the reduced capacity of the cortex. It is common for children impacted by trauma to have language delays, have limited vocabulary, have challenges communicating with peers, use less self-talk (a foundation of self-regulation), struggle with complex direction, use rapid talk of any type, and/or use complex language in conversation or books.

Impacts on cognitive development. Trauma impacts children's ability to symbolize, or to use words or symbols to represent concepts, a foundation for literacy and mathematical thinking. Further, trauma also reduces children's working memory (ability to store and retain new information), attention, focus, ability to see a situation from a point of view other than their own, and capability of having emotional and behavioral control. When children are constantly scanning their environment for signs of danger, they often focus more of their attention on nonverbal behavior (facial expressions and tone of voice) than verbal communication. This can mean that they do not process a lot of information communicated to them verbally.

> The teacher announces it is time to clean up and transition to circle time. One child continues playing and does not transition. It appears to the teachers that this child is intentionally not following instructions.

Impacts on health and physical development. Trauma impacts children's health and physical development in multiple ways. They often report somatic symptoms (e.g., headaches and stomachaches) and experience what, to an adult, can seem to be exaggerated levels of pain for minor injuries or accidents. Conversely, they may not register any signs of discomfort or pain when they actually are injured and sick. Challenges falling asleep, eating, and eliminating are common. Additionally, many children show signs of delays with both fine motor development (difficulty holding a crayon, picking up small objects, tying shoelaces) and gross motor development (climbing, jumping, throwing a ball, balancing on a beam), as well as sensory integration challenges.

> Malcolm is frequently bumping into other children and has difficulty managing his personal space.

Impacts on social emotional development. Trauma has profound and negative impacts on children's social–emotional learning and development. Most significantly, trauma impairs children's ability to build healthy relationships with peers and adults and for many children, trauma can leave them struggling to build trust that adults will keep them safe and take care of their needs. Children impacted by trauma can also struggle to identify their emotions and the emotions of others (they often misinterpret others' intentions including non-verbal behavior and facial cues), which makes it challenging to develop empathy and to regulate their emotions and access skills and strategies to help them cope with big emotions and sensations in their bodies.

> Miguel often plays by himself. When he enters the space of 1–2 other children to play, he indicates his need to play by scratching their back, sticking out his tongue, or grabbing a toy. Miguel wants to initiate play but has difficulty reading the social clues as to how to engage appropriately with other children.

Though each child's reaction to trauma is unique, trauma can impact every aspect of children's development and capacity to learn. Understanding the many ways that trauma can impair children's cognitive, social, emotional, and physical capabilities is the reason why creating trauma-sensitive early learning classrooms and school environments is so essential (Nicholson et al., 2021).

Many classroom schedules, curricular activities, and classroom management approaches are often ineffective for children impacted by trauma. They might require children to use skills they have not yet developed—due to developmental delays resulting from their exposure to trauma—or that they cannot access when their stress-response systems are activated, which for some children is continuous.

> Silvia has been asked two times to clean up her toys before she is allowed to go outside. Every time she is asked, she runs away from the teachers with a laugh or smile on her face. The teachers keep asking why she is not listening, "You have done this before so why are you not listening now? We know you understand what we said."

Using trauma-responsive strategies to guide all aspects of the early childhood classroom (relationship-building, curriculum, instruction, assessment, family engagement, etc.) can help children to calm their stress-response systems so they are able to learn and reach new developmental milestones. Safety, stable environments, and consistent caring relationships are the basic needs that are required for children experiencing trauma in the classroom. Early Childhood Mental Health Consultation can also provide an additional and valuable form of support when teachers or administrators have concerns about the behavioral or social–emotional challenges for an individual child or about classroom-wide behavioral management challenges.

REFLECTION AND DISCUSSION QUESTIONS

Since feeling safe is of primary importance to help children impacted by trauma, consider the following reflection questions:

- In what ways does your program provide predictable environments and routines every day to help children feel safe?
- How do you support teachers to not react to a child's dysregulated behavior and instead to look more deeply at what the challenging behavior is "communicating" about how the child feels and the type of support they need?

NEUROPLASTICITY IN THE EARLY YEARS

Though young children are the most vulnerable to the risks and negative consequences of early traumatic experiences, the developing brain is also the most able to recover and heal. *Neuroplasticity* refers to the brain's ability to change its structure and function in response to either external environmental changes or internal changes within a child's body. Neuroplasticity is most possible in the early childhood years, as this is the time when brain development is most influenced by environmental factors. Experiences, positive and negative, literally become the "neuroarchaeology of the child's brain" (Perry, 2001a, p. 14). Just as early traumatic experiences can interrupt children's typical brain development and lead to negative outcomes that can last a lifetime without proper intervention, children's brains can adapt and grow in positive ways in supportive conditions. Through healthy and caring relationships, environments that support children to feel a sense of safety, belonging, and personal agency, children can develop healthy synaptic connections that create a foundation for health and well-being.

Though young children are the most vulnerable to the risks and negative consequences of early traumatic experiences, it is also true that the developing brain is most able to recover and heal because of neural plasticity. Both of the following are true:

- A large number of young children are impacted by trauma.
- Children's brains can be rewired as a result of supportive relationships and environments. Every interaction with a young child is an intervention and provides an opportunity to build their resilience and support their healing.

CREATING TRAUMA-RESPONSIVE LEARNING
ENVIRONMENTS AND SCHOOLS

Principals and early childhood teachers have an important role in supporting children's early brain development. The combination of so many young children experiencing adversity and trauma and the fact that neural plasticity is most active in the early childhood years, reinforces the need for trauma-sensitive, trauma-responsive, early learning environments. Foundations of a trauma-responsive environment include:

Consistent caring relationships. All children who have experienced traumatic stress need to have at least one consistent and caring adult who is responsive to their needs and helps them to feel safe. When a child has relational and co-regulatory support, they are able to develop important coping skills and resilience.

> When it is time for Jeremy to be picked up by his dad, the teacher welcomes Jeremy's father and proceeds to share several positive things that Jeremy did that day to be helpful and friendly to others.

Understanding how stress and trauma impact children. When adults learn about how stress and trauma impact young children's development and capacity to learn, they understand that children's stress-related (fight, flight, or freeze) behaviors are automatically triggered survival responses that are involuntary. Using a trauma-sensitive lens, adults understand that all behavior is children's best attempt to communicate with adults about how they feel and the types of support they need. For children impacted by trauma, their challenging, surprising, and otherwise puzzling behavior is the automatic result of their brain's perception of being in danger, and they need teachers and other caregiving adults to help them calm their nervous systems and feel safe.

> Melinda's parents are going through a very contentious divorce. Ever since this started, Melinda has refused to eat snack or lunch. She can be found sitting and staring into space, rocking herself back and forth repeatedly. The teacher approaches Melinda at the table, gets down to her level, and with a calm voice says, "You are safe here at school with me. Would you like me to sit with you or would you like to go for a walk outside for a few minutes with teacher Romy?

Use a strengths-based approach. It is important not to categorize children as "traumatized," which defines them by the bad things that happen to them. Conversations about toxic stress and trauma should always be balanced with a consideration of the "whole child" and the topics of resiliency and healing. All children have strengths, and many who face adversity have developed a range of coping strategies and capacities. Further, because of neuroplasticity, children's brains have a tremendous capacity to reorganize and rewire if the child has access to supportive relationships and safe environments.

> In talking with a teacher who is reporting a child with challenges, the principal asks a few additional questions: 1. When do you notice the behavior does not occur? 2. Have there been any strategies that have worked? 3. Have you gathered input from the family? 4. What are some of the child's strengths?

Create environments that reinforce safety and predictability. A central characteristic of a traumatic event or experience is feeling a sense of danger or threat. Being safe and feeling safe are critical for children with histories of trauma and the only pathway to healing and interrupting the activation of their stress-response systems. There are many ways early childhood teachers reinforce feelings of safety for young children. Consistent and responsive relationships, feeling a sense of belonging in the group, predictable schedules and routines, as well as support with transitions are some of the ways that adults can support children to feel safe in their environment so that they can focus and learn new skills (these are discussed in Chapter 7).

> It is time to transition from outdoor high energy to indoor, where a calmer energy is required. The teachers used to rely on a verbal warning: "Five more minutes." This always resulted in several challenges after entering the classroom. They decided to create a ritual to provide children with a more predictable routine and a less abrupt transition that relied solely on a verbal cue. They asked one child to volunteer to walk around with a 5-minute visual cue (sign with a big #5) with another child ringing a bell and stating, "Five more minutes." Then, after the children line up to come in, the teacher leads them through a mindfulness activity from their Mindful Activity deck of cards to help their bodies go from high energy to calm before they enter the classroom.

Provide children with opportunities to feel a sense of agency and control. Another defining characteristic of traumatic events and experiences is feeling overwhelmed, combined with a total loss of control. An essential feature of a trauma-responsive environment is providing opportunities for children to feel a sense of agency and control and providing time and ongoing support to strengthen children's social–emotional capacities. This helps them build sensory and emotional literacy, friendship skills, strategies for managing their strong emotions, and problem-solving skills (see Chapter 7), which in turn supports children to build confidence and resilience so that they can manage their daily stressors and challenges.

Teachers Maria, Jarissa, and Monica have implemented an emotion check-in chart at arrival and drop off. Parents/caregivers and children both check in as to how they feel when they arrive and leave for the day. This offers an opportunity to provide relational connection during those key transition points in the day.

Actively prevent burnout and support stress-reduction in the workplace. Working with children and families who are affected by trauma is very emotionally impactful and puts early childhood staff at risk for burnout, compassion fatigue, and secondary trauma (Perry, 2014). Further, when teachers' stress systems are repeatedly activated, the neurochemicals they are exposed to can put them at risk for a range of health problems, including anxiety, depression, headaches, digestive problems, heart disease, disruption of healthy sleep, weight loss/gain, diabetes, and memory and attentional challenges (Cozolino, 2006; Pally, 2000; Stein & Kendall, 2004). And significantly, when teachers are stressed, they are less able to engage in the caring, responsive interactions with children that support their optimal learning and development, especially children whose stress-response systems are continually activated. It is important that early childhood staff have access to self-care and organizational care in the workplace to reduce their stress (see Nicholson et al., 2020, 2021).

KEY TAKEAWAYS FOR PRINCIPALS

- Early childhood teachers are increasingly serving young children and families impacted by many types of toxic stress and trauma. Trauma can impact every aspect of a young child's development and ability to learn. When observing children in early learning classrooms, it is helpful to know the various ways that trauma might impact young children's development, learning, and experiences in the classroom.
- The early childhood workforce is especially vulnerable to the negative impacts of unhealthy levels of stress and traumatic experiences and at risk for secondary traumatic stress or vicarious trauma as a result of working with a growing number of children and adults impacted by trauma.
- Though young children are the most vulnerable to the risks and negative consequences of early traumatic experiences, the developing brain is also the most able to recover and heal as a result of neural plasticity.
- Principals can work with early childhood teachers to create early learning and school environments that integrate trauma-sensitive policies, procedures, and practices and to support children and adults to reduce stress and calm their stress-response systems so that they are able to teach and learn effectively.

CHAPTER 5

Understanding Curriculum in Early Childhood

In early childhood education, the word *curriculum* can refer to a philosophy, an approach, or a set of specific materials and activities that are purchased as part of a standardized curriculum. Early childhood curriculum involves all the elements within an early childhood program that foster young children's learning and development. This includes:

- Goals for children's learning and development
- The concepts, skills, and dispositions that are desired for children's learning. Sometimes this is described as children's thinking, their feelings, and their dispositions to learn and relate with others
- The environments, activities, experiences, opportunities, materials, and strategies that teachers plan and implement to support children's learning and development
- Experiences and interactions that are both planned and that emerge spontaneously
- The contexts and environments in which teaching and learning take place

EARLY CHILDHOOD CURRICULUM LOOKS DIFFERENT FROM ELEMENTARY CURRICULUM

The curriculum with older children is approached very differently than with preschool-aged children. Typically, the curriculum with older children is organized by subject matter. Learning activities and experiences are organized by distinct subjects (e.g., reading, writing, science, or mathematics) and taught separately. Because of the integrated approach to learning in early childhood, preschool teachers do not structure the children's day with a sequence of subject-specific learning activities. Instead, they understand that the curriculum occurs in a wide range of learning contexts that support children to actively explore their environment, experiment with ideas and materials, and engage in a variety of interactions.

The curriculum in early childhood is expansive enough to include the wide range of learning experiences and everyday interactions that children have throughout a preschool day. The curriculum in early childhood occurs throughout the daily routine, in both planned and spontaneous learning moments. Table 5.1 outlines what a typical routine might look like.

Early childhood teachers understand that children are learning in important ways in all these moments and more in preschool classrooms. They thoughtfully plan a curriculum to support children to *construct concepts* (balance, gravity, friendship), *build skills* (negotiate with peers, communicate feelings, ask for help, express ideas verbally and symbolically), and *develop dispositions* (responsibility, flexibility, empathy).

A Continuously Evolving Process

Curriculum planning in an early childhood classroom is dynamic and continuously evolving (CDE, 2016). The curriculum is informed by children's interests, ideas, and capabilities, which are always developing and changing. Therefore, the curriculum adapts throughout the year and with every new group of children and families who enter the classroom. However, the concepts, skills, and dispositions for children's learning are more constant.

> All the children see a rainbow outside. They are so excited as they leap with joy trying to touch the rainbow. The teacher pulls out chart paper and brings it outside and invites the children to capture the image of the rainbow on the paper. Back inside the classroom, they all wonder "how is a rainbow made?" The teacher asks the children to think about it and then together they read a book about rainbows and learn about how a rainbow is made.

Constructed in Collaboration With Children and Families

In early childhood classrooms, children, teachers and families inform the development of the curriculum. Teachers listen to and continuously observe children to discover their ideas, interests, questions, concerns, and feelings. Teachers share what they are learning with parents and families as well as with the children themselves. This communication leads to a process of teachers, families, and children co-planning and co-constructing possible ideas for engaging children and deepening their learning experiences in the classroom. Sometimes teachers offer ideas for activities or experiences to extend children's learning. Other times, ideas emerge through conversations with family members or from the children as they are guided to reflect on, and talk about, their learning experiences.

> The Aguilar family shared with the teacher that they just got a new puppy they named Quinn. In school, Miguel is showing everyone a picture of Quinn. The children have so many questions and they all want to talk about dogs! The teacher builds on this "spark" of passion the children have to initiate a

Table 5.1. Example of a Preschool Daily Routine

Arrival time	• Saying goodbye to a caregiver at the beginning of the day, locating their cubby and putting their jacket and personal items away • Transitioning into the classroom, connecting with staff and friends, settling into a favorite activity
Morning circle time	• Joining in with songs, fingerplays, and greeting rituals • Listening to stories read aloud • Participating in class discussions • Sharing ideas and feelings with the group • Understanding feelings shared by others
Free-choice time	• Making decisions about which areas of the classroom to play in • Negotiating play with peers, sharing, deciding roles and themes, working together • Expressing ideas, advocating for own ideas, coming to consensus on shared play • Enacting ideas symbolically through dramatic play and imaginative play • Grappling with physical concepts such as spatial relationships, balance, volume, and density • Interacting with teachers about their play, responding to questions and prompts • Dictating stories to adults to transcribe • Asking for help from adults and/or peers when needed • Accessing, using, and putting materials away
Small-group time	• Participating in small-group activities planned by the teachers • Interpreting activity in own unique way • Talking with staff about discoveries or product • Asking for help from adults and/or peers when needed • Using tools such as scissors, staplers, glue sticks, and paints
Snack time	• Stopping play and transitioning to snack • Washing hands in preparation for snack • Joining in conversation at snack table • Making healthy food choices • Cleaning up after snack
Outdoor time	• Engaging in physical activity—e.g., running, jumping, climbing, balancing, pulling wagons, and riding trikes • Engaging in imaginative play • Engaging with nature (using magnifying glass in school garden, sorting leaves, watching weather signs) • Problem solving how to share materials, how to express needs and wants, and how to resolve conflicts
Departure time	• Participating in end-of-day circle time • Discussing events of the day, sharing experiences that happened during free play, small-group time, or outdoor time • Locating items to bring home (products, personal items) • Saying goodbye to staff and peers • Greeting caregiver and leaving the classroom

lesson on dogs: that dogs are mammals, that there are different breeds, and how to care for a new dog to help them feel safe in a new home.

Responsive to Children and Families, the Program/School, and Community

As an early childhood curriculum is informed by the interests and ideas of the children and their families, it is inherently responsive to the backgrounds, assets (e.g., cultural and language practices), and contributions of each group of students and families. The curriculum is also responsive to the unique aspects of the school and surrounding community.

> Although they share a common language with many of the families of children in the class, a bilingual teaching team is not familiar with common children's songs and rhymes in the families' countries of origin. They informally survey parents as they drop off their children and work up a list of songs and rhymes to learn so that they can teach the children. They ask parents to teach them the tunes, they write up the lyrics, and use these songs to develop children's phonological awareness.

As teachers design a curriculum for preschool children, they have to consider many factors. Early childhood teachers are responsible for creating learning contexts that:

- Support individual children's developmental patterns.
- Are responsive to children's diverse cultural backgrounds and linguistic assets.
- Incorporate family input and goals for children.
- Align with state standards and/or developmental benchmarks.
- Intentionally disrupt bias and inequity.
- Inspire children's joy, engagement, safety, and belonging.

Relationships: The Primary Focus of a Curriculum

Building positive relationships is the most important and foundational priority in early childhood classrooms. It is through experiencing consistent, responsive, and attuned relationships with primary caregivers and teachers that children learn to feel loved, to feel a sense of trust that their needs will be met, and a sense of belonging and connection to others in the world around them.

The Importance of Attuned Interactions With Young Children. Attunement is described as moments when adults are "tuned in" to children with such intentional and mindful focus that the child "feels felt" by the adult (Levine &

Kline, 2007), a process that communicates to the child that what they think and feel matter. Teachers practicing attuned relationships are continuously observing children to learn about them. In attuned interactions, adults focus in on a child's emotional state, verbal and non-verbal communication, and behavior without judgment or reactivity but instead, respond with interest, curiosity, empathy, and a desire to provide support. When they notice a child is displaying complex, puzzling, or concerning verbalizations and/or behavior, instead of being reactive, they ask themselves, *what story is this child communicating to me about how he feels and what he needs to feel safe?* The adult's mindful presence supports the child to feel a sense of belonging, safety, and protection (Nicholson, Kurtz, & Perez, 2019), which is necessary for the child to build trust in the relationship. These are foundations that allow children to engage in the learning process.

Healthy relationships are the solid foundation children need for all future learning and achievement. This is why early childhood teachers spend a significant amount of time supporting and guiding young children to develop positive relationships with adults and peers.

Interactions and Communication as Curriculum

Early childhood teachers know that the conversations and interactions that occur throughout the preschool day are essential elements of an early childhood curriculum. Conversations and interactions with peers and adults in different contexts provide many opportunities to support children's language learning, cognitive development, and social–emotional capacities. As children interact with others, they build awareness of the expectations, customs, and systems of cultural meaning that are valued in their early learning environments and community. Early childhood teachers build in many opportunities for children to have meaningful conversations and interactions throughout their day (e.g., through informal one-on-one or small-group conversations, large-group activities like singing or interactive book reading, conflict resolution when children have arguments, or collaborative problem solving as children face challenges in their play). As with all early childhood curriculum, teachers are responsive to individual children's needs and adjust the level of scaffolding and guidance they provide to children, depending on their unique needs.

Curriculum focused on interactions and conversations might look like:

A small group of children discover a line of ants crawling into the classroom. Teacher Ivy invites them to get magnifying glasses to investigate where they are coming from and what they want in the classroom. The children excitedly get to work and discover that the ants have discovered some food in the trash can. The teacher encourages the children to share ideas about what to do about the ants in their classroom. During circle time, the children share their ideas with the larger group, and they take a vote to decide on the option they prefer.

CURRICULUM PLANNING IN EARLY CHILDHOOD

Curriculum planning in preschool classrooms looks different than lesson planning with older children. The specific format and content of preschool teachers' plans differ widely for programs with different philosophies and approaches. Even with this variability, early childhood curriculum planning should maintain openness to allow the key characteristics of curriculum in the preschool classroom—its flexible and evolving nature, constructed in partnership with children and families, and responsiveness to each group of children—to be realized. When preschool teachers write curriculum plans, they recognize that they are seen as:

> holding 'possibilities' for children's inquiry, rather than delivered as an activity focused solely on a particular skill. A responsive plan may be proposed as a question—'What might happen if we . . . ?' or, 'In what ways will the children explore . . . ?' When posed as a question, the plan prompts teachers to observe what ensues and to record what delights, surprises, amazes, or puzzles the children. Mindfully noting children's responses adds to teachers' understanding of how children are thinking and making sense of the experience. A responsive plan is more than simply the proposed activity written on a planning form. It includes observations of what occurs and teachers' interpretations of what children appear to be thinking and feeling during the experience. (CDE, 2016, p. 55)

Preschool teachers write curriculum plans for different groupings of children. Sometimes curriculum plans are tailored for individual children, and other times a plan is focused on a learning experience for a small group of children, but most frequently, curriculum plans are developed for the entire group of children in the classroom. All curriculum plans should "hold possibilities" while also remaining open to the emergent quality of children's learning in a preschool classroom.

Identifying Learning Goals

An essential part of planning a curriculum for young children is identifying desired goals that are individualized and developmentally, culturally, and linguistically responsive for each child in the classroom and for the group as a whole. Learning goals:

- *Address all domains of development* (physical, social, emotional, linguistic, and cognitive) and several content areas, including but not limited to language, literacy, mathematics, social studies, science, art, music, physical education, and health.

- *Align with state early learning standards or other mandates* (e.g., Head Start Performance Standards).
- *Are developed and continually adapted with input from different individuals* including the classroom teacher(s), parents and families, support staff (e.g., speech and language specialist, early interventionist, etc.), and the children. School staff are responsible for ensuring that this process is accessible to all families (e.g., having interpreters available for families when appropriate and translating all written materials).
- *Follow Universal Design for Learning principles* and proactively provide multiple means for young children's learning and engagement, multiple means of representing their developing skills and knowledge, and multiple means of taking action and expressing what they are thinking, feeling, and learning.

> Once goals are determined, they need to be communicated to all engaged parties (e.g., families, teachers, administrators, and interdisciplinary team members) in a manner that is easy to understand and accessible.

Curriculum Planning Cycle

Curriculum planning for young children is a dynamic process (CDE, 2016) that is continually emerging and taking shape in response to the individual and collective needs, interests, cultural backgrounds, and lived experiences of the children and families enrolled in the program. In order to remain responsive, engaging, and meaningful, curriculum planning involves an iterative process that teachers are involved in on a daily basis. The different elements of this process include:

- Observation
- Documentation
- Planning
- Implementation
- Continuous reflection and dialogue with children, families, colleagues, and supervisors

Observation. Teachers begin the curriculum planning process by observing children's daily experiences in the classroom, including the topics that interest them, their conversations with peers and adults, the types of play they engage in, the materials and areas of the learning environment (indoors and outside) in which they show interest and gravitate toward, the worries or concerns they have, what brings them joy and engagement and what they avoid, and the information they communicate (through words, drawings, play, etc.) about their families, cultures, and communities. Often teachers use specific criteria or inquiry questions to guide their observations ("How are children showing evidence of number sense in their play? What questions and ideas emerge in children's conversations as they explore in the class garden?"). As teachers are gathering this information, they are continually comparing what they see a child is capable of doing alone or independently and what is possible within their zone of proximal development (with the assistance of peers or adults or in the context of play).

Teachers' observations provide important information about the skills, knowledge, and dispositions children are displaying. Observations inform teachers' ideas about what they believe each child knows and can do and the different types of experiences they believe could deepen and extend the children's learning. Teachers understand that what they observe does not necessarily reflect all of a child's capacities. For example, a child may demonstrate a skill in a different context that is not seen at preschool (e.g., a child is able to recite a long prayer at church but does not show this type of memory recall in the classroom).

Documentation. As teachers are observing children throughout the day—as they play, engage in conversations, interactions, and conflicts, participate in daily routines, and transition between activities—they document moments that reflect children's skills, knowledge, dispositions, and learning experiences through note-taking, video or audio recordings, and photographs and by collecting examples of children's work (drawings or other artistic expressions, writing samples, etc.). They might audiotape a conversation between two children negotiating how to share the soap while washing their hands, take a photograph of a symmetrical design a child created using pattern blocks, or videotape a group of children joyfully taking turns navigating through an obstacle course during outdoor play.

In the curriculum planning process, documentation is then used to consider different options for extending children's learning. Teachers often share documentation with the children, their teaching team, other colleagues, and family members to gain greater awareness about how children are constructing meaning as they learn—what they are thinking, how they are feeling, and the way they approach problem solving. These discussions and the range of interpretations and insights they inspire are used to inform ideas for deepening children's thinking and supporting their continuing mastery of new developmental skills and capacities.

Planning. Teachers use their observations, documentation, and what they learn through continuous reflection and dialogue to inform their ongoing planning of a curriculum to support learning for every child in the classroom. As they plan, they consider what they have observed when children work independently and in small groups and when they interact with the whole class. They consider how to build and strengthen children's relationships with their peers and with adults, how to arrange the environment to inspire children's curiosity and exploration, and what types of activities to provide to support children's learning across developmental domains and the different types of support/scaffolding individual children need to feel challenged just slightly beyond what they are currently capable of doing independently. Planning also requires that teachers consider what will help children feel a sense of safety and what adjustments are needed to reduce potential threats that lead some children to trigger their stress-response systems (e.g., reducing or limiting loud sudden noises, strangers arriving unannounced, etc.). Taking all of these factors and more into account, teachers plan experiences for children that hold possibilities for their learning while always maintaining a strong focus on the goals they have for each child's and the group's learning and development.

Implementation. The next step in the curriculum planning process is implementation, where teachers arrange the environment, gather the materials, and guide children to engage in the learning experiences they have planned. Teachers will have various roles—observing, collaborating, and/or leading children through activities and experiences all designed with specific learning goals in mind. Teachers continually monitor how different learning contexts are supporting children's development of specific skills, knowledge, and dispositions and the appropriate level of support and scaffolding they should provide. Adjustments to the curriculum plans—both in the moment and for the following day or the future—are made in response to what teachers learn as they observe children engaged in different learning contexts.

Continuous Reflection and Dialogue. Every part of the curriculum planning process includes the processes that support teachers' reflection and professional learning. Central to professionalism for teachers is making their practices "public"—for example, sharing stories and evidence of their teaching practices with colleagues and supervisors in order to deepen their self-awareness (e.g., about their beliefs, assumptions, and biases that influence their beliefs and behavior) and the level of thoughtfulness and intentionality they bring to their work with children and families. Whether engaging in private reflection (in the action as well as outside the action; Schön, 1983) or reflecting in collaboration with colleagues (e.g., coaching, Communities of Practice, Reflective Supervision, attendance at conferences, etc.), teachers are using reflection and dialogue to continually inform the curriculum planning and implementation process. They might do private reflection while observing a child or share documentation with a child's family, meet as a classroom team to do collaborative planning, or share implementation highlights of the children's study of butterflies in a Community of Practice with other preschool teachers. Each moment of reflection and dialogue informs the teacher's understanding, which in turn influences the cyclical curriculum planning process.

The examples that follow illustrate two types of curriculum planning: Figure 5.1.1 shows a section of a plan for 1 day in a preschool classroom and Figure 5.1.2 shows a section of a curriculum plan for 2 weeks. The teacher provides a general description of the activities planned throughout the day/week. She also includes some of the concepts, skills, or specific knowledge that the activities are intended to address (e.g., number concepts, color names, self-help skills, rhyming words) and discussion prompts for various literacy activities. The right column in Figure 5.1.1 includes links to indicators from state preschool standards as well alignment with the Common Core.

The Limitations of Using a Prewritten Scope and Sequence

If preschool teachers are required to use a standardized curriculum with a predetermined scope and sequence of instructional learning contexts and activities, creating an integrated curriculum that is flexible and responsive to children's interests, preferred forms of engagement, and developmental levels is much more difficult. If using a prewritten scope and sequence of activities is necessary, it is important that teachers have flexibility to modify the content and activities:

- To meet the diverse developmental levels and abilities of children
- To ensure that the topics are meaningful and connected to children's daily lives and reflect what is valued and familiar within their families and communities (culturally, linguistically, and contextually)

DIFFERENT APPROACHES THAT INFORM CURRICULUM IN EARLY CHILDHOOD EDUCATION

Developmentally Appropriate Practice

The National Association for the Education of Young Children (NAEYC), the largest professional organization in the United States for early childhood professionals serving children birth through age 8, has published four editions of a position statement on Developmentally Appropriate Practice (DAP). The statement provides guidance on how to plan and implement intentional, developmentally responsive learning experiences that promote children's social and emotional development, physical development and health, cognitive development, and general learning competencies.

Figure 5.1. Examples of Two Preschool Curriculum Planning Documents

Figure 5.1.1: Daily Curriculum Plan

Example of Daily Planned Activities in a Preschool Classroom, Developed by Maria Allis

Timeframe	Focus	Learning Domains
8:45 A.M.	Arrival / Welcome / Health Check / Sign In	
8:55 A.M. / 9:30 A.M.	**Community Gathering / Morning Meeting: Focus—Literacy (Rhyming) and Math Concepts (Number Concept—Focus on connecting counting to cardinality)**	
	Mon: *The Itsy Bitsy Spider* song and book (book by Iza Trapani)—focus on rhyming words	Common Core—English Language Arts—Reading: Foundational Skills (CCSS. ELA-LITERACY.RF.K 2.A) PLF Vol. 2—Music: 2.2 / 3.2
	Tues: *Pretend You're a Cat* (book by Jean Marzolo & Jerry Pinkney)—focus on rhyming words	Common Core—English Language Arts—Reading: Foundational Skills (CCSS. ELA-LITERACY.RF.K 2.A)
	Wed: *Feast for 10* (book by Falwell)—number concept— focus on connecting counting to cardinality	Common Core—Counting & Cardinality (CSS.MATH. CONTENT.KCC.B4—4.A through 4.C and B.5)
	Thurs: *Graceful Elephant* song in English and Spanish from *Arroz Con Leche*—number concept— focus on connecting counting to cardinality numbers in Spanish	Common Core—Counting & Cardinality (CSS.MATH. CONTENT.KCC.B4—4.A through 4.C and B.5)
	Fri: *Fiesta* (book by Guy & Moreno)—planning a party	Common Core—Counting & Cardinality (CSS.MATH. CONTENT.KCC.B4—4.A through 4.C and B.5) Speaking and Listening (CCSS. ELA-LITERACY.SL.K 1 through 6)
9:30 A.M.	Journal Writing—Individual Work	
	Mon: Drawing and writing related to the story: *The Itsy Bitsy Spider* song and book (book by Iza Trapani)—focus on rhyming words	Common Core—English Language Arts—Reading: Foundational Skills (CCSS. ELA-LITERACY.RF.K 2.A) Speaking and Listening (CCSS. ELA-LITERACY.SL.K 1 through 6)

(Continued)

Figure 5.1. (continued)

Timeframe	Focus	Learning Domains
	Tues: Drawing and writing related to the story: *Pretend You're a Cat* (book by Jean Marzolo & Jerry Pinkney)—focus on rhyming Words Prompt: If you were an animal, what animal would you be?	Common Core—English Language Arts—Reading: Foundational Skills (CCSS. ELA-LITERACY.RF.K 2.A) Speaking and Listening (CCSS. ELA-LITERACY.SL.K 1 through 6)
	Wed: Drawing and writing related to the story: *Feast for 10* (book by Falwell)—number concept—focus on connecting counting to cardinality Prompt: If you were making a feast for your families, what foods would you include?	Common Core—Counting & Cardinality (CSS.MATH. CONTENT.KCC.B4—4.A through 4.C and B.5) Speaking and Listening (CCSS. ELA-LITERACY.SL.K 1 through 6)

Figure 5.1.2: 2-Week Curriculum Plan

FAIRFAX-SAN ANSELMO CHILDREN'S CENTER~ PRESCHOOL CLASSROOM

Curriculum Planning Based on DRDP Observation Evidence. 8/7/18–8/23/18

Observations of Children Interest and Needs	Developmental Objectives and Goals
Based on our observations of children's play for the past 2 weeks, the children's major interests have been: 1. Learning to do new things on their own (tasks, milestones, self-help skills) and team building, i.e. teaming up with someone to clean up or help someone new in the classroom. 2. Role-playing (parents/caregivers, family roles, playing with babies, feeding them, soothing them, etc. . . .) 3. Exploration of colors /mixing colors—discovering how to make secondary colors	Regarding children's interests and needs: 1. Encourage younger children to partner with older children to learn new self-help skills / create a book "Now that I am three years old, I can . . ." / "Now that I am four years old . . . I can . . ." 2. Check out library books and read during nap time / circle time re: different family compositions. 3. Continue to provide exploration of colors, primary to secondary with varied materials. Provide continuous experiences in the art area and outdoors where children can discover secondary colors, using primary colors. Also introduce the notions of tints and shades.

Figure 5.1. (continued)

Observations of Children Interest and Needs	Developmental Objectives and Goals
4. Shapes concept through puzzles, play dough materials, and treasure hunts (initiated by the teachers)	4. Offer puzzles and other small-motor and math activities that explore the concepts of: shapes, colors, and number sense 1 – 10.
5. Counting and one-on-one correspondence	5. See #4.
6. Pretend cooking	6. Involve the children in real cooking experiences / recipes from home / make a recipe book with families' recipes (incorporate math concepts) / make play dough from scratch.
7. Treasure hunt	
8. Exploring basic physics: ramps, stopping the flow of something, speed, gravity in the block area and outdoors	
9. Music and dance	
10. Bingo and matching games	7. Using social-science concepts from The Preschool Learning Foundations, use the map of our school and go on treasure hunts around our school:
Based on our observation of children's strengths, developmental needs, and capabilities, the teachers have noticed: (numbers below correspond to children's interests on page 1):	Partner younger children with older ones to go on a treasure hunt to find . . .("I spy . . ."):
1. Older children being role models for the younger ones, supporting their self-help skills and partnering with them to support them.	• Places around our school • Items around our classroom and our outdoor environment (based on our areas and activities)
2. Children's concepts of families could expand to include different types of family compositions.	• Letters of the alphabet hunt, color hunt, shape hunt, numbers hunt
3. Children's abilities to use colors and to combine materials to make a representation (with paints, crayons, pastels, pencils, scissors, glue, and collage materials). We have introduced secondary colors and now the children have just begun to be introduced to the concepts of tints and shades.	8. Continue to promote the exploration of basic physics: ramps, stopping the flow of something, speed, gravity in the block area, and outdoors.
4. Children's ability to recognize shapes: We have taken the children on treasure hunt walks, looking for shapes.	9. Offer music and dance from different parts of the world. Ask families to provide music from their countries of origin.
5. Children's ability to count, making one-to-one correspondence (1–12) / subitizing.	10. Create small group opportunities for older children to engage in "games with rules."
6. Children's ability to create pretend recipes. The teachers have offered opportunity for the children to make play dough.	

WHAT IS THE DEFINITION OF DEVELOPMENTALLY APPROPRIATE PRACTICE?

NAEYC (2020) defines DAP as:

Methods that promote each child's optimal development and learning through a strengths-based, play-based approach to joyful, engaged learning . . . to be developmentally appropriate, practices must also be culturally, linguistically, and ability appropriate for each child. (p. 5)

The DAP framework is an approach to teaching and working with young children and families that is the most influential resource informing early childhood curriculum and instructional practices across the country.

NAEYC (2020) recommends that a developmentally appropriate early childhood curriculum should:

- Build on an understanding of the integrated nature of learning for young children and support all domains of children's development—physical, cognitive, social and emotional, and linguistic (including bilingual or multilingual development)—as well as approaches to learning.
- Emphasize play and active engagement with the environment to promote joyful learning and foster children's development of self-regulation, language, cognitive, and social competencies as well as content knowledge across disciplines.
- Be flexible enough to be individualized, as children's development and learning occur at varying rates and children have different interests, abilities, and skills.
- Build on each child's assets by connecting their experiences in the classroom or learning environment to their home and community settings.
- Integrate technology and interactive media as valuable tools for supporting children's development and learning.

When early childhood teachers use the DAP guidelines to make decisions about their work with children, they are encouraged to consider the following factors together:

Commonality. Research findings and understandings of processes of child development and learning that apply to all children. For example, understanding that all development and learning occurs within specific social, cultural, linguistic, and historical contexts or that all child development occurs in the context of relationships.

Although K–5 students are dropped off for school by their families and enter the building on their own, the preschool teacher recognizes the transition between home and school for parents of young children. A preschool teacher schedules a 30-minute morning transition time at the beginning of the day during which parents and families are invited to stay and ease their student into the preschool day. Adults join in with their students' free play, interact with one another, talk, and share anecdotes about their child with the preschool staff. Some parents participate in this transition time every day, others occasionally, some not at all.

Individuality. Characteristics and experiences unique to each child, within the context of their family and community, have implications for how best to support their development and learning. Examples include children's various social identities, interests, strengths, and preferences; their personalities, motivations, and approaches to learning; and their knowledge, skills, and abilities related to their cultural experiences, including family languages, dialects, and vernaculars as well as special needs or disabilities or other individual learning needs.

Preparing for a conference with Kayla's family, teacher LeRon looks through drawings, photos, and observation notes he has collected. He reads through his collection of anecdotes and chooses some highlights to share with her family. He thinks about Kayla's strengths and wants to ask her family how they have inspired her so he can follow through in the classroom.

Context. Recognition that our current body of evidence highlights that all human development and learning is embedded within and affected by social and cultural contexts. Therefore, as social and cultural contexts vary, so do processes of development and learning for children. To fully support each child's optimal development and learning in an increasingly diverse society, early childhood educators need to understand how contexts inform children's learning. This includes children's *personal cultural context* (the ways of knowing and being in the world that reflect the traditions and values of their families, caregivers, and communities) and the *broader multifaceted and intersecting cultural contexts* (e.g., social, racial, economic, historical, and political) that impact every aspect of their lives.

Early educators recognize that young children's development and their experiences of learning are always influenced by their social identities (race or ethnicity, language, gender, class, ability, family composition, and economic status, among others). Additionally, teachers work to build self-awareness of the impact of their own social identities on their work with children and families and intentionally strive to discover and disrupt any biases that may compromise a child's positive development and well-being.

A child who recently immigrated from a war-torn country regularly enacts a scenario during outside time in which she is being chased and must rally others around her to escape. Teachers recognize that this is an important outlet for the child to gain confidence that she is safe and that she is now in a situation in which she has support.

Critiques of DAP. Despite its widespread use and popularity, DAP has been critiqued for decades for important reasons:

- Concerns that DAP is based on theories, conceptions of children and their development reflected in White and Western norms of childhood development presented as "neutral" and universal. DAP has historically "ignored power relations and context, such as gender, race, home language(s), home culture(s)" in descriptions of what optimally supports children's development and learning and how early childhood educators should care, teach, and guide them (Berman & Abawi, 2019, p. 166).
- Critiques that the research and empirical base that informs DAP is founded on data collected with White, middle-class, able-bodied, English-speaking children, which is problematic given the significant and growing diversity of children and families. Critics have noted that divergence from this dominant norm have been historically viewed as deficits and deficiencies perpetuating cycles of oppression and maintaining structural inequities (Berman & Abawi, 2019; Lubeck, 1994).

The fourth edition of DAP (NAEYC, 2020) attempts to address these concerns. The authors acknowledge "multiple tensions" about the information they present in the DAP document. The most recent edition no longer uses the term *best practices* to describe DAP. Instead, DAPs are referred to as *guidelines* for early childhood educators' professional practice. This reframing acknowledges, that the term *best* "has historically reflected the dominant culture's assumptions," which in the United States has "historically and generally speaking been that of white, middle-class, heterosexual, Protestant people of northern European descent" (p. 34). The authors state that "what is best is a dynamic and creative set of practices that embrace and build on the varied assets children bring to the learning community" (p. 34).

REFLECTION AND DISCUSSION QUESTION

- How can you use the recommendations of developmentally appropriate practice in a way that supports, but doesn't limit, your preschool program? Specifically, in what ways can the notions of "commonality, individuality, and context" be used in the preschool classroom to promote rich and equitable early childhood experiences?

Emergent Curriculum/Inquiry-Based Approaches

Emergent curriculum is a philosophy of teaching and approach to planning a curriculum in early childhood that is child-initiated, inquiry-driven, play-based, collaborative, and responsive to children's interests and needs. Teachers use observation, documentation, and conversations with children in the classroom to identify what interests and engages them. The curriculum emerges from the topics and experiences that fascinate children, from their questions, interests, experimentation, and theories about how the world works instead of prescriptive lesson plans with predetermined outcomes.

Key features of an emergent curriculum include:

- Trust in teachers as professionals with skills and abilities to create meaningful learning experiences for children.
- Images of children as strong, capable, and actively engaged learners.
- Flexible environments that allow teachers to be responsive to the emerging and dynamic interests of the children.
- Observation of children and their interests as springboards for developing curriculum.
- Because curriculum is rooted in children's interests, content is responsive to the values and cultural backgrounds and practices of the children, their families, and their communities (MacLachlan et al., 2013).

Teacher Mayra planned a lesson on reptiles for the week. But Monday morning, those plans were temporarily diverted when she observed the children at recess excited about observing a squirrel who was gathering nuts and bringing them repeatedly up the tree to a nest. They were so fascinated that Mayra could not help but build on that interest by bringing in the concept of squirrels and why they gather nuts in preparation for the cold winter, when food may no longer be as readily available.

An emergent curriculum does not mean a lack of intentionality or "anything goes" (NAEYC, 2020). Implementing an emergent curriculum requires a high level of professional knowledge and skill for early childhood teachers.

- Teachers must be skilled observers who listen carefully and identify what fascinates and engages children.
- Once they have discovered children's interests, teachers need to know how to arrange the classroom and provide materials and activities that invite children to explore their interests in meaningful ways at a level that challenges them and promotes their development.

- Effective early childhood educators continually make connections between emergent curriculum, preschool learning standards, and authentic assessment of each child's developmental progression in skills and knowledge across domains.

USING INQUIRY IN EARLY CHILDHOOD EDUCATION

Emergent curriculum approaches are based in inquiry. Inquiry is an approach to curriculum and instruction in early childhood that involves children asking questions, exploring the natural and material world, testing their ideas, and making discoveries in a dynamic learning process.

Inquiry begins by inviting children to ask questions, explore topics, ideas, experiences, and solutions to problems of great interest to them (Souto-Manning, 2013). By starting with children's questions, teachers do not preplan themes or introduce topics that have no relevance or meaning to the children's lives. Instead, when the curriculum is continually informed by children's questions, by design, the content is responsive to their interests, interactions, and lived experiences, and it changes with each new group of students and families. Using inquiry is one way that teachers can intentionally implement a curriculum that is culturally and linguistically responsive to the specific group of children in their classroom.

Inquiry-based classrooms are filled with the engaged sounds of active conversation and adults and children learning in collaboration. Teachers do not determine in advance the amount of time a particular question or topic will be explored. Instead, children's level of engagement is what drives the length of an inquiry, as teachers want children to explore ideas and topics in depth to maximize the learning opportunities.

Inquiry can enhance equity by supporting children to develop critical-thinking skills and positive attitudes toward diverse ideas, experiences, and perspectives (Souto-Manning, 2013). As children explore questions that interest them, there are many opportunities to draw on a range of resources, stories, and diverse perspectives—especially input from the children and families in the classroom and individuals from their communities—to inform their thinking and learning process. In this way, children can experience firsthand why it is valuable to have many different people contributing to a project or thinking through a challenging problem to construct an effective and meaningful solution.

The Reggio Emilia Approach

The Reggio Emilia approach in early childhood education is very popular across the United States and widely considered to reflect high-quality early childhood pedagogy. Early educators from around the world have been inspired by the

Reggio Emilia early childhood programs for many years. Teachers and administrators regularly travel to the Reggio Emilia region in Italy to see firsthand the schools that have inspired a range of adaptations of the methods and materials used in the Reggio preschools in American early learning settings. Reggio Emilia is described as a philosophy or approach to working with young children and their families and not a specific prescriptive curriculum.

The Reggio Emilia philosophy is very complex. Many comprehensive books and resources are available for educators interested in learning about the Reggio schools in Italy, as are programs that have adapted and implemented the approach in early childhood programs within the United States. Though Reggio-inspired programs in the United States do not all look the same, the following ideas are central to the Reggio philosophy and are commonly observed in programs guided by this approach (Lewin-Benham, 2008):

The image of the child. Our "images of the child" reflect cultural beliefs about what we believe children should know and do at specific ages, what we think they are capable of, and what motivates them to learn or to behave in certain ways and the skills and outcomes we value for their achievement and development (Rogoff, 2003). The image of the child that continues to inspire Reggio-influenced programs everywhere is a powerful learner who is curious, engaged, and capable of co-constructing their own learning process. The image of a child in early learning programs is critical, as the way we perceive children impacts how we interact with them and the way in which we arrange the environment and implement the curriculum.

Relationships, dialogue, and interaction as central to learning. The Reggio philosophy emphasizes that children learn in the context of relationships, and Reggio schools become a central meeting place where relationships between children, teachers, families and the surrounding community are built and nurtured. Conversation and collaborative play and project work in small groups—typically groups of 3–6 children with one or two adults—are important features of Reggio Emilia pedagogy.

The role of the teacher. Teachers have complex multifaceted roles in Reggio classrooms: they are partners, nurturers, guides, and researchers. Reggio teachers consider themselves researchers, and they observe and listen to children more than talking to them or formally directing their learning. These teachers observe children's use of materials and listen to their conversations to learn about the questions children are grappling with, the ideas and hypotheses they are exploring, and the theories of the world they are constructing. Teachers are also guides who wonder and hypothesize with children and explore the use of materials or different solutions to problems in collaboration with children. Teachers also ask open-ended questions and intentionally introduce provocations to spark children's interest and to deepen their exploration, dialogue, and discovery. Teachers also have an important role in arranging the environment—materials, use of space, and time—to be a "third teacher."

> A teaching team launched a provocation using "beautiful junk," collections of found materials that each family sent to school with their child in a small brown lunch bag the teachers provided. The children gathered around excitedly as each child presented their bag and dumped the contents in the middle of the circle. "How can we sort these things? What goes together?" one of the teachers asked. "I see a white bottlecap and a white straw," one child responded as she put those objects together. "I see a tall feather and a long stick, they are both tall," another piped in.

WHAT IS A PROVOCATION?

The Reggio Emilia philosophy of early childhood (Edwards et al., 2011) is the inspiration for the concept of provocations. Using provocations in an early childhood setting, teachers invite children to explore and discover new ideas, relationships, questions, and experiences. Provocations build on children's current knowledge and skills, "provoking" children to deepen and expand their thinking and understanding of the world through discussion, creative exploration, and experimentation and diverse expressions of their ideas through play, text, sound, drawings, and other formats.

Provocations are open ended and invite children's participation and engagement by reflecting the children's interests and the themes and topics under investigation in the classroom. Examples of simple provocations include:

- Loose parts found in nature
- An interesting photograph, book or piece of art
- Items that have cultural and specific meaning to the children's families and/or local communities
- An emerging interest, hypothesis, or question from one child or a group of children
- A school or community event, celebration, or classroom visitor
- Art materials (especially new or unknown materials that invite creativity and exploration), objects, and artifacts

Example provocations:

- What will the children do when they discover mirrors and paints with many different skin tones at choice time?
- How will the children respond when they see colored paper, pens, and tape in the block area?
- What conversations and questions will take place when the children see various Guatemalan textiles on the walls of the classroom?

Curriculum based on children's questions and interests. Teachers in Reggio classrooms do not use a standardized or published curriculum. Instead, the curriculum in Reggio classrooms is emergent, focused on children's engagement in long-term in-depth projects, and collaborative. A curriculum begins with teachers' observations of children. Teachers listen to children's conversations and observe their play to identify what they are curious about, what they talk about in their conversations with peers and adults, what interests them (e.g., topics, materials, concepts), and what problems they want to solve. Teachers use what they learn from the children to plan in-depth project work that children engage in over a period of time, typically in small groups. The curriculum is dynamic and evolves over the course of the year as the children's interests and skills change as well as with each new group of children entering the classroom. The curriculum is co-constructed with teachers who work in collaboration with the children, their families, and the community.

> When children returned from a dance class and it was time to put their shoes back on, a couple of children purposely put on two different shoes. Others followed and soon there was riotous laughter as they mixed up all the shoes. Teachers noticed their delight in talking about buckles, shoelaces, decals, colors, and how much they enjoyed adhering the Velcro fasteners. The teachers decided to launch an investigation of shoes the following week and planned a series of explorations of shoes—making paper shoes, setting up a shoe store in the dramatic play area, and interviewing people in the school about their shoes.

The environment as third teacher. Educators in Reggio Emilia consider the learning environment as a "third teacher." They are very intentional about how they arrange the environment to support children's learning and knowledge construction. Teachers create many opportunities for active engagement with materials, for social interactions with peers and provocations that push them to go deeper in their thinking, and for exploration of a phenomenon (e.g., shadows, balls and ramps, birds, etc.). In addition to the indoor and outdoor classrooms, all Reggio schools have a spacious well-resourced art studio (the atelier), and a large central gathering area (the piazza) that is used for group activities and for children's independent play. The Reggio classroom is designed to invite the children into a space that inspires interaction with peers and provides them with many opportunities for agency and control as they explore materials based on their interests, skills, and internal motivation.

Arts and aesthetics are valued. An atelier (artist's studio) and atelierista (artist/studio teacher) is in every Reggio school. Atelieristas are knowledgeable about supporting children to bring a diverse range of materials into their play and project work to support the expression of their interests and evolving ideas and exploration of theories and relationships about how the world works. Reggio teachers spend a lot of time creating aesthetically beautiful environments for children and adults to spend time in. Everywhere you look there are natural materials, abundant natural light and connections to nature, and the outdoors. Examples of children's artistic expressions are intentionally displayed throughout the school, accompanied by written documentation to tell the learning stories associated with each creative construction.

The metaphor of *The Hundred Languages of Children* is central to Reggio schools and their value for the arts (Edwards et al., 2011). The 100 languages refers to the many ways that children express what they are thinking, feeling, learning, and interested in sharing in communication with others. Examples of these languages include discussions, playing, painting, working with clay, drawing, poetry, music, singing, movement, building, sculpting, songwriting, and many other forms of artistic and creative expression.

Documentation as communication. Documentation is a significant element of the preschool environment in Reggio schools. Because teachers are considered researchers, they are continually documenting children's thinking and learning processes as they engage in the exploration of ideas, topics, or questions in their long-term project work. Documentation aims to capture important moments in children's learning. Teachers take photographs and video recordings of children's exploration of materials, their constructions, and artistic expressions, and other work samples (e.g., drawings, paintings, etc.). They record children's conversations and create transcripts that document their questions, wonderings, theories, solutions, and the many details of their conversations with peers and adults. This research data is mounted and displayed on the walls or assembled into portfolios and then shared with the children, families, visitors, and community members. Documentation is used to better understand children's thinking and to inform ongoing curriculum planning, teachers' professional development, and communication with families about their children's experiences in the classroom, and their progress in learning new skills and expanding their knowledge.

Parents as partners and engagement with the community. The central focus on relationships extends to families and the larger community surrounding the Reggio schools. Families are welcomed to participate in every aspect of the life of the schools. They participate in decisionmaking; inform the curriculum, environment, and documentation of children's learning; and are seen as essential to the interdependent relationships nurtured within the school. Similarly, community members are regularly involved with the school and inform the dialogue, topics, and issues addressed and the collective care of the children.

REFLECTION AND DISCUSSION QUESTIONS

- The Reggio Emilia approach challenges us to think about our "image of the child." What is your view of the child? What is your preschool staff's view? How does it compare to Reggio's view of the child as strong, curious, and capable?
- Reggio-inspired programs adopt elements that enhance their work with children. What elements of the Reggio Emilia approach do you think might enhance the program at your site?

Anji Play

Anji Play is a fairly recent approach to early childhood education that is rapidly gaining popularity with early childhood teachers across the United States and among interdisciplinary scholars and childhood advocates around the world. In fact, many early childhood experts describe Anji Play as one of the most inspiring approaches to high-quality early childhood in the world today.

Anji County, a mountainous mostly rural area in eastern Zhejiang Province in the People's Republic of China, is the birthplace of educator Cheng Xueqin, the Director of Early Education, Anji County Department of Education. Ms. Cheng is the creator of the Anji Play approach to early education currently used in public kindergartens across China serving children ages 3–6 years. She was committed to creating an early education program in which children and their teachers would experience joy, love, and authentic engagement. Anji Play is rooted in a deep commitment to social justice and equity and a belief that it is every child's human right to experience True Play (True Play is child self-determined play). Creating opportunities for True Play in the Anji kindergartens is, in Ms. Cheng's words, "a way of returning the right of play back to the child" (Cheng, 2015).

Anji Play is an "ecology of learning" rooted in relationships between children, teachers, administrators, families, policymakers, and communities. The five guiding principles of Anji Play are *love, risk, joy, engagement, and reflection* shared among the children, their families, and their teachers. These principles are supported through several foundational beliefs and practices implemented in Anji Play early childhood environments. Observers visiting Anji Play kindergartens will see:

Children's self-determined play. The concept of self-determined play is rooted in a belief that children are most engaged in their learning when they are supported to have agency and control in every aspect of their learning process. The teachers in the Anji kindergartens believe it is children's right to be fully responsible for their learning through play. As a result, in the

Figure 5.2. Risk Taking in Anji Play

| Figure 5.2.1: Balancing on Wood | Figure 5.2.2: Jumping from a Ladder |

Anji kindergartens, children guide every aspect of their play—the direction, flow, use of materials, playmates, plans, and outcomes. Children are trusted to ask and explore their own questions, to define and solve their own problems, and to make meaning of their world through active engagement with materials and collaboration with peers.

Children taking risks (see Figure 5.2). Children in Anji kindergartens are given freedom to manage the amount of risk they take while learning and playing. The teachers observe the children at play and intervene in extraordinary situations, but most of the time, the children manage risk on their own. Teachers believe that children are capable of effectively engaging in self-assessment of risk, so they are allowed to determine what they can handle when exploring materials, solving a problem, or experimenting with an emerging skill or idea. It's common in Anji kindergartens to see children having conversations and even debates about safety and risk. They problem solve with one another about how to make adjustments in their play constructions and activities to improve safety or to increase the level of challenge. Ms. Cheng states, "without risk, there is no ability to solve problems. Without problem solving, there is no learning" (Cheng, 2015).

The role of the teacher (see Figure 5.3). Teachers in Anji Play programs see themselves as responsible for creating environments that support children's deep learning and to continually strive to build awareness about children's insights and understandings about the world. A fundamental part of the teacher's role in Anji Play is to be a careful observer. The teachers in

Figure 5.3. The Role of the Teacher in Anji Play

An Anji teacher documenting children's block play using a tablet to capture video clips and photographs.

the Anji kindergartens do not lead or guide children through preplanned or sequenced learning experiences. Instead, they are asked to step back and to observe play without interrupting or interjecting their own ideas or directing children's play toward certain outcomes. Teachers offer as little help as necessary and intervene only on rare occasions to ensure the children's safety and well-being. Teachers are continually documenting children's play by recording photos and videos of children's activities and materials; conversations and interactions; interests, questions, dilemmas, conflicts, experimentation, hypotheses, and problem-solving efforts; and discoveries. This documentation is used to guide children's reflection and discussion about their learning.

Minimally structured environments. The indoor and outdoor environments in Anji Play are intentionally very minimally structured in order to support the expression of children's interests, ideas, and self-determined play. The environment is organized to support children's flexibility to move freely from one area to another and to have opportunities for collaborative play with peers as well as solitary play. A wide variety of materials are organized in bins and containers on the perimeter of the outdoor environments. They are entirely open ended, with no specific directions for their use; instead, children are trusted to let their interests guide not only which materials they select for their play, but also how they use these materials within their environment. Common materials in Anji Play kindergartens include ladders, wooden stilts, wooden blocks in various shapes and sizes, tires, ropes, soft mats, PVC pipe, balls, scarves, blankets and sheets, baskets and bowls, scoops, buckets, shovels, magnifying glasses, boxes, and bins of all shapes and sizes.

SELECTING MATERIALS IN ANJI PLAY KINDERGARTENS

Teachers select materials that support children to engage in True Play. After introducing a new material, they spend time observing how children use it. Several questions guide their assessment of materials:

- Does it encourage children's collaboration with peers?
- Does it support problem solving and the expression of creativity? Imagination? Symbolic thinking?
- Does it support children's risk taking?
- Does it support engagement and children's expression of joy?
- Does it support children to bring their own meaning to the play?
- Does it have cultural relevance to the children and families? Can the materials be found within the local community?

Teachers engage in a continuous cycle of observing children's use of materials in the environments, reflecting on what the children are learning and discussing their observations with their colleagues and then adapting the materials and environment based on what they learn about the children. If a certain material is not leading to complex and collaborative play, they may decide to remove it and consider an alternative. In contrast, if materials support children's self-determined play, collaboration, and learning, they are more likely to keep them in the environment.

Sharing and play stories: children's co-construction of meaning of their play (see Figures 5.4). After their extended periods of morning play and clean up, children return inside to their classrooms and teachers lead them through a process they call "play sharing," in which children are provided with space and time to collaboratively discuss, analyze, and reflect on their "stories of play." During play sharing, teachers carefully select photographs and/ or video clips just captured that morning during their observations of the children's play. The teacher asks the children open-ended questions and she encourages them to discuss the details of their play together ("Tell me about your play. What were you talking about here?"). This dialogue and reflection support the children to interpret and co-construct meaning about their play with their classmates. It also makes visible for the teachers and the children all the complex ideas children are thinking through, the questions they are asking, the hypotheses they are testing, and the various skills they are learning within their play. Teachers allow and encourage the children to engage in discussion and debate and they hold back from offering their own opinions and perspectives (see Figure 5.4.1).

Children are also invited to sit at round tables in small groups and asked to draw a picture or a "play story" that documents their morning play (see Figure 5.4.2). Children choose which aspects of their play they would like to document. As the children draw their play stories, they talking with one another, and they often retell a story verbally while also drawing it on paper. Creating the play stories supports the children to continue to co-construct meaning of their play with their peers while also helping them learn how to represent their experiences symbolically. Teachers often compile these stories into books that are shared with parents and family members, and teachers use this documentation for their own professional learning.

Anji Play is an innovative approach to early childhood that places children's right to play at the center. Anji Play supports complex learning and self-regulation through self-determined play. Many teachers in the United States are learning about Anji Play and are actively exploring ways to integrate elements of this approach into their early childhood classrooms.

REFLECTION AND DISCUSSION QUESTIONS

- What elements of Anji Play could you envision in the preschool at your school? Ask your teachers to take some pictures of their students playing. Then ask them what aspects of the five guiding principles of Anji Play (love, risk, joy, engagement, and reflection) they observed.
- Consider the criteria for choosing materials in the Anji Play classroom. Which criteria would you like to see used when selecting materials for the preschool at your site?
- Anji Play sees a productive role for risk taking in play. What level of risk taking do you feel optimally balances learning and safety?

Antibias Education

Young children notice differences. But it is the adult world that assigns value to those differences, and children quickly pick up on those values. As young children construct their unique identities and find their place in the world, the early childhood classroom can embrace differences in a way that is full of wonder and curiosity without assigning judgment. Children also notice unfairness. They can be vigilant about routine things like taking turns, who goes first, and who got a bigger ball of playdough, but they also notice who gets reprimanded, who is excluded, and who the teacher feels more comfortable with. Children notice that some people's identities have more status, more

Figure 5.4. Play Sharing and Play Stories

Figure 5.4.1: Play Sharing

The teacher projects a photo taken during the morning play session and asks the children in the picture to stand up one at a time and describe what they see. She then asks, "Have they explained it completely?" and invites the children who were not in the photo to describe what they see happening. The following day she shares a minute-long video clip and ask all the children, "What is happening in this play? Tell us the story of your play."

Figure 5.4.2: Play Stories

A child in an Anji kindergarten sharing her play story with peers.

power, and more opportunities than others. It is no surprise, then (as noted in Chapter 3), that young children are already aware of racial differences, are learning racial stereotypes and biases from their environments, and, sadly, many have already experienced racism and bias directly (see Chapter 7 for discussion of exclusionary discipline and racism in early childhood).

WHAT IS THE ROLE OF PRESCHOOL IN EDUCATION FOR SOCIAL JUSTICE?

Social justice starts with affirming each child's identity and an awareness of others. Ensuring that every child is validated for who they are, who their family is, and the communities they belong to provides a foundation for embracing the identities of others. Being curious about other people and discussing how we are both alike and different supports the development of empathy and solidarity that provides the basis for considering justice and fairness.

Antibias education (ABE) is a perspective, not a curriculum that is intended to influence every aspect of early childhood education—including teachers' interactions with children, families, and colleagues (Derman-Sparks et al., 2020). ABE strives to "identify and prevent, as much as possible, the harmful emotional and psychological impacts on children from societal prejudice and bias" (p. 4). ABE diverges from what educators may know as "multicultural education" through goals that address justice as well as identity.

Antibias education aims to support children to develop:

- A confident sense of their identity without needing to feel superior to others
- Respect for and comfort with human diversity
- An understanding and approach to talking about fairness and justice
- The ability to stand up for themselves and others (Derman-Sparks et al., 2020)

ABE Goal 1: Identity. Each child will demonstrate self-awareness, confidence, family pride, and positive social identities. Early childhood teachers have an important responsibility to support young children to develop a sense of pride in themselves and in their families and communities. This includes guiding each child to develop positive associations with their social identities. This might look like:

"I like to wear my braids like this, like my mom. She is soooo beautiful!"

"I love my family; they work a lot and I can help them."

PERSONAL IDENTITY VERSUS SOCIAL IDENTITY

Just like adults, children have multiple intersecting identities that reflect their individuality as well as their membership in social groups (Derman-Sparks et al., 2020). These identities carry both positive and negative connotations in the larger society, resulting in privilege as well as stereotyping and bias. As individuals, children have unique personalities, interests, abilities, preferences, approaches, and personal relationships. At the same time, they are members of various social groups defined by gender and racial identity, culture, language, religion, citizenship status, and socioeconomic class, among other social categories.

ABE Goal 2: Diversity. Each child will express comfort and joy with human diversity; accurate language for human differences; and deep, caring human connections. Early childhood teachers can guide children from their earliest years—and while their brains are developing—to create positive associations with diversity. This happens when teachers regularly talk about and expose children to human differences in the classroom and reinforce messages that all people's social identities, families, and cultural ways of knowing, lifestyles, and differences have value and should be respected.

> "Alex is transgender and a boy."

> In a conversation about favorite foods, Kenji shares that he ate rice for dinner the preceding evening. Krystal excitedly shouts out, "I had rice, too! I ate it with gravy." Juan adds, "I had rice with beans."

ABE Goal 3: Justice. Each child will increasingly recognize unfairness, have language to describe unfairness, and understand that unfairness hurts. Preschool teachers guided by ABE are keenly aware that they have a responsibility to guide children to learn about justice and injustice. They help children learn language they can use to talk about justice and injustice not only within their classroom but also within their communities and world around them. Preschool teachers guide children to learn about justice and injustice by observing and responding to the language, topics, ideas, perspectives, and concerns that children bring into their play, conversations, and daily interactions in the classroom.

Early childhood classrooms inspired by ABE intentionally and consistently build children's awareness that unfairness hurts and that we all have a responsibility to learn about how we contribute to harming others through the language we use, the stories we tell, and the actions we take. Preschool teachers intentionally intervene when they observe children excluding others based on social identities (e.g., "Nobody with brown skin can pull the wagon.") or using stereotypes (e.g., "Only boys can run fast."). Children are also taught that our society is unjust and that some individuals and groups are treated differently based on their social identities.

ABE Goal 4: Activism. Each child will demonstrate empowerment and the skills to act, with others or alone, against prejudice and/or discriminatory actions. Early childhood teachers in ABE-inspired classrooms go beyond teaching children about injustice; they support them to become advocates for themselves and others, speaking up and acting in response to unfairness. The goal is to be honest and transparent with children about the existence of injustice but also to teach them that they have agency and can take actions—individually or working together with others—to make positive changes about the things that matter to them.

> An older student teases a preschooler's attempt to climb to the top of the play structure. Another young child notices and speaks up, "He can do it. Don't bother him."

> Ronan arrives at school upset; he has been noticing more and more people living in tents or vans. The class, with the help of their teacher, decide to write to their city to ask for more food and services for their community.

How can the picture books we read impact children's concepts of diversity and inclusion? The stories we tell through the books we read influence children's concept of what is "normal," acceptable, and valued in the world. If children are read a steady diet of books with only White characters in conventional middle-class settings, both White children and children of color begin to establish Whiteness as an unexamined standard. This makes nonrepresented groups into "others" that deviate from the norm.

In her classic essay, "Mirrors, Windows, and Sliding Glass Doors," Bishop (1990) calls on educators to ensure that all children see themselves represented in books. Windows to other worlds are important; but too often, BIPOC (Black, Indigenous, and People of Color) children are provided only windows. All children need mirrors of their lived experience and the people dear to them. They need to see the joy of their communities represented in contemporary real-life settings rather than as an exoticized version of their culture or a portrayal of victimization absent resilience and resistance.

What if the children are all White? If children are in an all-White environment, it is even more crucial that they are provided with "windows" that expand their awareness of diversity because "if they see only reflections of themselves, they will grow up with an exaggerated sense of their own importance and value in the world—a dangerous ethnocentrism" (Bishop, 1990, p. 3). As we have seen throughout this book, children are active and self-motivated learners; this applies to social concepts, values, and categories as well. Discussions of race and racism and bias have become more commonplace in recent years but, sadly, racism in everyday interactions as well as systemic racism is a daily reality of life and permeates every aspect of children's lives. As Derman-Sparks and Ramsey (2011) ask, what are the children learning? If children don't see their parents interacting with BIPOC children and adults as friends, neighbors, and colleagues or, if they observe people making derogatory comments based on the color of someone's skin or another social category of identity, what ideas about diversity are the children learning about themselves and others? This type of question is central to preschool classrooms that integrate an antibias approach to education.

RESISTING A STANDARDIZED AND SCRIPTED CURRICULUM

Commercial textbook series adopted for elementary grades attempt to ensure equity of access by standardizing the scope of sequence of content as well the pedagogical approach outlined in units and lesson plans. Some textbook products go as far as scripting dialogue for teachers to deliver to students. Standardized and scripted curriculum products have trickled down to the preschool level, leaving principals to consider whether these materials would support efforts to offer a high-quality preschool program at their sites.

RIGID, SKILLS-FOCUSED, TEACHER-SCRIPTED CURRICULA ARE **NOT** DEVELOPMENTALLY RESPONSIVE

The NAEYC (2020) warns, "Rigid, narrowly defined, skills-focused, and highly teacher-scripted curricula that do not provide flexibility for adapting to individual skills and interests are not developmentally appropriate (p. 25).

> A standardized curriculum that is designed to replicate outcomes often eliminates all possibility of spontaneous inquiry, stealing potential moments of learning from students and teachers in a cookie-cutter approach to education in the classroom. Given the diversity of the children we teach, accepting a canned recipe for teaching, evaluation, and assessment is problematic at best. Each child we teach is unique, requiring us to use our own judgment, instead of rules, to guide our teaching practice. To teach well, educators must ensure that creativity and innovation are always present. Although good teaching requires organization and routines, it is never inflexible and rarely routine. It dances with surprise. It pursues wonder. It finds joy at every turn. (Biermeier, 2015)

A Standardized Curriculum Limits the Potential of a Preschool Program

Educational publishers are in the publishing business, so they strive to create products that appeal to a mass market. This means that they take generic approaches to curriculum content and teaching practices they perceive as "safe" but may not relate to the children in any specific program. This limits children's ability to build new knowledge based on their prior knowledge. Preschoolers are immersed in rich worlds that they are observing and learning from every minute. They blend their prior knowledge with new information to create or challenge new knowledge. For example, a standardized curriculum might feature a unit on "snow" during the winter months. However, a child in the state of Washington is stomping in puddles and hanging on to an umbrella on a windy winter day. The snow unit misses the opportunity for children to build concepts and vocabulary based on familiar experiences and instead focuses on something that is quite abstract to them. While it is important to expose children to phenomena new to them, deeper learning is built by expanding existing schema.

By directing teachers to use specific dialogue, a scripted curriculum limits the potential for interaction between children and teachers. Preschool children are associative, and a word or an idea mentioned in a lesson or story prompts them to make a connection to their lives. These are rich connections that teachers can capitalize on to build oral language and related concepts. The scripted approach also conveys a lack of confidence in teachers to "read the room" and build on the moment. It suggests that there is a "correct" way to deliver a lesson and devalues modifications based on what teachers know about their students as individuals. It shifts teachers from professionals to technicians.

How Can We Use Our Adopted Preschool Curriculum as a Resource Rather Than as a Script?

Teachers personalize their approaches based on their own expertise, preferences, and knowledge of the assets and needs of their students. Rather than forcing them "underground" or making excuses for departing from the curriculum, principals can encourage innovation. An adopted curriculum provides ideas, structure, and approaches that teachers may not have considered and can be used as a valuable resource. However, principals can give the strong message that the teacher is the expert on their group of students and is trusted to make instructional decisions based on their knowledge.

REFLECTION AND DISCUSSION QUESTION

- Explore the curriculum that you have adopted. Ask your teachers to identify a concept or skill that they are expected to teach. Then ask them how they made modifications to the scripted materials so that the teaching and the learning was meaningful to their children.

KEY TAKEAWAYS FOR PRINCIPALS

- Principals can remind teachers that an adopted curriculum should be used as the springboard for concepts they are already planning to teach. They should encourage teachers to be creative and to develop lesson plans that are truly developmentally and culturally appropriate for the children they serve.
- To select curriculum, principals and teaching staff can carefully examine a proposed curriculum to determine whether it:
    - » Is developmentally appropriate.
    - » Is adaptable/flexible enough to meet the needs of the children being served, including the needs of emergent bilingual/multilingual learners.
    - » Is culturally diverse and mirrors the lives of the children, families, and community.
    - » Accommodates different learning modalities (audio, visual, kinesthetic, etc.).
    - » Addresses equity and includes antiracist and antibias content and teaching strategies.
    - » Allows the teacher to develop and learn new skills and strategies to become an effective educator (versus being scripted).
    - » Was developed solely by experts or also included teachers, families and others in the field of early childhood and/or community.

CHAPTER 6

Instruction in the Early Childhood Classroom

Preschool teachers arrange the environment to support a variety of learning formats and contexts.

Each type of learning format—individualized, large-group, small-group, and learning centers—has its own characteristics and value in supporting young children's learning and development. A typical preschool day is arranged to provide children with opportunities to participate in a variety of formats. Preschool children spend the majority of their time in small-group and center work, as these are the most appropriate contexts to support their learning. Circle time and large-group instruction are less effective with young children and scheduled for only short periods of time to match their developmental capabilities and attention spans. The environment is planned with an understanding that children need physical activity and movement throughout the day.

Each learning format offers benefits for young learners. Preschool teachers consider which learning context will help an individual child to experience a sense of joy and engagement while they are making progress on their personal learning goals. Preschool environments are arranged to invite collaboration and peer interaction and provide many opportunities for children to support each other's learning in pairs or in small groups (NAEYC, 2020).

THE IMPORTANCE OF INDIVIDUALIZING

Preschool teachers arrange the environment to create meaningful, accessible, and responsive learning experiences for every child. They consider each child's unique interests, prior experiences, skills and abilities, relationships, and individual learning goals when selecting materials and learning activities for the classroom. Teachers understand that every child should "see" themselves and their families—their cultures, language(s), and communities—represented in the classroom. Additionally, working in consultation with children's families, school staff, and when appropriate, interdisciplinary specialists, preschool teachers make adjustments to the environment to be inclusive of any child with special needs and/or disabilities.

Large-Group Activities

Large-group activities typically include the whole class and are the least effective format for supporting and engaging young children. The value of large-group activities is primarily in supporting children to come together to build a sense of community with one another or to have a shared experience— reading a storybook together, taking a class vote, sharing highlights from the day's playful activities, or participating in a movement activity together (yoga, mindfulness, freeze dance, etc.). Large-group activities should invite children's active engagement (e.g., singing, movement, sharing ideas, or turn and talk with classmate). Preschool children should not be asked to sit still and listen to the teacher talk for long periods of time. Similarly, asking children to wait while every child in the class takes a turn talking (e.g., show and tell) is not developmentally appropriate for this age and should be avoided or limited.

Small-Group Activities

Working with a small group of children (typically 4–8) is a common format in preschool classrooms and a very effective way to support young children's learning. Small groups allow teachers to work with children in a more intimate manner. Teachers can carefully observe children's exploration of materials, facilitate a conversation, guide children's problem solving, introduce a new idea or skill, and individualize the type and amount of support they provide to each child as they engage in different activities.

Use of Centers or Interest Areas

Another format used to support learning in an early childhood classroom are learning centers (sometimes called "interest areas"). These are areas in the classroom where children learn about a particular subject or have opportunities to engage in certain types of play or to use specific learning materials. Examples of preschool centers or interest areas include:

- Block play area
- Dramatic play area
- Sensory play area (e.g., sand and water play)
- Art area

- Computer/technology center
- Listening center
- Library/book nook area
- Cozy/calm-down area
- Games and puzzles area
- Math manipulative area
- Literacy/writing area
- Discovery area or science center
- Music and movement center
- Readers' theater center (playing with puppets)

As children engage with the materials and activities within a center, teachers are:

- Observing, listening, and documenting what they see
- Asking thoughtful questions
- Offering support when needed
- Talking with the students to better understand their ideas and feelings
- Scaffolding as appropriate to help children make discoveries and connections
- Sharing information

PLAY AS A PRIMARY CONTEXT FOR TEACHING AND LEARNING

Play is so important to optimal child development that it has been recognized by the United Nations High Commission for Human Rights as a right of every child. (Ginsburg et al., 2007, p. 183)

Play is the primary way preschool children learn, and it has always been at the center of the preschool curriculum. Play supports children's development and learning in many ways. Through play, children:

- *Learn about their interests, strengths, and capabilities, and experience joy.* As they play, children also gain new knowledge, build and extend their skills, and develop essential dispositions needed for learning in school, and for living a healthy and happy life.
- *Explore their identities.* Children experiment with the messages and social norms in society. Through play, children make sense of familial, cultural, and societal roles and norms—exploring what it feels like to conform and to resist as they experiment with different

possibilities. Children communicate in play their perceptions of who they are and what they desire and imagine as future versions of who they can become.

- *Learn about what is valued in their families and communities and the society around them.* They are also trying to make sense of inequities they observe all around them related to social identities including race, ethnicity, gender, ability, income, and other factors.

- *Manage and communicate big and overwhelming feelings and cope with the stressful or traumatic experiences and events in their lives.* Many times, during play is the only time children can bring their big emotions (fear, worry, sadness, anger) and concerns, as they do not have language to talk about them, their stress-response systems are activated, and they don't have access to their higher brain function, including language, or talking about the topic or experience is too overwhelming or frightening.

- *Learn about other children's feelings, thoughts, ideas, values, and unique differences.* Through play, children can learn that others have different ideas, thoughts, feelings, or opinions. And through play, children can explore different ideas, perspectives, and ways of thinking.

- *Build social connections and friendships and navigate the complexities of relationships.* Children learn to read social cues; have two-way conversations; play with others; listen to, respect, and value differences; negotiate social dilemmas; and build problem-solving skills in the context of relationships.

PLAY-BASED LEARNING ACROSS A CONTINUUM

Play-based learning is an approach to curriculum and instruction in the preschool classroom that emphasizes the use of play to support children's learning across all domains of their development. Teachers carefully plan for play *and* they allow for flexibility and invite children's spontaneous play and emergent interests and discoveries (Gronlund & Rendon, 2017).

There are many different types of play-based learning experiences that are supported in a high-quality preschool classroom. Teachers have different roles and responsibilities in each. It is helpful to think of the diverse play-based learning contexts as falling along a continuum that includes child self-determined play, adult–child collaborative play, and adult-planned and directed play (see Tables 6.1, 6.2 and 6.3; Jensen et al., 2019; Zosh et al., 2018). Preschool teachers plan for children to engage in all types of play-based learning across the continuum, as each form offers distinct opportunities for children's growth and development.

Preschool teachers consider several factors when making decisions about the frequency and balance of different types of play across the continuum. Teachers have to thoughtfully consider:

- The developmental needs and interests of the specific group of children
- The philosophy of their school or early childhood program
- The cultural backgrounds and goals of the children's families
- The events happening in society (health pandemic, natural disaster, etc.)
- The group's emerging interests

We know from research that preschool children need:

- Many opportunities to engage in child self-determined play
- Daily opportunities to be guided through adult–child collaborative play
- Limited time spent in teacher-planned and teacher-directed play

It is helpful to think about children's play as representing different points along a continuum (see Figure 6.1; CDE, 2021a, Jensen et al., 2019; Zosh et al., 2018). In high-quality early childhood classrooms, teachers plan for children to participate in a variety of different types of play across this continuum. Young children need many opportunities to participate in self-determined play, and early childhood teachers continuously scaffold their learning through adult–child collaborative play. In contrast, adult-planned and directed play should be limited in early childhood programs. Each program and school will establish the right balance of these different types of play as they consider what approach is responsive to the developmental levels, interests, and cultural backgrounds of the children they are serving, in addition to the goals of the families, the state or district learning standards, and the philosophy of the early childhood program or school. Effective teachers will consider all these factors when planning for the integration of different forms of play to support children's learning throughout the day.

Child Self-Determined Play

Child self-determined play is a foundation of young children's healthy learning and development (CDE, 2021a). It is essential that children in early childhood classrooms have daily opportunities to engage in self-determined play. Table 6.1 describes the characteristics and teachers' roles in this form of play.

Figure 6.1. Play-Based Learning Continuum

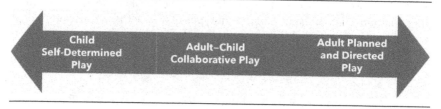

In a preschool classroom, child self-determined play looks like the following:

> A child in the classroom takes all the books off the shelves and sets up a library. She makes special library cards for children to check out her books. She even makes a sign that says "SHHH (Quiet)" and says to the other kids playing with her, "I am going to be the librarian and you are all checking books out from me at the library."

> It just rained and a few of the children decide to make "mud pies" with their small tins. They build a whole store where they sell their mud pies to other children.

> Using the tub of Unifix© cubes, two boys work together to make a line of cubes that stretch the entire length of the classroom.

Adult–Child Collaborative Play

In adult–child collaborative play, teachers are entering children's play to provide different levels of support and guidance—minimal, moderate, or

Table 6.1. Child Self-Determined Play

CHILDREN:	TEACHERS:
Have freedom, responsibility, and agency to direct their own play. Children make choices about the direction, focus, and learning goals associated with their play. Children select the play activities and materials that most interest them. Through their self-directed play, they explore materials, ideas, hypotheses and questions, and solutions to problems. In doing so, they make discoveries and construct knowledge individually and in collaboration with others.	Observe and listen to children as they play in order to discover and document the topics, interests, and problems they are exploring. Arrange the environment and plan the curriculum in ways that support and extend children's interests, learning, and development. Extend and deepen children's play through additions to the environment and curriculum based on the children's interests.

Table 6.2. Adult–Child Collaborative Play

CHILDREN:	TEACHERS:
Initiate and have agency to inform the focus and direction of their play experiences. They choose the types of play, materials, and roles based on their interests and internal motivations.	Carefully observe and follow the children's lead and interests. Build on and extend children's ideas, exploration, problem solving, creative thinking, and discoveries. Might participate in a selection of activities, materials, and play partners. Provide different levels of support and guidance based on children's developmental needs and children's requests or to offer support, increase engagement, or extend their thinking and learning (skills, knowledge, and dispositions).

more intensive (CDE, 2021a). Together, children and adults contribute to the direction, flow, and outcomes associated with the play. Table 6.2 outlines the characteristics of adult–child collaborative play and teachers' roles and responsibilities in this play.

In a preschool classroom, the continuum of adult–child collaborative play looks like the following:

Minimal guidance. A teacher sits on the rug next to a child who is building with Legos. She narrates what she sees the child doing, "You put a green Lego on the very top of the building." Or, the teacher introduces a large cardboard box to the dramatic play area and observes how the children incorporate it into their play.

Moderate guidance. After children keep asking if they can save their block buildings instead of cleaning them up each day, a teacher brings in wood scraps and white glue and invites them to construct buildings that they can keep. Or, after observing children's interest in insects during their outdoor play, the teacher offers magnifying glasses and introduces books on insects into the classroom library or reads a story about insects during circle time.

More intense guidance. After Halloween, a group of children continue to be very interested in spiders. The teaching team collects informational texts featuring spiders and invites the students to page through the books and tell them what they see. One teacher takes dictation on a chart as students share their discoveries. Or, for some children with disabilities, the teacher might provide more intense guidance (e.g., helping them enter and participate with a group of children exploring with paints or playing at the water table), allowing the children to have more autonomy in their play.

"If a child initiates a context for play and then an adult intervenes to direct the play within that context, we enter co-opted play, not guided play. The child might have been interested in building a circus out of blocks, yet the well-intentioned [adult] swept in to declare that the animals were at the zoo, redirecting the child's vision and robbing her of some agency in the play experience. When adults initiate and direct using playful elements, the scene more closely resembles direct instruction—even if it is dressed up in playful 'clothing' (Zosh et al., 2018, p. 3).

Adult-Planned and Directed Play

In adult-planned and directed play, adults are in charge and lead children through preplanned activities directed toward the development of specific concepts and skills (CDE, 2021a). Table 6.3 describes the characteristics of adult-planned and directed play and teachers' roles and responsibilities in this play.

In a preschool classroom, adult-planned and directed play looks like the following:

> After students have shared the characteristics of spiders they noticed in informational texts about spiders, a teacher provides playdough and pipe cleaners and asks the children to create spiders. She shows a detailed photograph of a spider and leads children in counting the legs. She asks if they can put that many legs on the spider.

> A teacher reads the story *Brown Bear Brown Bear, What Do You See?* by Bill Martin Jr. and Eric Carle featuring a series of animals (brown bear, yellow

Table 6.3. Adult-Planned and Directed Play

CHILDREN:	TEACHERS:
Follow along with adult directions. Should be actively engaged in the play activity/experience.	Plan, initiate, and direct the children's play. They direct the focus, rules, direction and outcomes, and learning goals associated with the play.
	Plan and prepare environments, materials, and activities that encourage children to practice specific concepts, skills, and dispositions, expand their understanding of specific information, and result in predetermined outcomes.
	Provide different levels of guidance and support, depending on the intended learning goal and children's developmental levels and skills.

duck, blue dog, etc.). He has prepared a copy of the illustration for each animal from the book. He asks children to retell the story by acting it out using the copies of the illustrations.

Children listen as a group during circle time and follow the directions to a freeze dance song in order to strengthen their listening and self-regulation skills.

THE BENEFITS OF PLAY FOR CHILDREN'S LEARNING AND DEVELOPMENT

Play supports children's learning and development across every domain of their development. As discussed in Chapter 2, decades of research reveal that children learn best when several conditions are present, all of which are possible through play:

- They are active and engaged and have opportunities for exploration, hypothesis testing/problem solving, experimentation, and discovery.
- They feel safe, their social–emotional needs are met, and they have many opportunities to interact with responsive and caring adults and peers.
- New information builds on what they already know and reflects their daily lives and familiar language(s) and family, cultural, and community practices.
- The process is emphasized as much as the outcomes.
- Their diverse and individualized interests and needs are supported.

Play builds and strengthens children's cognitive development (Fisher et al., 2013; Reikeras et al., 2017), language and literacy development (Roskos & Christie, 2007; Souto-Manning & Yoon, 2018), social and emotional development (Barker et al., 2014; Bodrova & Leong, 2007; Knight, 2009; Ramani, 2012), physical development (Van Hoorn et al., 2010), and beliefs about diversity, fairness, equity, and social justice (Adair et al., 2017; Derman-Sparks et al., 2020). More specifically, the following skills and dispositions are developed through play:

Cognitive Development

- Language and communication skills
- Problem solving
- Mathematical and scientific thinking
- Perspective taking and empathy
- Abstract thinking and representational abilities

- Attention and memory skills
- Imagination and creativity

Language and Literacy Development

- Symbolic processes and attaching meaning to objects
- Vocabulary
- Narrative structure
- Language behavior in play is related to literate language

Social and Emotional Development

- Social skills (e.g., taking turns, collaborating, following rules)
- Labeling and expressing emotions
- Self-regulation and executive functioning skills
- Positive identity and self-esteem

Physical Development

- Muscle development
- Coordination
- Health hygiene
- Reduces/prevents obesity

Beliefs About Diversity, Fairness, Equity, and Social Justice

- Awareness and respect for diversity in themselves and others
- Confidence and ability to express opinions and make choices/decisions individually or in collaboration with others
- Strengthens ability to solve conflicts or problems peacefully through conversation, negotiation, or voting on a solution
- Awareness about what is fair/unfair, how it feels to be harmed, and inequality in the world around them

DIFFERENT TYPES OF PLAY THAT SUPPORT LEARNING AND DEVELOPMENT

Children need opportunities to engage in many different types of play, as each play context supports development of different types of skills and dispositions (see Table 6.4). Creating preschool environments with different types of play experiences and allowing children to have opportunities to choose the types of activities that most interest them enhances their engagement and motivation to learn. Scholars and practitioners have grouped play in different ways. The categories listed in Table 6.4 are often used to represent the different types of play in early childhood (Brown & Vaughn, 2009; CDE, 2021a; Frost et al., 2012).

Table 6.4. Different Types of Childhood Play

Physical Play (Body play and movement)	Physical play incudes activities such as running, jumping, riding a tricycle, or climbing a play structure or playing games that require movement (tag, hide and seek). Children develop many skills through physical play, including muscle strength and coordination. *Examples of Physical Play in Preschool* • Riding tricycles • Pushing heavy logs or pulling a wagon around the yard • Throwing a ball • Climbing play structures • Building an obstacle course
Object Play	Children imagine, build, and create things with a range of materials, explore objects, discover patterns, experiment with and test their ideas, and solve problems. *Examples of Object Play in Preschool* • Building a tower with Legos • Creating an intricate pathway of roads throughout a town using blocks • Crumpling up paper and using tape to make a soccer ball and playing soccer with it outdoors
Social Play	Children interact with others in social play. They develop and strengthen interpersonal skills, friendships, communication skills, negotiation skills, self-regulation, persistence in solving problems, turn-taking, sharing, competition, and cooperation. Social play also supports children to increase their understanding of their unique identities and how they are similar to and different from others. *Examples of Social Play in Preschool* • "Let's race . . . ready, set, go . . ." • "Let's pretend we're at the grocery store. I'll be the shopper and you be at the checkout."
Imaginative or Pretend Play	While engaged in imaginative play, children explore a range of roles, possibilities, and situations that often expand beyond what they are familiar with in their everyday lives. Pretend play provides many opportunities for children to be creative, be imaginative, feel powerful, and learn to process and express their emotions. Imaginative play is also an important context in which children can learn new vocabulary or experiment with new languages and deepen their understanding of a wide variety of information and ideas.

(Continued)

Table 6.4. *(continued)*

	Examples of Imaginative Play in Preschool
	• A group of 3-year-olds asks the teacher for some cardboard boxes. They're playing "moving," they announce. Tiffany is the mother. Romana is her sister. They fold the dress-up clothes and then pack them and the doll's dishes in the boxes. As they play together they are using both English and Spanish words. • A child may get out a toy bowl and spoon, pretend to pour cereal into the bowl, add some milk, and serve it to a doll. • A child pretending to be a doctor might say to another child, "I'm the doctor, you be the patient, OK? Where does it hurt?" Or a child pretending to be a police officer pulls other kids off the road to give them a ticket.
Storytelling–Narrative Play	Children learn a tremendous amount about themselves, their families, communities, cultures, and the larger world by listening to others' stories, telling their own stories or retelling stories they've heard, and acting out stories. Children's stories in play are sometimes real, sometimes imaginary, and often a combination of both. *Examples of Storytelling–Narrative Play in Preschool* • Brian says, "My big brother works at McDonald's and we get free hamburger and french fries. One time I went to visit him, and he gave me an ice cream that was the best. I want to work at McDonald's, too."
Creative/Expressive Play	Creative and expressive play supports children's self-expression of their thoughts, feelings, ideas, questions, wonderings, dreams, and more through various forms of art, including digital art, music, dance, theater, poetry/spoken word, writing, and other artistic forms. *Examples of Creative/Expressive Play in Preschool* • A child in the classroom recently experienced falling into a pool but was saved immediately by their parent. However, throughout the week, the teachers noticed she drew several pictures of pools of water with a child under the water. The teachers knew that she was expressing her experience through her drawings.

Table 6.4. (*continued*)

Virtual/Digital Play	Many children engage in play that involves the use of digital technologies, including video and computer games, Internet sites, electronic toys, mobile technologies, cellphones, tablets, and the creation of digital content (e.g., playing *Minecraft* on a computer; using digital apps; texting, sharing, and creatively enhancing photographs and video clips on the phone). Digital play can be solitary, though it is most often social in nature. *Examples of Virtual/Digital Play in Preschool* • Marissa and her dad are using an app to take a photo of themselves and turn their faces into funny dogs or cats. She shares these funny creations with her teachers.
Language Play	Language play involves children's playful and often inventive use of sounds, rhymes, poetry/spoken word, riddles and jokes, and songs. Language play is also seen when children create new words, phrases, and sounds, or combine and express language in creative ways. Children often combine more than one language in their language play and use silly or nonsense words that have meaning only to the specific child/children involved in the play. *Examples of Language Play in Preschool* • Three kids in the classroom are laughing. The teacher asks, "What is so funny over there?" The kids reply back, "Bee bop boop ball." Then they laugh with one another. (They decided that day to invent their own language so no one else would understand.)

OPEN-ENDED MATERIALS AND LOOSE PARTS

The flexibility of open-ended materials supports children's development of agency, self-expression, imagination, and problem solving. This is because these materials can be used in innumerable ways, and there is no one right way. Open-ended materials allow children to be in control and to decide how the materials will be used and for what goal or purpose. One popular type of open-ended material often used in preschool classrooms is loose parts. These can be:

found objects and materials that children can move, manipulate, control, and change while they play. . . . [C]hildren can carry, combine, redesign, line up, take apart, and put loose parts back together in almost endless ways. The materials come with no specific set of directions, and they can be used alone and combined with other materials. . . . [C]hildren can turn them into whatever they desire: a stone can become a character in a story; an acorn can become an

ingredient in an imaginary soup. These objects invite conversations and interactions, and they encourage collaboration and cooperation. Put another way,
loose parts promote social competence because they support creativity and innovation. (Daly & Beloglovsky, 2014, p. 3)

The following is a list of many different types of loose parts:

- Rope, wool, ribbon
- Funnels, water, buckets
- Wood (sticks, stumps, boards, coins, branches, wood chips,
  cinnamon sticks, pegs, beads)
- Jar lids, yogurt cups
- Shells, leaves, pinecones
- Plastic bottles and tops
- Seeds (acorns, nuts, dried beans, seed pods)
- Flowers, petals, corks
- Buttons
- Sand, stone
- Dirt (mud, sand, clay)
- Grasses (hay, straw)
- Textiles (hemp, cotton, wool, felt, silk)
- Newspaper, cardboard, paper tubes (Daly & Beloglovsky, 2014)

Richard Louv (2008) reminds us that nature is the richest source of
loose parts. Loose parts in nature support children's imagination, exploration, creativity, and inventiveness. The following are examples of loose
parts in nature: trees, bushes, long grasses, bugs, water, sand, stumps, rocks,
and pebbles.

OUTDOOR PLAY

Outdoor play is an important element of the preschool curriculum. When
children play outdoors, they engage their whole bodies and have opportunities to support growth in every domain of their development. Outdoor play
is educationally valuable for many reasons:

Children have opportunities to engage in big body play and movement (e.g.,
running, jumping, playing catch, riding a tricycle, walking across a balance beam, climbing a structure, and more) not typically available inside
the classroom. Big body play creates feelings of joy and happiness for most
children and supports children to regulate their stress-response systems and
to maintain an optimal level of arousal, which supports the use of their

cortex and the higher-level brain processes needed for learning. These so-matosensory activities (involving movement and the senses) also provide an appropriate outlet for children impacted by trauma to release the excess energy they have in their bodies after trauma reminders trigger the activation of their stress-response systems.

Promotes health and physical development. When children are running, jumping, skipping, swinging, riding tricycles, pulling wagons, rolling down hills, playing with balls, and climbing on play equipment or child-size rocks, they are using their large muscles and developing oculomotor skills (eye–hand coordination). Outdoor play strengthens bone and muscle development, and aerobic activity helps to prevent obesity and to maintain cardiovascular health.

Supports imagination, flexible thinking and experimentation. Young children's outdoor play frequently reflects a wider range of play themes and forms of inquiry than seen with indoor play (Corsaro, 2011; Perry, 2001b). Often, the natural materials available to children in outdoor play spaces invite their imagination, exploration, and experimentation. Children can gather leaves that become money in a pretend store, or pebbles and sticks are used to create a magic castle, while sand, water, and wood chips are combined to create any number of possibilities (Perry, 2004, 2008).

Provides many opportunities to build and strengthen social skills. Outdoor play typically provides children with more autonomy and opportunities for agency in decisionmaking than they experience inside the classroom. Children must make decisions about where to play, who to play with, how to collaborate with peers to co-construct rules for their play, and how to respond as challenges and conflicts arise.

Recommendations for Outdoor Play and Recess

Following are recommendations informed by research on young children's outdoor play as well as studies on recess in elementary school. These suggestions are provided as guides for teachers and principals to create effective outdoor play environments that enhance instructional learning and development for young children:

Preschool children need access to active play—best supported in outdoor environments—throughout the day. All children should have:

60 minutes or more per day of strenuous or moderate physical activity that includes aerobic activities (e.g., running, jumping); muscle-strengthening activities (e.g., climbing on play structures, riding tricycles); and bone-strengthening

activities (hop scotch, hopping, skipping, jumping, jumping rope, basketball, tennis, gymnastics). (U.S. Department of Health and Human Services, 2018, p. 8)

Preschool-aged children (ages 3–5 years) should have opportunities to be physically active *throughout the day* to enhance growth and development. (U.S. Department of Health and Human Services, 2018)

Outdoor environments need to be as thoughtfully and intentionally planned and arranged as indoor environments (Perry, 2001b; 2015). Play equipment and a variety of materials, including loose parts (e.g., balls, jump ropes, hula hoops, recycled materials like boxes, soda bottles, and cardboard tubes), should be available to children to encourage child self-determined play. Children should have agency to make their own play choices and have options for active play (swinging, riding tricycles, playing with balls, etc.) as well as sedentary and individual activities (digging in sand, talking with friends, drawing with chalk).

Teachers provide guidance for children's outdoor play with the same level of intentionality as they do inside the classroom. Teachers also take an active role in looking for, and removing, any hazards, as well as supporting children as needed to resolve conflicts, and identify solutions to problems that arise as they play.

Outdoor play/recess should never be withheld from a child as punishment for any reason (e.g., as a consequence for missed schoolwork or misbehavior). The American Academy of Pediatrics and leading national associations for school administrators, educators, and parents do not recommend withholding recess as punishment (Jarrett, 2019).

PLAY IS DISAPPEARING

Though play is essential for children's healthy learning and development, *play is disappearing* from early childhood programs and in elementary schools across the United States at an alarming rate.

- Opportunities for children to play—inside and outside school—are profoundly declining for American children (Ginsburg et al., 2007; Hirsh-Pasek et al., 2009; Miller & Almon, 2009).
- Low-income and poor children are least likely to have access to play, especially opportunities to engage in child self-determined play (Milteer et al., 2012). This pattern is a factor contributing to the opportunity gaps that deepen inequities and harm children's well-being.

The American Academy of Pediatrics (AAP) is so concerned about the negative consequences of the loss of play for children's healthy development and potential to learn, that they have released three reports urging families, early childhood programs, schools districts, and communities to recognize this trend and reverse it (see Resource section).

Play must be a right of every child. Not a privilege. After all, when regarded as a privilege, it is granted to some and denied to others, creating further inequities (Souto-Manning, 2018, p.1).

REFLECTION AND DISCUSSION QUESTIONS

- What examples of child-directed play, child–adult collaborative play, and adult-directed play do you see in the early childhood program at your site?
- What role does play have in your elementary program? Could more play enhance elementary students' learning as well as preschool students' learning?

KEY TAKEAWAYS FOR PRINCIPALS

- Teaching in a high-quality early childhood play-based classroom looks different than teaching in older grades.
- When principals understand what teaching and learning look like in a preschool classroom and the complex role of preschool teachers to continuously guide, scaffold, and direct children's learning through play, they are able to provide ongoing support and constructive feedback to their early childhood staff.
- When principals are effective early learning leaders, they understand how teachers engage in continuous cycles of observing, documenting, planning, and implementing dynamic and responsive curriculum and the different contexts and formats that support children's learning in preschool. They are also aware of special factors, including the impact of trauma on children's learning and the importance of risk taking in children's healthy development.

CHAPTER 7

Creating a Caring Community of Learners

The Collaborative for Social Emotional Learning (CASEL) defines social–emotional learning (SEL) through five core competencies: self-awareness, self-management, social awareness, relationship skills, and responsible decisionmaking. Defined in terms of competencies that are intrinsically motivated for the student rather than the result of compliance behaviors, the framework develops young children's voice and agency. Recently, CASEL updated its framework to more explicitly connect the five competencies with empowering young students to confront inequity and injustice (Neimi, 2020).

As preschoolers, children are challenged to manage the emotions involved in sharing materials, forming friendships, negotiating imaginative play with others, following classroom routines, and expressing their needs and wants. Children need social–emotional skills and capacities, including self-regulation skills in order to focus, to pursue interests, and to persevere in learning. Importantly, SEL competencies and self-regulatory capabilities are associated with academic achievement in first grade (Rhoades et al., 2011). SEL competencies can be intentionally fostered by families, teachers, and caregivers in supportive environments, and they form the significant foundation for all curriculum and instruction in preschool classrooms.

THE TEACHING PYRAMID MODEL

The Teaching Pyramid was developed in 2003 by the Center on the Social and Emotional Foundations for Early Learning (CSEFEL, n.d.; Fox et al., 2003). In 2014, the Pyramid Model Consortium was founded to continue this work as a systems-based approach. The framework provides guidelines for establishing a nurturing environment for young children that promotes social competence, which in turn reduces challenging behavior. Rather than focusing on managing behavior, the pyramid design emphasizes preventive strategies that create a positive learning community.

The Teaching Pyramid model is a tiered approach based on establishing a foundation of social–emotional well-being in the classroom and explicitly

Figure 7.1. Social Emotional Foundations for Early Learning (SEFEL) Pyramid Model

teaching prosocial behaviors (see Figure 7.1). The framework is organized into four tiers:

- Nurturing and responsive relationships (foundational layer)
- High-quality supportive environments
- Targeted social emotional supports
- Intervention (top layer of the pyramid, smallest in size)

The successive layers of the Pyramid Model signal that the foundational layers help to mitigate challenging behavior, which is why intensive intervention is represented by the smallest layer at the top.

Strategies in the "Promoting and Preventive" Tiers

Relationships. The foundational tier, "nurturing and responsive relationships," begins with establishing rapport with every child and family. This means an affirming relationship in which every child's identity as an individual, member of a family, and member of a cultural community is acknowledged and validated through practices such as greeting each child and family daily, checking in with each child on their feelings as they arrive for the day and throughout the day, acknowledging children's positive behaviors, and accomplishments, and so on. While these strategies may already be familiar, the Pyramid Model highlights their critical contribution to the well-being of every child.

> A preschool teacher relates to each student as they arrive each day by connecting to their interests. He knows that Yovani, one of his students, is very attached to Blanco, his new puppy, and that he has responsibilities for Blanco's care. Every morning when Yovani arrives, the teacher asks about Blanco—what funny things he did, what Yovani fed him, what they played together.

> At preschool orientation, the teachers photograph each child with their family members. They ask each family to write their hopes and dreams for their child in their home language on a card they provide. Later that week, they create a display in their classrooms with each family's photo and their aspirations for their student. These displays remain in the classrooms all year.

What Is Positive, Descriptive Acknowledgment, and How Does It Validate and Affirm Children?

Positive, descriptive acknowledgment (PDA) is the process of "describing children's positive behaviors using explicit and specific language" (Fish & Zercher, 2017, p. 1). Teachers literally describe what the child is doing and refrain from adding praise or evaluative statements.

> "Megan, you are sharing your blocks with Eduardo."

PDA can include additional information, including "the impact of the child's behavior on others, the feelings or emotional state of the child/children, or the character trait linked to the behavior observed. When used in this way, it is called PDA Plus" (Fish & Zercher, 2017, p. 1).

> "Christopher, you are being patient as you wait for your turn with the tricycle." "Sonya, you are helping Zakir put away the blocks. It looks like you feel happy when you can help your friends at cleanup time."

When teachers use PDA, they are describing the positive behaviors they observe a child taking loudly enough so that a child hears their narration. The focus of PDA is on children's efforts, as research documents that

children's persistence with solving challenging problems and/or completing difficult tasks is more likely when they are acknowledged for their effort versus praised or corrected based on outcomes. The goal of PDA is
to support children to develop focal attention (a foundation of higher cognitive processes including self-regulation) and to learn to recognize the
relationship between their behavior, their emotional states, and positive or
desired outcomes (Fish & Zercher, 2017).

Supportive environment. The second tier focuses on the role of a stable,
predictable, stimulating environment in eliminating stressors to children.
This tier sets classroom norms for how adults and children will treat one
another with kindness and respect. Routines and schedules are explicitly
introduced, posted with child-friendly visuals, and practiced. For example,
what to do during transitions is clear through signals and songs. Materials
are organized and accessible, and there is adequate space for children to
work and to pass through the classroom.

A mother asks her 4-year-old to clean up her toys at home and hears the
child humming a tune. She realizes it is the cleanup song from her child's
preschool.

Knowing the importance of the physical environment for learning, a principal
schedules time before the school year begins to devote to classroom setup.
The preschool team carefully considers how to organize the areas of their
classroom and where to place materials. They cover bulletin boards but
do not post commercial decorations. These will be filled with the photos,
stories, and artwork of the incoming students.

A child is anxious about when her mother will come to pick her up. Her
friend shows her a teacher-made poster illustrating the times in the preschool day in photographs. He points to the photo of snack time toward the
end of the day and says, "Your mom is coming after snack."

Regular Schedule

Having a regular schedule and limiting changes in the schedule as much as
possible helps create a sense of safety for young children. When changes are
needed in the daily schedule, it is helpful for teachers to provide children
with advance notice whenever possible, with additional emotional support
throughout the time of change.

Using a visual schedule provides support for children who feel anxious
or are new to a program (see Figure 7.2). A visual schedule is posted at

children's eye level and includes photos for each activity that occurs during the day (e.g., arrival, circle time, free play, reading, small-group activity, lunch, outdoor play, departure). Throughout the day, children can be guided to see what comes next on the visual schedule. Visual schedules not only help children feel a sense of predictability by understanding what is coming next in their day, but research also shows that these schedules can reduce children's anxiety, tantrums, acting-out behaviors, misunderstandings and miscommunication, and dependence on verbal prompts (Mesibov et al., 2005).

Figure 7.2. Visual Schedule

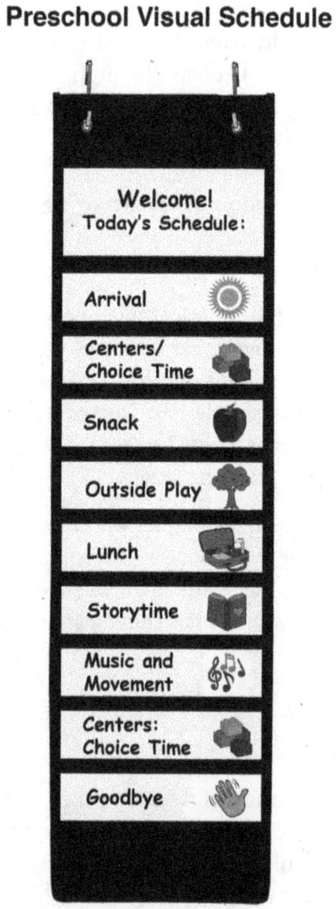

Preschool Visual Schedule

Welcome!
Today's Schedule:

Arrival

Centers/
Choice Time

Snack

Outside Play

Lunch

Storytime

Music and
Movement

Centers:
Choice Time

Goodbye

Also see: How to Use Visual Schedules to Help Your Child Understand Expectations, https://challengingbehavior.cbcs.usf.edu/docs/backpack/BackpackConnection_routines_visual-schedules.pdf (also in Spanish on website).

Predictable Routines

Routines are the small steps followed in sequence associated with each activity included on the daily schedule. Establishing a routine for every activity with a sequence of tasks helps children understand what to expect during each event that occurs in the classroom. An example of one routine: cleanup time with song → transition activity → outdoor play. When children use consistent routines throughout the day, they develop a clear understanding of classroom expectations, and the sense of regularity can help reduce their anxiety

Supporting Children Through Transitions

Transitions between activities in the daily schedule ask children to interrupt what they are involved in and move to a new activity based on an externally designed timetable. Transitions can be sensitive and challenging for children, especially when they have histories of trauma. Moving from the known to the unknown can cause an internal feeling of anxiety and loss of control. Reducing the number of times children are required to transition throughout the day is important, although every classroom will have several transitions.

One way to support children through the change points in the daily schedule is to create a ritual or routine for each transition. These routines are like stories with a beginning, a middle, and an end. If you write a story for every transition you have throughout the day, children will begin to know what is expected when the beginning of the routine is introduced.

A TRANSITION "STORY"—CIRCLE TO HANDWASHING TO LUNCH

Let's look at a classroom that had a transition from circle time (beginning), to the handwashing station (middle), to lunch (end). At the end of circle time, a teaching team gives each child a triangle, square, or circle shape. The teachers then disburse, with one remaining at circle, one going to the handwashing station, and one waiting at the lunch tables. The first teacher sends children one group at a time to the handwashing station by calling groups by shape and waiting briefly between each one; for example, all the "Squares," then "Triangles," then "Circles." He keeps the children engaged in circle time until it's time for their group to go to handwashing. Meanwhile, the teacher at the handwashing station engages children in conversation and humor while providing individual connection and attention. The children are then released to the third teacher at the lunch tables. Creating a routine for this transition substitutes wait time and long lines and potential social anxiety with extra time for personal interaction, language development, and mathematical thinking about shapes.

Strategies that support children to keep their stress-response systems calm during transitions include:

- Songs that signal when a transition is coming (for example, a cleanup song). It's most helpful when the same song is used every day to create safety and predictability.
- "Game-ifying" the transition (try to cleanup or line up in 5 minutes, etc.).
- Using verbal cues paired with visual cues (announcement "5 more minutes" and holding up a sign showing the number five).
- Providing adult one-on-one support.

Targeted social-emotional supports. Young children are learning how to interact with others outside their homes. The third tier focuses on explicitly teaching children how to "navigate peer relationships, understand and regulate their emotions, respond to the emotions of others, and engage in problem solving" in age-appropriate ways (Dunlap & Fox, 2015). Children learn how to describe their feelings and the feelings of others, how to calm down, how to read social cues, how to be a friend, how to share, and how to solve conflicts with peers. Developing children's "sensory and emotional literacy" helps them identify and communicate about the sensations in their bodies and how they are feeling.

A "feelings chart" is posted in the area where community circle is held. The chart shows a range of emotions using simple illustrations. During morning circle, children share how they are feeling as they begin their day.

During outside time, Jayden tells the teacher that a group of classmates told him he can't play with them. The teacher suggests, "Let's go tell them how you feel." While walking over to the group, the teacher asks Jayden what he would like to say and affirms his feelings by restating what he has said.

REFLECTION AND DISCUSSION QUESTIONS

- Is your program using the Teaching Pyramid model or another approach that emphasizes the importance of creating a foundation of social-emotional well-being in the classroom and school? Are teachers encouraged to spend time building children's social-emotional competencies?

> • How much emphasis do you and your staff put on building nurturing
> and responsive relationships with children? Creating supportive
> environments (using visual schedules, predictable routines, providing
> support for transitions, etc.)?

Teaching Conflict-Resolution Skills

Early childhood teachers see conflicts as a ripe context for young children
to build and practice social–emotional capacities. Teachers' respect for children's varying interests, feelings, perspectives, and ideas informs their approach to resolving conflicts when they emerge throughout the day. They
approach children's conflicts with an attitude of empathy and belief in children's abilities to solve their problems with appropriate levels of guidance
and support from adults. When conflicts emerge, teachers:

- Remain calm and regulated and use their calmness to co-regulate
  children.
- Maintain responsibility for children's physical safety.
- Acknowledge, accept, and validate all children's feelings and
  perceptions of the "story" they share about the conflict (see "Name
  It To Tame It" text box).
- Help children verbalize or communicate (through drawings,
  emotion cards, or other means) their feelings, desires, or needs
  to those involved in the conflict and to listen to each other's
  perspectives.
- With young children, adults often need to provide simple language
  to help the child clarify and state the problem.
- Invite children to suggest their ideas and solutions. Children
  enjoy this process and often surprise adults with imaginative and
  creative suggestions.
- Propose solutions when children do not have ideas.
- Model and reinforce the value of identifying ideas, solutions, or
  statements that are points of agreement.
- Model for children how they can respectfully reject or disagree with
  a proposed solution. When this happens, encourage everyone to
  keep brainstorming ideas.
- Use language that communicates that all the children and adults
  involved have some level of responsibility in both the conflict and
  its resolution.
- Reinforce the importance of repairing relationships, but do so
  without forcing children to be insincere (for example, directing
  them "say you're sorry").

- Over time as children's social–emotional skills develop, gradually decrease the amount of support provided and reinforce to children that they becoming more capable of resolving conflicts without adult support (DeVries & Zan, 1994).

"Name It to Tame It"

Dr. Daniel Siegel, an expert in interpersonal neurobiology, explains that when teachers invite children to share stories about their feelings and experiences, they are helping them to calm their stress-response systems. When someone shows compassion and takes time to listen to a child's story (told verbally, through drawings, or play), this calms the emotional intensity within the right side of their brain. After a child is able to share their story and emotions in a context where they feel heard and supported, they will become visibly more relaxed, appear calmer, and more self-regulated. This process is often referred to as "Name It to Tame It."

Source: Siegel & Payne Bryson (2012)

Intervention. Despite these preventive features, there will be times when a young child becomes angry, impulsively acts out, loses control, or withdraws. The top of the Pyramid Model adds individualized approaches for children who require additional and intensive intervention and support.

Transitions times are often difficult for Jason. For example, when the class gathers to go inside after outside play time, he continues to run around the playground. The class watches and waits while one of the staff chases and cajoles him to join the group. The teaching team discusses how transitions trigger him and makes a plan to announce 10-minute, 5-minute, and 3-minute warning times before transitions.

A teacher complains to the principal that a child is particularly "difficult." When asked what specifically is difficult, the teacher cannot explain exactly what is troubling. The principal suggests that the teacher keep a log of the child's behavior the teacher feels is difficult over a week's time. After a week, they will analyze the data together to make an action plan that supports both the child and the teacher, which may include asking an early childhood mental health provider to collaborate with them on how best to support the child.

During a small-group activity led by the teacher, Luis puts his head down on the table and refuses to talk or participate. The teacher asks Luis if he feels sick or sad and he doesn't respond. Knowing Luis, the teacher realizes that this is a change in his behavior. She plans to start noting when he withdraws and to ask Luis's mother if she has seen this at home. She contacts his mother and asks if she is available to work with her to understand this new behavior.

EXCLUSIONARY DISCIPLINE IN PRESCHOOL CLASSROOMS

Preschoolers are expelled from child-care programs and preschools at rates that are up to 13 times higher than the rates for K–12 students (Gilliam, 2005, 2016; Gilliam et al., 2016; Malik, 2017). Even more troublesome, exclusionary discipline does not affect all children equally. Young boys of color, especially Black boys, are systematically expelled from early childhood programs at rates that are at least 3.6 times higher than the rates for White students (see Figure 7.3). In preschool, this means that despite Black boys representing only 19% of all students, they comprise 47% of all out-of-school suspensions (U.S. Department of Education, 2016).

These data are alarming, as we know that the exclusion of young children from early childhood programs has harmful consequences for children's education and development, interfering, for instance, with early intervention screenings and access to supports, disrupting the child's sense of identity and self-worth, depriving them from the very educational and social–emotional opportunities they deserve and might need, and often causing trauma and severe distress for the child's family (CDE, 2021b).

Figure 7.3. Disproportionate Rates of Exclusionary Discipline by Race in Preschool

Black Boys' Enrollment vs Exclusionary Discipline

Black Children Are 19% of Preschoolers Enrolled
(1.9 of every 10 preschoolers)

But Comprise 45% of Preschoolers Suspended One or More Times
(4.5 of every 10 preschoolers)

Exclusionary Discipline Looks Different in Early Childhood Settings Than in K-12

Early childhood teachers and principals may not use words such as *suspension* or *expulsion* to refer to their actions; however, certain practices may effectively have the same result—the removal of children from the classroom as a form of punishment. Following are examples of the different ways exclusionary practices are enacted in early childhood (Schachner et al., 2016).

In-school suspension. Sending the child out of the classroom, for instance, sending the child to the playground, to the school nurse, to an outside bench in the hallway (with supervision, but out of the classroom), or to the principal's office. While in many of these instances the child is supervised, the effective result is that the child is no longer receiving support in the classroom and is being separated from the opportunities that come from being in an early childhood setting.

Out-of-school suspension. This includes calling the family and asking them to pick up their child because of behavioral issues (e.g., biting, hitting, not following directions, etc.) (Schachner et al., 2016). Consider this example:

> It's Marisa's 4th birthday and all the kids in her class sing Happy Birthday except Gabriel who starts making raspberry noises, throwing himself on the floor, and kicking the chairs. Teacher Michelle asks him to stand up and stop the noises, but Gabriel doesn't stop. Michelle then loses her patience and asks her assistant to take Gabriel out of the classroom and to call his mom. "If he doesn't know how to behave in the classroom, he should not be here," she states.

Expulsion. Telling a family that they need to find another program or school because this is not a "good fit" for the child or because they "cannot provide adequate support" to their child (Schachner et al., 2016) instead of trying to learn what the child's needs are and preparing supports to ensure that the child can remain safely and thrive in the program.

"Soft" expulsion (sometimes referred as "push-outs"). This is an indirect way of forcing families to leave the school by making it really difficult for them to stay. Consider Chris's experience:

> Chris and his wife have started to look for a new early childhood program for their son Devin after months of frustration. He says, "It seems it is almost every other day that we receive a call in the middle of the day and are asked to pick him up because of one thing or the other. I am afraid I will lose my job! I know Devin needs to learn to deal with his emotions in a different way,

but we are trying! It just seems the school has given up on our boy. They are making all of us feel uncomfortable about staying in the program. This is no longer sustainable."

Seclusion. The practice of placing a child in a room that they cannot exit as a reaction to perceived behavioral issues (i.e., door is blocked by staff, furniture, equipment, or is locked) (Butler, 2019). There are documented cases of the use of seclusion in early childhood settings including one preschooler placed in a closet until his mother arrived to pick him up. Such instances are a true failure of teachers' commitment to the welfare, education, and care of the children they are charged with.

Physical restraint. Physically restraining a child as a reaction to behaviors such as moving around too much, taking their shoes off, getting out of a chair, not doing their work, or other similar activities (Butler, 2019).

It is important to note that all of these practices are harmful to children and contrary to the values of responsive, equitable, and caring education.

The Problem With "Challenging Behaviors"

At the core of exclusionary discipline are what are often described as children's "challenging behaviors"—behaviors that are experienced by teachers and administrators to be disruptive or even dangerous for the child or for others. Yet many behaviors described as challenging are actually age-appropriate and expected elements of young children's learning and developmental processes. It is important to remember:

- The ability to regulate emotions and behaviors is a long-term process for humans that continues to develop well into adulthood. Imposing a zero-tolerance rule for behaviors that are developmentally appropriate (i.e., tantrums, not following rules, etc.) not only doesn't solve the problem, it fails to support a child to learn important social–emotional skills.
- Defining what counts as a "challenging" behavior is subjective, biased by adults' values, beliefs, mental states in the moment, and often by implicit racial and gender-based biases, as will be described later (Gilliam, 2016; Gilliam et al., 2016). Research documents that educators frequently judge a behavior as "challenging" or even violent when observed with children of color, especially boys of color but are less concerned and reactive when the same behavior is displayed by White children.
- In addition, "challenging behavior" labels are never the result of a reflective inquiry about the causes that are leading to the behavior or about the supports a child might need—practices that align with a supportive early education program. Instead, the label of

"challenging behaviors" can be stigmatizing to a child and may, therefore, harm their development and learning.

- Importantly, in some cases, behaviors described as "challenging" are actually a result of the activation of children's stress-response systems as a result of trauma reminders or trauma triggers (see Table 4.3 in Chapter 4). In this case, children already perceive the world to be a dangerous place, and they desperately need the adults around them to help them feel safe and to feel a sense of love and belonging.

Several program and personal factors are associated with increased exclusionary discipline practices in early childhood. These include:

- High teacher-to-child ratios
- Long school/program days
- Lack of consistent availability of mental health support for teachers and children
- Teacher stress
- Programs that are too structured and those that are not structured enough
- Lack of training and use of reflective practices
- Lack of knowledge of child development
- Implicit bias

The Role of Implicit Bias

Implicit bias refers to automatic and unconscious stereotypes and attitudes that drive people to behave and make decisions in certain ways. It is this kind of quick, involuntary, and unconscious bias that can bring a teacher to interpret the same behaviors in significantly different ways depending on the race, ethnicity, and gender of the child. For instance, a teacher who sees a Black, 3-year-old boy taking a toy from the hands of another child might be perceived to be "out of control" whereas, this same behavior is often seen as "normal for his age" and an "opportunity to teach" when observed with a White child.

IMPLICIT BIAS

- Implicit biases are not based on objective, observable behavior, but on our society's history of stereotypes (based on gender, age, race/ethnicity, religion, ability or disability, etc.).
- Implicit bias plays a role in all human behavior. People of all races, ethnicities, genders, and cultures have implicit biases.
- Though having biases is human, it is the responsibility of everyone to become self-aware and to take action to unlearn their biases.

We now have several important studies documenting the role of implicit bias in the disproportional expulsion rates for young boys of color, especially Black boys (Gilliam, 2016; Gilliam et al., 2016). Black infants, toddlers, and preschoolers, especially if they are boys, are consistently perceived to be significantly older than they are and less innocent than their White peers. This is problematic, as a Black preschool boy who accidentally bumps into a peer might be perceived to be "aggressive" or "doing it on purpose" while the same behavior in a White child might be seen through a more developmental perspective, "he is a very active preschooler who needs some outside time" or "sometimes he loses his balance." The significant role of implicit bias in the inequitable care and education of young children, especially young boys of color, is why Dr. Gilliam (2017) states, *"Preschool expulsion is not a child behavior. It is an adult decision."*

All teachers, administrators, and staff need to learn about and address implicit bias, especially as it influences their approach to communication and discipline. All children deserve to feel safe and protected in school. Interrupting the effect of biases that are ingrained in our society does not have a quick and easy solution, and research on the topic is still developing. However, research studies are documenting that *early childhood mental health consultation* is an effective intervention that provides teachers with additional support to reduce their stress and increase their responsiveness and empathy for young children (Reyes & Gilliam, 2021). Additionally, the California Department of Education (2021b) has published a free and comprehensive resource that describes a range of research-based strategies for addressing bias and improving equity in early childhood classrooms.

REFLECTION AND DISCUSSION QUESTIONS

- Reflecting on your school practices, how familiar are you with the rates of exclusionary practices in your school? What about on the breakdown by gender and race/ethnicity of these rates?
- Now that you have read the definition of "soft expulsions," do you see instances in your practice where your school's actions might have contributed to such actions? If so, what could be done differently to support teachers in providing the best education and support for children?
- Examine your site's disciplinary data (office referrals, soft suspensions/expulsions, suspensions/expulsions), including preschool data. What trends do you notice? Do the data give you any specific information about the program's disciplinary practices? What types of guidance, policy, or goals does your school district offer as it relates to equity?
- Through your school district and/or community, what types of mental health support are offered to your staff, the children, and the families they serve?

- If this is not already the case, how would incorporating professional development opportunities focused on racial and implicit biases into your district and school site plans be beneficial to the students and families you serve?
- How often do you explicitly talk about reinforcing strengths-based messages to staff and children? Can this be incorporated into staff meetings and walk-throughs?
- How are your school's goals and policies, including suspension and expulsion, conveyed to teachers and parents?

KEY TAKEAWAYS FOR PRINCIPALS

- High-quality early learning classrooms establish a foundation of social-emotional well-being in the classroom through nurturing relationships, supportive environments, and targeted social–emotional support. They explicitly teach prosocial behaviors such as self-awareness, self-management, social awareness, relationship skills, and responsible decisionmaking.
- Expulsions, suspensions, and other practices that separate children from the educational opportunities brought by schools occur more frequently in early childhood than in K–12 students; in fact, infants, toddlers, and preschoolers are expelled from child-care programs and preschools at rates that are up to 13 times higher than the rates for K–12 students.
- Boys of color in early childhood are disproportionately expelled and suspended as compared with their White peers, with research showing the role that implicit bias (and racism more generally) plays in this disproportionate application of disciplinary actions. Providing guidance, mental health support, professional development, and self-reflection time for teachers can be transformational for both teachers and the children they serve.
- Principals should be informed of these data and ensure that teachers and staff have the time and resources necessary to learn about the impact of implicit bias, to reflect on their own cultural assumptions and biases, and to plan for a more equitable approach to children's behavior.
- Principals can articulate their program/school values for teaching over punishment and emphasize that the school values teaching social-emotional skills—when children have self-regulation breakdowns—versus punishment and that children need long-term practice with guidance and support from adult caregivers to develop self-regulation.

- Principals should reinforce strengths-based messages to staff and children that every day provide new opportunities to learn and practice self-regulation. An important responsibility of school leaders is to talk about these values on a regular basis and to integrate them into the culture, policies, and practices of the early learning program and school.
- Principals can work with teachers to develop a clear process for supporting children who need extra help with self-regulation. The process should be clearly described to staff and families and consistently used in the program. All plans should include support for teachers to address implicit bias, analyze the learning environment to identify potential stressors that lead to dysregulation for a child, and adapt to address their individual learning and developmental needs and intentional teaching and scaffolding of social–emotional skills.
- Principals can identify community resources, especially early childhood mental health consultation services, and support teachers to have access to them as needed.
- It is important that principals engage with families and parents up front about discipline policies. They should communicate openly and transparently with families about their program policies and values ("We are not a school that relies on suspension and expulsion. We have a process and we emphasizes compassion and teaching").

CHAPTER 8

A Closer Look at Powerful Learning in Early Childhood Classrooms

In order for principals to be effective early learning leaders, they need to have a strong sense of the look and sounds of powerful learning in preschool classrooms. This chapter invites principals into micromoments within an early childhood learning environment to see examples of developmentally responsive curriculum and instruction in action. Through brief vignettes, readers are guided to see how play-based learning and the integrated nature of learning happens in high-quality preschool programs. Through intentional planning and implementation of meaningful learning experiences, the following descriptions highlight how early childhood teachers support children to develop a wide range of skills, knowledge, and capacities through play-based activities. Building on the ongoing cycles of observation, documentation, implementation, and reflection/adaptation to inform curriculum development, these examples highlight how preschool teachers use children's interests as foundations from which to extend and scaffold their development of new skills and capacities.

PROMOTING COGNITIVE DEVELOPMENT

As Vygotsky (1978) stated, play creates a zone of proximal development for young children and many opportunities for them to demonstrate skills, behaviors, and dispositions that go beyond what they can do outside of the play context. In play, it is as if children are a "head taller" than themselves (Vygotsky, 1978, p. 102). Research documents how children learn a wide range of cognitive skills through play. For example, studies of dramatic play in early childhood find that spontaneous use of mathematics is frequent, with a wealth of teachable moments that early childhood educators can notice and build on (Clements & Sarama, 2014; van Oers, 1996).

The following is an example of a powerful teaching and learning moment in a preschool classroom where three 4-year-old boys are creating a game as they play together with wooden blocks (see Figure 8.1). Their teacher, Maria, encourages agency in the boys in leading the play themes and use of materials to explore their ideas and make discoveries together.

However, as she observes their play, at opportune moments, she asks them questions that are intended to deepen their thinking and problem solving while not co-opting or taking over and directing their play. Maria uses teachable moments that emerge spontaneously in the children's play to offer small provocations to promote the children's cognitive development, including their learning of mathematics.

> Lucas, Pablo, and Connor play with blocks together and build daily in the block area of the classroom. They love the hollow blocks, and as engineers, they frequently collaborate on constructions. The photos show one morning during which they worked together to create a game using the blocks. First, they started with a slanted ramp (see Figure 8.1.1 and Figure 8.1.2) and then a straight runway that had a tunnel at the end (see Figure 8.1.3 and Figure 8.1.4). In the beginning, the boys explained that to win, they had to roll a wooden ball down the ramp across the runway and to send it through the tunnel, rules the boys created. As the game went on, they changed the rules to reflect the discoveries they were making about the ball and its trajectory on the runway (see Figure 8.1.10). Throughout their block play, the boys are not only building and strengthening important cognitive capacities, they are also practicing social–emotional skills and supporting their physical (fine motor and gross motor) development.

An Example of Integrated Learning

As discussed throughout this book, young children learn new skills and gain knowledge in an integrated (versus subject-specific) manner. We can see the integrated nature of learning with Lucas, Pablo, and Connor's block play. By observing their interactions to create a game in the block area, early childhood teachers would also see evidence of the following:

Cognitive Development.

- Creating rules of a game with a clear goal
- Learning about the concepts of balance, stability, gravity, cause and effect, speed/force
- Developing spatial understanding: vertical, horizontal, and "bridging space" in which they perceive the space between two blocks and then choose an appropriately sized block to fit in that space
- Developing understanding of equivalencies among the differently sized block units and measurements of length, height, and depth of the structure (comparing and measuring objects)
- Making predictions and testing them
- Learning about cause-and-effect relationships

Figure 8.1. Lucas, Pablo, and Connor Playing Blocks

Figure 8.1.1: Pablo Checking Alignment

Pablo is checking the alignment of the blocks on the slanted ramp so that the ball will have a smooth run from the ramp to the tunnel. He is pushing the blocks together in preparation for taking a turn to roll the ball.

Figure 8.1.2: Prepared to Start the Game

Pablo is prepared to start the game. He has a cylinder to hit the ball down the ramp.

Figure 8.1.3: Teacher Maria Asks a Question

Teacher Maria asks: What do you think is happening when the ball doesn't go through?
Boys: You lose.
Lucas then tells Maria the rules of the game: We need to go again if we lose.
Pablo: I've already went two times [he holds up 2 fingers].

Figure 8.1.4: Here Is Where the Ball Goes

Pablo: And here is where the ball has to go through. It has to go through the hole.

Figure 8.1. (continued)

Figure 8.1.5: Going Through the Tunnel

The ball begins going through the tunnel as seen in Figure 8.8.5, but the boys discover that the ball often rolls off the runway. They begin to problem solve.

Figure 8.1.6: Their First Idea

Their first idea is to make sure the blocks are aligned correctly as seen in this photo.

Figure 8.1.7: Pablo Eliminates the Ramp

Next, Pablo eliminates the ramp and sits closer to the tunnel. He uses the cylinder block to hit the ball, but once again, the ball goes off the runway and rolls onto the carpet.

Figure 8.1.8: Placing a Ball on Top of the Tunnel

Lucas places one of the balls on the top of the tunnel.

(continued)

Figure 8.1. *(continued)*

Figure 8.1.9: Pablo Tries Again

Figure 8.1.10: The Ball Ricochets

Pablo tries again. This time, the ball hits the middle of the two blocks.

The ball ricochets off the side of the runway onto the rug.

Teacher Maria asks: What happens when it hits the middle?

Pablo: You win a trophy!

Lucas: You win!

These comments reflect a quick collaborative shift in the rules of the game. As the boys were learning that it was much harder to get the ball to go through the tunnel than it was to hit the center of the tunnel, they decide to shift the rules of the game so they can be "winners."

Figure 8.1.11: Shifting the Blocks

At this point, one of the boys shifts the boards on the runway to add some more challenge to the game. Now, the two tunnel blocks are shifted so that they are not aligned.

Lucas announces: Now we got to start all over again. Remember?

- Developing dispositions of experimentation, curiosity, and open-mindedness
- Seeking information through active investigation
- Having firsthand experiences with quantity and counting
- Learning about weight (heavy and light)
- Developing creativity by considering different ways to play their game and adapting the rules and goals based on what they discover in their play
- Developing several language- and literacy-related skills: concept development (cause and effect, games with rules); expressive language (ability to put thoughts into words and sentences) and receptive language (ability to understand the words, sentences, and the meaning of what others say as they talk about the game)

Culturally and Linguistically Responsive Practice. It is important to note that Lucas and Pablo are both emergent bilingual (Spanish/English) language learners and articulate their ideas in both languages during their play. Additionally, they each have construction workers in their family and often play with construction themes, an example of integrating their families' funds of knowledge (Moll et al., 1992) into the classroom curriculum.

Social and Emotional Development.

- Turn-taking, patience, and self-regulation as they wait for their turn (an example of the boys acting "a head taller than themselves" [Vygotsky, 1978] in the context of play
- Cooperating with others/teamwork as they develop the rules of the game and adapt them in response to their discoveries and peers' ideas.
- Playing with the concepts of winning and losing without any concern or disappointment if they or their peers do not "win"—for example, developing a growth mindset (Dweck, 2007)
- Showing initiative and self-direction in their actions
- Developing confidence and the ability to make decisions and take agency while working with others
- Communicating (listening and expressing oneself, exchanging ideas, building vocabulary through social interactions) in English and Spanish
- Problem solving

Physical Development.

- Figuring out how to position their bodies in the space (moving with balance and control) and coordinating their movements in the midst of other children and blocks

- Practicing eye–hand coordination (oculomotor skills)
- Developing fine motor coordination as they use the cylinder to hit the ball down the ramp

Approaches to Learning.

- Approaching the process with flexibility and inventiveness
- Displaying persistence in problem solving and sustained attention with the task over a period of time
- Showing eagerness and curiosity as learners and engagement in their learning over a period of time

---

PLAY AND DEVELOPMENTALLY RESPONSIVE SEQUENTIAL INTENTIONAL GROUP WORK

High-quality mathematics throughout early childhood does not involve pushing elementary arithmetic onto younger children. Instead, good education allows children to experience mathematics as they play in and explore their world. (Clements & Sarama, 2014, p. 2)

The early years are a critical time for young children to develop an interest in math. Research studies document that the mathematical-thinking skills and knowledge that children learn from birth through preschool are important predictors of their mathematics and reading achievement in future years (Duncan et al., 2007; Duncan & Magnuson, 2011; Clements & Sarama, 2014).

Mathematics in early childhood should always be taught using a developmentally responsive, playful, and joyful approach. Research evidence is clear that children are most successful in developing mathematical knowledge when they have regular opportunities for play *and* intentionally planned, sequentially ordered play-based group activities in which adults guide and support children to discuss and think about the math concepts they are learning through their play (Chien et al., 2010; Clements & Sarama, 2014).

Clements and Sarama (2014) make the following recommendations—based on a comprehensive analysis of the empirical research—for supporting young children to learn mathematics:

- When instruction is only teacher-led, and children do not have opportunities for agency and self-determined choices, they are not developing critical self-regulation skills that are essential foundations for all children's successful learning and achievement.
- Child-centered approaches, including play and small-group discussions, make important contributions to children's

development of mathematical thinking, especially when they are scaffolded by adults.

- Children learn best when they are supported to explore materials and problems first (before any explicit instruction). Children should be encouraged to engage in discussion with their peers and to create and describe their own solutions and methods to solve problems and to describe and compare different solutions.
- Children benefit from a range of teaching strategies (e.g., play, projects, direct instruction, etc.); however, guided discovery (adult–child collaborative play) should be prioritized. Teachers should encourage children to explain their own ideas and then intentionally introduce children to mathematics vocabulary and concepts. Teachers can provide children with feedback that is strengths-based—building from their ideas and knowledge—to extend their thinking or to guide them to new interpretations and understandings.
- Support children to use manipulatives, "concrete" representations, real materials, and authentic lived experiences as they play and learn about math. Research documents that students of all ages, ability levels, and grades learn math and retain their knowledge to a greater degree when they are able to use manipulatives and concrete materials. Young children need manipulatives/concrete materials to solve problems and learn about mathematical structures and processes (e.g., counting, patterns, shapes, arithmetic, etc.).
- Many math concepts (e.g., subitizing, counting, comparing numbers, naming shapes, etc.) are learned through practice or *repeated experiencing*. To learn mathematics, young children need repeated experiencing or frequent opportunities in a variety of learning contexts with different types of activities where they can practice the new skill or learn the new concept in meaningful ways. All these learning contexts should reflect the conditions that support young children's learning—they should not feel like decontextualized drills of facts or skills.

EXAMPLES OF REPEATED EXPERIENCING WHEN LEARNING ABOUT PATTERNS

- Creating and extending a pattern with Uniflx© cubes or other manipulatives
- Creating patterns with language (rhymes, poetry, storybooks with repetitive patterns)
- Creating and extending patterns with songs or musical instruments
- Making patterns with materials from a nature walk

What Principals Should Observe in Preschool Teachers' Use of Intentionally Sequenced Math Curricula

- Opportunities to reenact ideas from math curricula in their play by providing materials, time, and informal interaction by adults.
- Balance between math experiences in play and intentionally sequenced math curricula in terms of both time and the value placed on the two approaches.

Preschool children should *not* be spending time in decontextualized or abstract activities and drills (e.g., completing worksheets, reciting numbers, sitting for long periods of time while the teacher talks about the calendar). *The most successful pedagogical approaches with young children include play or play-based activities.*

REFLECTION AND DISCUSSION QUESTIONS

- What was your first reaction in reading about Lucas and Pablo's block play? What feelings or thoughts come up for you? What new ways of looking at how play supports children's cognitive development and mathematical thinking in preschool were sparked by this vignette?
- What did you notice about Teacher Maria's role in the boys' play?
- How comfortable are you supporting this type of play-based cognitive learning in your preschool classroom?

PROMOTING LANGUAGE DEVELOPMENT AND THE EMERGENCE OF LITERACY

Literacy emerges from children's earliest experiences with language. Babies listen to the sounds around them and begin to sort out and imitate meaningful speech sounds by babbling. Children come to preschool already filled with the language of their homes and communities. They recognize the sounds, rhythms, and cadences of their home language. As they are exposed to print, preschoolers begin to understand that speech can be written down and read back. This milestone is called the "alphabetic principle" and along with "phonological awareness," it underlies their later understanding of phonics.

Dominick is an avid 3-year-old "reader" who is read to frequently at home. When he picks up a book that he is familiar with, he is able to show how to hold a storyline, which is often very consistent with the storyline in the book (see Figure 8.2). He has book knowledge. He knows the title of the book and the front and back of the book. He reads from left to right, tracking words with his fingers as he reads (see Figure 8.2.1 and Figure 8.2.2). He also turns the pages while reading. Dominick has learned to use intonation in his voice for the different parts of the story (see Figure 8.2.3 and Figure 8.2.4), and he recognizes and shows through his expressions the climax of the story (see Figure 8.2.4). He demonstrates a love of reading and a huge sense of accomplishment when he says, "The end" (see Figure 8.2.5).

At Dominick's preschool, book reading is an important part of the children's daily experiences. There is a book area in the classroom as well as an outdoor book corner, which is set up daily by the teachers. During outdoor time, Dominick picked up one of his favorite books and began reading. Dominick shows not only a sense of pleasure as he turns the pages, keeping up with the storyline, but he also shows confidence in his ability to "read" the text. Dominick has already mastered many of the skills he will use when he begins to read print. Even more importantly, he is engaged with reading as a personally pleasurable experience. He already sees himself as a reader who is motivated, skilled, and sees reading as a personally satisfying experience.

WHAT TO LOOK FOR IN PRESCHOOL CLASS LIBRARIES

- Books that reflect the experiences of students in the class
- Books that include languages of students in the class
- Informational text on range of topics as well as storybooks
- Access to books that adults have read aloud to them so they can "reread"

Emergent Writing in the Preschool Classroom

Writing begins with storytelling (Horn & Giacobbe, 2007). Prompted by read-alouds, teachers ask children about their stories on related topics; "Where do you like to go with your family?" "Did you ever feel like (the main character)?" "What's your dog's name?" Asking children about their experiences, drawing out details by asking questions, and restating their ideas demonstrates to them that they have stories to tell.

Storytelling and oral language development are further fostered by providing time, materials, and teacher support for drawing. What may look like a random scribble comes alive when an adult asks a child to tell them about the story. As children gain fine motor control, scribbles begin to take the form of spirals. By taking dictation from children about their stories in English or in their home language, caregivers model that spoken language can be written down and read back. Spirals spin off into circles, and forms emerge that represent people. Children attempt to label the objects and people in their drawing using letter-like forms, often a line of sticks and lines with some letters and numbers mixed in.

Figure 8.2. Dominick's Emergent Reading

Figure 8.2.1: Go. Dog. Go.

"Go, Dog, Go." (Points to "Dog Go.")

"That spells A, B, C." (Points to "Go.")

Figure 8.2.2: That Guy Is Running

"And that guy is running. [turns page] And that guy's hat off [pointing at top left picture]. And two of those have a scooter (pointing to bottom left picture]. And that guy is dragged down the hill [pointing to bottom right picture]. And those guys, [looking over all pictures on page. Then turns page]. And that guy is in the water. Throw me in the water [Points to character diving into water. Turns page].

Figure 8.2.3: That Guy Says Stop

[Looks at picture and notices red light.] "And that guy says STOP!" [Uses hand gesture to show "STOP" while saying the word.]

Figure 8.2.4: A Great Party

"And a great PARTY!" [intonation goes up on the word "party"]

Figure 8.2. *(continued)*

Figure 8.2.5: The End

"The End." [He says, "The end"
while slowly closing the book and
then looks up.]

One of the most meaningful representations in print for young children is their name, specifically the first letter of their name. As they write approximations of their names, their friends names, and their family's names using what they know about print, children see the communicative power of writing. Caregivers encourage children's understanding of how print works by talking with children about the letters in their name, comparing their name to other names ("You and Joshua both have the letter J."), and modeling the writing of names on class charts and on children's work. Some centers have children "sign in" as they arrive each day by providing a class list where children write their name adjacent to their name on the list.

Figures 8.3 and 8.4 highlight a preschool classroom environment where children are encouraged and inspired to draw, write, talk, and exchange while creating stories through pictures and words.

Materials That Support Emergent Literacy in the Preschool Classroom

Access to books as mirrors (Bishop, 1990). Books and stories help to describe and explain the world. When children see their families and their experiences reflected in the books in the classroom, they are welcomed as a member of a community of readers and they learn that books are for them. This contributes to the development of their identity as a reader.

> Every morning when she arrives at the center, Jada rushes to the Book Area to read her favorite book, *Hair Love* (Cherry & Harrison, 2019). As she examines each page, she retells the story of an African American father styling his daughter's hair and says, "My daddy fixes my hair, too."

Figure 8.3. Examples of Emergent Writing

Figure 8.3.1: Symbolic Representation

As Vygotsky (1978) pointed out "first drawings arise from gestures of the (pencil equipped) hand, and the gesture constitutes the first representations of meaning" (p. 110). Vygotsky emphasized the importance of symbolic representation in learning to write. In this classroom, the teachers agree with this view and have adopted a practice that supports this theory. As you can see in this and the following examples, as children draw, teachers engage with them in dialogue about what they are doing and encourage them to write words that come directly from their story pictures, supporting children in a transition "from drawing things to drawing speech" (Vygotsky, 1978, p. 115). These written words are chosen by the children, and since they are part of their story pictures, they are meaningful to them. During Choice Time, 3-year-old Inti was working in the Art Area. He focused for an extended period of time in order to draw this picture of a ghost. His teacher observed his ability to add details to the drawing, to use his pencil to make zigzag lines and to describe what he drew using an animated voice. He explained, "A ghost with teeth that goes, 'ooh!' and eats people up. He lives in a scary gooey house that has spiderwebs. The ghost likes zombies." When Inti's teacher asked him what the lines on the side of the ghost represent, he said, "This says ghost." (indicated by zigzag line above arrow in Figure 8.3.1).

Figure 8.3.2: Hand

Joanna, 4 years old: "That's a hand and it has sharp nails."

Figure 8.3.3: Nails

Joanna, 4 years old: "Nails."

Figure 8.3. (continued)

<table>
<tr><td align="center">Figure 8.3.4: Playground</td><td align="center">Figure 8.3.5: Grass and Flower</td></tr>
</table>

Audrey, 4 years old: "This is a playground with a green slide."

Audrey, 4 years old: "That's the grass. And this is the flower."

Access to books as windows to other worlds (Bishop, 1990). Young children are gathering information about the larger world. Informational text on a range of topics as well as books featuring children and families who are different than the children in the class provide the background information and vocabulary on which they will draw for later reading comprehension.

> Matthew has never been on a public bus but is fascinated by the toy bus in the Block Area. His teacher pulls out "Last Stop on Market Street" (De la Peña, 2015) and asks him if he'd like her to read him a story about a little boy on a bus with his grandmother.

Access to materials to draw and write. Writing emerges from talking and drawing. Children tell stories as they scribble. As they gain more motor control, scribbles become drawings. As drawings become more complex, children start to label their pictures using letter-like forms and/or the letters and sounds that they know. Teachers can encourage emergent literacy development by providing materials that encourage children's exploration with drawing and writing (see Figure 8.5).

Access to real objects as well as toys. Children are interested in objects from the real world—natural specimens like seeds, sticks, nests, and feathers; tools such as magnets, pulleys, magnifying glasses, and staplers; and sensory materials like sand, water, ice, and slime. Experiences talking about, and playing with, real objects build background knowledge and vocabulary.

> Stocked with materials to examine and explore, the Science Area sparks a wide range of conversation among children. Playing at the water table, children debate what will "sink" and what will "float." As they sort leaves

Figure 8.4. Angelee's Card

Angelee frequently chooses to spend her time in the Writing and Art areas during Choice Time. She engages in both drawing and writing. She often creates small books or cards out of her stories. In this example, Angelee started with a picture of Fairyland (a children's amusement park) but most importantly, she wanted to point out the letters she had made (see Figure 8.4.1). She then folded the paper in half, making a card. She turned the paper over and wrote letters and numbers (see Figure 8.4.2). When she began to read what she had written, she realized she had written it upside down, exclaiming: "Oops, I made it upside down, but that's okay" (reflecting her growing understanding of the concepts of print and how to read books). Angelee then made a choice to create her card again. She used another piece of paper on which she drew almost the exact same drawing, except this time, she drew Fairyland without the sprinkles. She also wrote the same letters (see Figure 8.4.3). She then turned the page in the correct direction and on the back, she wrote the same exact letters she had written on Figure 8.4.2. Angelee is demonstrating that she knows that print is used to communicate, that letters are oriented in a particular direction, that details (like sprinkles) make a difference when conveying meaning, and that text can be edited by authors.

Angelee had a goal of completing her self-chosen task in a way that satisfied her own expectation. When children engage in self-chosen literacy experiences such as these, they are able to express their ideas through gestures, words, graphic representation, and writing within a rich context in which written language is used to communicate with a purpose instead of writing that focuses only on specific bits of knowledge or skills in isolation.

Figure 8.4.1: Letters

"I made letters." (Letters: "m" "o" "Y" "I" "L"). "This (is) Fairyland, the water, the land, and sprinkles."

Figure 8.4.2: Upside Down

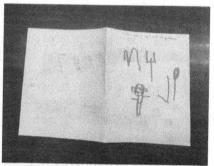

"Oops, I made it upside down, but that's okay."

(Letters: "l" "r", number "8", letters "Y" and "m").

Figure 8.4. *(continued)*

Figure 8.4.3: Fairyland

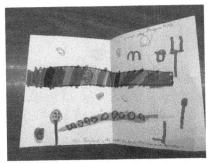

"It's Fairyland again. That one has no sprinkles cause it's a regular Fairyland."
  "So I can read it, I used the letters." (Letters: "M" "Y" "L" "i").

Figure 8.4.4: Right-Side Up

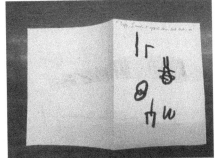

"This one I did not do upside down."

and seed pods and describe what they see, the teacher supplies the words "stems" and "veins," which they quickly incorporate into their discussion. "We saw stems in the book about plants you read yesterday," a child remarks.

What About "Reading Readiness?"

The term *reading* readiness refers to an outdated belief that children need to reach a certain level of maturity to be taught to read. In the past, some programs administered tests to children to assess their readiness levels. There was a fear that introducing formal literacy too early would be ineffective, if not damaging. This belief did not recognize the ways in which children were developing an awareness of sounds and print all along. We realize now that

Figure 8.5. Materials That Support Emergent Literacy

Figure 8.5.1: Paints and Paper

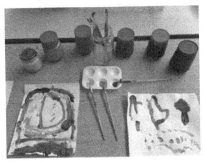

Figure 8.5.2: Paper, Letters, and Crayons

we can support emergent literacy from birth in child-centered ways that lay the foundation for both literacy skills and literacy engagement. The concept of emergent literacy has replaced reading readiness.

How Do Early Childhood Programs Support Emergent Literacy?

Literacy is a social practice. We communicate with others through speaking, listening, reading, and writing. This can take the form of gestures, symbolic play, sign language, drawing/artistic expression, and adaptive formats as well. A child asks for a story to be read again and again, draws a picture as a gift for a loved one, or pretends to write a grocery list in dramatic play. Adults sometimes think of technical aspects of literacy such as decoding print and spelling, and that will come later. Communication is the motivator for children's interest in literacy. A literacy-rich early childhood environment provides talk, text-related materials, and time.

Talk. Passing by a preschool classroom, we hear talk—children talking to one another, self-talking as they pretend and solve problems, commenting to adults, and asking questions. We hear adults narrating what they see children doing, reading aloud, labeling objects and feelings, asking and answering and exploring children's questions in collaboration (Souto-Manning & Martell, 2016). Talk in children's home languages as well as in English contributes to their oral language development.

Time to engage in literacy-related play (see Figure 8.6). Young children observe adults using print and digital tools and imitate these behaviors in their play. In pretend play, we see children acting out literacy behaviors like reading to stuffed animals, checking messages on play phones, and following recipes while engaged in pretend cooking. These activities are building their understanding of the purpose of print.

> Young children are symbol makers and symbol weavers, linking 'play, pictures and print' (Dyson, 1990, p. 50) . . . through play, young children attend to storylines, settings, and characters . . . in the early years, play is literacy . . . play is the grounds in which literacy skills develop. (Souto-Manning & Yoon, 2018, pp. 29, 33)

What Literacy Understandings Begin to Emerge in Preschool?

So much happens in a child's literacy development before we get to the ABCs. And so much needs to happen so that the ABCs have any meaning at all to children. Exposure to literacy-rich experiences is the foundation that builds two key understandings—phonological awareness and print awareness.

Figure 8.6. Examples of Literacy in Children's Play

Figure 8.6.1: Following a Recipe

A 4-year-old child identifies the green bell pepper following the recipe in the book.

The preschool children were interested in creating recipes to use for their pretend cooking the dramatic play area. The teaching team looked for books that had healthy choices that could be used both in pretend cooking as well as for real cooking projects. They made sure that the items in the book reflected the plastic food items that were in the kitchen area. After a few weeks of using this book, the children not only knew the recipes by heart, but they were also able to recognize many written words in the book.

Figure 8.6.2: Making Dinner

In the Dramatic Play area, Natalie, Lucas, and Augustus (all 4 years old) make their plates for a nice dinner. Augustus (standing) patiently waits for Natalie and Lucas to finish serving themselves before he sits down. They talk about how tasty the food is and how much they have on their plate. They use a combination of pretend store-bought foods and other items, such as "yarn" for spaghetti.

(continued)

Figure 8.6. *(continued)*

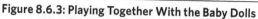

Figure 8.6.3: Playing Together With the Baby Dolls

Santino (3 years old) and Juan Pablo (3-and-a-half years old) often play together in the block area. In addition to pretending they are block builders and construction workers, they also take on roles of members of a family, such as fathers. In this scenario, they have built a house (the enclosed building behind them), and they are now caring for their babies. Using the felt pieces (available in the Block Area as accessories), they make beds for their babies and use blankets to wrap them so they can go to sleep. You often hear them saying "Sh," Sh," "Sh," as they rock their babies to sleep. They have also added two rocking chairs to their play area, which they use as needed when their babies wake up.

Figure 8.6.4: Santino Rocking His Baby Doll

Santino is rocking his baby doll after getting help from the teacher to dress the baby. Once he puts the baby to sleep, he is able to "save" the baby with his "Saving card" so that he can play with it later (see Figure 8.6.5). In this preschool classroom, the teachers have established with the children a system that supports children as they move from one activity to another during Choice Time. The

Figure 8.6. (continued)

children are able to "save" their items and /or creations in order to come back and revisit their experience. This system provides continuity to the children, and it encourages them to come back again and again to an area or an activity of interest. This also supports children's attention span as they are motivated to continue something they had started earlier in the day.

Figure 8.6.5: Using a Saving Card

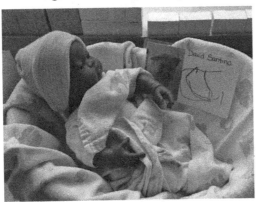

Phonological awareness. In order to understand sound/symbol corre-spondence, children must first be able to hear and manipulate sounds. *Phonological awareness* generally refers to the ability to hear and make rhymes, isolate individual speech sounds in words (for example, recognize the beginning sound of a word), segment words into sounds, and blend sounds back together into words. All cultures have traditional forms of word play—riddles, sayings, rhymes, songs, poems—that attune children to the sounds of their language. Early childhood programs fill children with word play to develop their ability to hear and manipulate speech sounds that they will later use to break words apart in order to decode and spell.

The ability to hear and manipulate speech sounds transfers across lan-guages. When families play with words through songs and rhymes in their home language, the auditory discrimination that children develop applies across languages (Yopp & Stapleton, 2008). Phonological awareness is not learned through drills and worksheets but through playful activities that use the sounds of language.

As part of their daily sing-along, teachers incorporate songs that focus on rhyming. Singing "Down by the Bay," they contribute rhymes to finish each stanza. Lead by the teachers' voices, the group sings, "Did you ever hear a goose talking to a . . ." and stops expectedly. A child shouts out, "Moose!" and the group sings "moose" and continues the song.

Print awareness. With access to books, time to peruse them and frequent read-alouds by adults or older children, young children begin to retell stories from the illustrations. If readers point to the print on the page as they read, children begin to understand that the words on the page carry meaning and how to track print across the page.

How Is "Interactive" Read-Aloud Similar to and Different From Reading a Story?

> If we can make all read-alouds more interactive, and also increase the amount of talk at higher levels of cognitive thinking, then those read-alouds can contribute more to students' long-term language and literacy development. (Price & Bradley, 2016, p. 8)

- Choose the book you will read aloud purposefully. What's exceptional about your book?
- Review the book ahead of time and identify opportunities for participation.
- Design an engaging introduction; connect to children's identities, interests, and experiences.
- Plan possible stopping points to elicit comments, ask questions, or explain a word or idea.
- Emphasize sounds (rhymes, alliteration, onomatopoeia), stretch sounds.
- If reading a "big book," track print with your finger, wand, or pointer.
- Be dramatic with your voice, your eyes, and your pacing. Create suspense.
- Invite children's participation through talking, questioning, repeating refrains, and movement.
- Offer sentence frames to scaffold participation for emergent bilingual/multilingual language learners.
- Think aloud—describe what you're thinking about as you read.
- Read the book again and again. Bring out a new teaching point each time. Visit old friends.

Can Emergent Literacy Be Accelerated to Meet the Demands of Kindergarten?

Reviewing schoolwide data indicating that many students are struggling with reading in the intermediate grades, some teachers urge that reading instruction should be started in preschool. Preschool teachers explain that the strongest contribution they can make to later literacy development is not by pushing down the curriculum but by enhancing children's exposure to language and content. They increase opportunities for developing oral language and vocabulary by planning project-based activities in which preschool children will investigate various phenomena such as life cycles, forces and motion, light, and gardening. They model how print works by taking dictation and writing group stories about their experiences. They make up songs about what the children are learning set to familiar tunes.

There is a tremendous opportunity cost in using time in the early childhood classroom for formal literacy instruction rather than children's literacy play. Less time and/or less emphasis on oral language development, experiential learning, and phonological awareness can leave students with gaps in their understanding of print that cause them to struggle with reading and writing. Focusing on the technical skills of literacy rather than developing a love of reading and writing can impact students' engagement with reading later.

WHAT TO LOOK AND LISTEN FOR WHEN PASSING BY PRESCHOOL CLASSROOMS

- Children talking
- Movement around the classroom
- Teachers' talk in response to children's questions and needs
- Materials that are accessible and in use
- Children absorbed in play (individually, in pairs, and in small groups)

REFLECTION AND DISCUSSION QUESTIONS

- Children are actively constructing their ideas about reading and writing through their play. Take a moment to pop into the early childhood classroom during free-choice time. What literacy activities do you notice them engaging in that demonstrate how literacy is "emerging"?
- Early childhood educators enrich children's literacy play by reading aloud, engaging in conversation, leading singing and rhyming games, demonstrating how to express ideas through drawing and writing, and providing materials that support emergent reading and writing. How does the preschool classroom at your site reflect this notion of "literacy throughout the day"?
- Imagine that a preschool teacher at your site is concerned about later reading achievement and feels that it's important to introduce structured literacy activities such as worksheets and phonics lessons at an early age. How would you talk with the teacher about child-centered approaches to supporting emergent literacy?

PROMOTING CREATIVITY AND ARTISTIC EXPRESSION

The preschool classroom is an environment where young children's 100 languages (Edwards et al., 2011) come to life. Preschool teachers design curricula that provide opportunities for children to express their thoughts, feelings, desires, fears, wonderings, and theories about how the world works in many different ways. Children are supported to show what they know and can do through conversation, play, painting, dance, drawing, poetry, music, singing, movement, building, sculpting, songwriting, and many other forms of artistic and creative expression. Open-ended materials allow children to engage in exploration, experimentation, and discovery. The following is a small sample of the types of individual and collaborative experiences in preschool classrooms that support young children's development of creative thinking and artistic expression (see Figure 8.7).

PROMOTING ANTIRACIST, ANTIBIAS EDUCATION

Many early childhood educators have historically been silent on the topic of race, racism, and inequity in early childhood classrooms for a range of reasons, including:

- As discussed in Chapter 3, they may incorrectly believe that children are too young to notice race or to participate in exclusionary behavior.
- They do not have the language or know-how to talk productively about racism and other forms of oppression in a developmentally responsive way.
- They don't know what, if anything, they can do about racism and other forms of oppression, and they worry about creating feelings of anxiety and worry for children.

Although talking about race, racism, and other topics that address inequity and bias can be scary and challenging, it is important that all early childhood professionals educate themselves on how to do so, as this is the only way they will be able to create caring, inclusive, and safe environments for children. What can early childhood teachers do?

Be Prepared to Talk With Children About Race and Racism

Educators need to begin by tuning inward and building self-awareness of their own experiences with race, racism, prejudice, and privilege (Parris et al., 2020). Using reflection, reading, building knowledge, and dialogue, educators can identify their beliefs, discover their biases, and learn strategies

Figure 8.7. Artistic Expression in the Preschool Classroom

Figure 8.7.1: Jade's Drawing

Jade (4 years old) was very interested in finding, among different skin color crayons, the ones that matched her skin color. She also spent a considerable amount of time and focus in order to draw her hair, matching exactly what she looks like. When children are given high-quality materials and time to work on a project, the results show.

Figure 8.7.2: Welcome Sign

The mixed-age (3–4 years) group of children are working on a Welcome Sign for a Parent Meeting of incoming preschool parents and families. When children engage in real-life situations in the classroom, they are being active and important members of that community. In this classroom, art is a medium often used as children engage in real-life situations and events happening within the school.

(continued)

Figure 8.7. *(continued)*

Figure 8.7.3: Easel Painting

Painting with white paper and a range of colored paints is a common preschool activity. Children can explore the mixture of colors and symbolically represent a wide range of feelings and ideas on the paper as they work alone or with others.

Figure 8.7.4: Weaving Painted Gauze

This child is weaving painted gauze through a wooden loom, a group project that children in the class contributed to throughout the day. As children engage in this activity, they are strengthening their fine motor skills, developing eye–hand coordination, and developing a sense of agency and confidence as they learn that they are capable of creating a colorful weaving.

The self-portrait sequence in Figures 8.7.5, 8.7.6, and 8.7.7 took place at a preschool where the children were reading about people with different skin colors. The children had opportunities to look at themselves in small mirrors and then draw their self-portraits using colored pencils that represented a wide range of skin tones.

Figure 8.7. (continued)

Figure 8.7.5: Making Self-Portraits

Figure 8.7.6: Looking in the Mirror

Figure 8.7.7: A Closer Look

to disrupt them. White educators need to learn about and acknowledge their privilege, and all educators need to educate themselves about Black and Indigenous histories, and racism in America. This is hard work that principals can encourage through ongoing support for professional learning opportunities. Understanding the different pathways to regulation is important (see Chapter 4), as teachers need to be able to manage their own triggers and feelings that result from children's language, behaviors, and interactions about race, racism, and inequity. Adults need to be calm and regulated to guide children effectively through antiracist/antibias work.

Do Not Silence Children's Discussions About Race

Teachers working in high-quality early childhood classrooms should not silence or shut down children's conversations about race (Parris et al., 2020; Winkler, 2009).

> If adults go silent about things that children are seeing and trying to understand, children absorb the emotional message that the subject is dangerous and should not be talked about. This leaves children with an undercurrent of anxiety and unease, which are the earliest lessons about bias and fear. Silence is a powerful teacher. (Derman-Sparks et al., 2020, p. 52)

Principals should see open, honest conversations about race, racial differences and all forms of inequity that are facilitated and guided by the teacher. Figure 8.8 provides an example of what this might look like in a preschool classroom.

Be Honest and Accurate About the Existence and Impact of Racism

Sometimes adults simplify conversations about race with young children because they believe that children will not understand the seriousness and complexity of the issue. What this has done is created a focus on heroes, holidays, and cultural celebrations that are superficial and ignore the reality of structural racism in society. Children should be presented with accurate and honest information that is stated in an age-appropriate manner so that they learn to understand inequality and learn how they can take actions to disrupt it (Hirschfeld, 2008; Parris et al., 2020; Winkler, 2009). Van Ausdale and Feagin (2001) explain

> Don't encourage children to believe that negative racial talk or discriminatory action is the conduct of only 'sick' individuals or that it indicates a peculiar character flaw or just 'bad' behavior. Talk about the fact that the social world we live in is often unfair to people of color simply because they are people of color and that these inequalities are wrong and unfair. (p. 208)

Figure 8.8. The Skin You Live In

Teacher Shawn walks up to the easels where two children are painting next to each other. Micah, who is White, asks Sahara who is Black, "Why is your skin so dirty?" Instead of ignoring the conversation and remaining silent, Teacher Shawn leans down to the two children and says, "Micah, Sahara's skin is not dirty. Her skin is as clean as your skin, it's just a different color because she has more melanin than you do. Just like people in our classroom have different hair colors and different eye colors, people also have different skin colors." Later that day, Teacher Shawn reads the book *The Skin You Live In* (Tyler & Csicsko, 2005) and introduces the word *melanin* to the children.

Talking about race and racism in a manner that emphasizes what children and adults can do to address discrimination helps children to feel a sense of agency and hopefulness about the world around them. For children of color, these conversations can support resilience, strength, psychological well-being, and a healthy sense of racial identity and self-esteem. All children need adults who will guide them to learn about skin color/race and racism, through intentional instruction and open conversation, as these experiences are foundations for healthy identity development. Teachers will also need to reassure children that the adults will keep them safe at school. Derman-Sparks and colleagues (2020) provide several examples of honest, accurate, and age-appropriate language that adults can use in these discussions. For example,

'Sometimes people are treated badly because of the color of their skin or where their family came from, or how they talk, or because they are experiencing homelessness or because they have a disability. That is never okay.' or 'If someone is mean or unfair to you or to someone else, you can do something. You can help turn unfair into fair. You can tell people to stop! You can explain that unfairness hurts. You can be a friend to someone . . . you can ask a grownup to help you.' (p. 18)

Take This Topic Seriously

Many adults incorrectly believe that young children are incapable of being prejudiced or behaving in ways that hurt and exclude other children based on social categories of identity. Yet this is not true, and if adults downplay language or interactions where children are being discriminatory, this will only reinforce the development of prejudice (Aboud, 2008; Hirschfeld, 2008; Van Ausdale & Feagin, 2001; Winkler, 2009). As a result, it is really important that conversations about race, racism, privilege, and inequity start in early childhood, as this is the time when shame, fear, anxiety, and bias are first learned (Parris et al., 2020). The following are suggestions for addressing negative racial statements that young children make (Cellano et al., n.d.):

- *Ask them in a nonjudgmental tone, "What makes you say that?"* Try not to jump to conclusions (see Table 8.1). Listen to children, validate their feelings, and strive to understand what is underneath the statement. Teachers can then build from what the child says to address generalizations or talk about an idea that hurts.
- *Read books that introduce children to diverse people and characters and that talk about race, racism, and social justice topics.* Ask questions while reading to help children develop empathy for the characters who experience racism or other forms of prejudice/bias (e.g., How do you think Jesse feels when they talk about him that way/when they say he can't be the leader because he has dark skin?).
- *State very clearly and consistently that it is wrong to treat another person (adult or child) differently because of their race.* Children need to hear this message reinforced by the adults around them during their early childhood years, when they are developing foundational beliefs about diversity.
- *Make a rule that it's never okay to tease, reject, or be unfair to someone for any reason, including because of their identity.*

Emphasize That People Are Complex and Have Many Different Parts/Dimensions

Preschoolers often think about people in either/or categories, for example, "all good or all bad." An evidence-based strategy that reduces prejudice is

Table 8.1. Clarifying Conversations in Preschool

The following excerpt is from Derman-Sparks et al. (2020):

> *Selina and Habiba (4 years old) are playing with blocks. Katya (who has burn scars on her face and arms and has limited use of her hands) tries to join their play. Selena declares loudly to Habiba, "I hate Katya; she's ugly."*

Step 1. Find out what the child thinks. "Selina, I heard you say that Katya is ugly. That is a hurtful thing to say. What makes you say it?" (p. 156).

Step 2. Tell the truth. "Selina and Habiba, Katya has scars on her face and arms because she was in an accident when she was a baby . . . some hot oil in a frying pan spilled on her and burned her and it hurt the muscles in her hands" (p. 156).

Step 3. Clearly state the issue of justice. "It's okay to want to know about Katya's scars, but is it not okay to say she's ugly or not let her play with you" (p. 157).

Step 4. State your values. "Remember that in our classroom I expect us all to work and play together. Let's all four of us play with the blocks together" (p. 157).

to encourage young children to recognize human diversity by paying attention to many different characteristics or social categories of identity of a person instead of just focusing on their race (Aboud, 2008; Cellano et al., n.d.; Winkler, 2009). Also, helping children learn about a person as an individual—learning details about their interests and lives—is an effective way to reduce the impact of racial bias (Ispa-Landa, 2018).

> 'Benjamin acts like a baby. He doesn't talk right, and he doesn't even know how to write his name,' observes 5-year-old Rebekah. 'Benjamin isn't a baby, Rebekah,' his teacher says. 'He is 5 years old, just like you. Benjamin can do many things that you can do. He can ride a bike, run, play ball, and climb. He will be able to talk more clearly and learn to write his name, but it will take him longer.' (Derman-Sparks et al., 2020, p. 155)

Create Opportunities for Children to Have Agency and Voice

Teachers should acknowledge the reality of racism while also communicating messages about hope for future change, people who are committed to helping, and the value of participating in working for positive change (Cellano et al., n.d.; Winkler, 2009). It's essential that teachers reassure children that even though we have big problems in society, there are many ways that people work individually and with others to make things better.

READ BOOKS THAT TELL STORIES OF HOPE AND CHANGE,
ESPECIALLY OF CHILDREN WORKING FOR CHANGE

The following are several age-appropriate suggestions:

- Campoy, F. I., & Howell, T. (2016). *Maybe Something Beautiful: How Art Transformed a Neighborhood.* Houghton Mifflin Harcourt.
- Chin, K. (1995). *Sam and the Lucky Money.* New York: Lee & Low Books.
- Robinson, C. (2020). *You Matter.* New York: Atheneum Books for Young Readers.
- Woodson, J. (2018). *The Day You Begin.* New York: Penguin Random House.
- Smith, G. (2017). *You Hold Me Up.* Victoria, BC: Orca Books.

Learn Together

Teachers working to create racially literate students and classrooms committed to antiracist/antibias should not feel isolated and alone in their efforts. Building community is important, and principals can help (Hooven et al., 2018). Create opportunities for teachers to meet with colleagues to reflect on and discuss this work together or create a statement of diversity at the school site that communicates to parents the value that is being placed on antibias education at the site.

Be a Good Antiracist/Antibias Role Model for Children

Teachers and principals can model for children how to treat everyone fairly and how much they value diversity in the students, staff, and families at the school. They can also talk openly about how they are committed to listening and learning from children and families about what is unfair/unjust and taking actions to make the school and the world fairer and kinder.

Derman-Sparks et al. (2020) recommend four steps to guide these conversations with young children:

- Take time to listen and ask clarifying questions to better understand what a child is thinking, feeling, and understanding about an issue.
- When discussing the topic, use language children will understand, but always be honest and provide accurate information. Observe how children are making sense of what you share and make sure to provide clarifications as needed.

- Clearly and accurately help children see the connection between the issue and how it impacts people differently. Who is hurt and why? What about this issue is fair? Unfair?
- Reinforce the importance of fairness, kindness, respect, and inclusiveness in the classroom/school that everyone is expected to uphold. Help the children see the relationship between the issue and these agreements, "Here's how we treat people in our school...." (p. 55)

REFLECTION AND DISCUSSION QUESTIONS

- Many adults are not used to talking with children about race and antiracism. Reflect on your own perspective. How comfortable and prepared do you feel to address this topic? Open this conversation with the preschool staff at your school. How comfortable and prepared do they feel? What support do they need?
- Work with the preschool teaching team at your school to do an inventory of their classroom library. Do the books reflect the children in the program? Does the library include books making children aware of other groups?
- Work with the preschool staff to do an inventory of classroom materials. Do art supplies reflect various skin tones? Does the dramatic play area include household items common to various cultures? Do figurines in the block area reflect different racial groups?

PROMOTING TRAUMA-RESPONSIVE PRACTICE

Siddhi is riding a tricycle at her preschool when she hears the loud siren of an ambulance driving by the school. She starts to cover her ears and scream repeatedly "no, no, no, no" over and over. Her preschool teacher, Chen, walks over to Siddhi, bends down to her eye level and using a calm and reassuring voice tells her, "Siddhi, you are safe, you are here in preschool and the teachers will take care of you. That loud sound was an ambulance with helpers who are going take care of someone. There is nothing dangerous. You are safe. I will stay with you. Let's take three deep breaths together. After they finish their deep breaths, Teacher Chen asks Siddhi, "Do you want to continue riding on your tricycle or would you like to play in the sandbox or listen to a storybook with Teacher Lisa?"

Teacher Chen observed that Siddhi's stress-response system was activated when she heard the ambulance siren. She saw signs of a freeze, fight, or freeze survival response as seen in how she covered her ears and screamed within a split second after hearing the loud noise. After talking with Siddhi's father about this interaction, Teacher Chen learned that Siddhi's family recently experienced a very scary house fire that left her mother with minor burns. During that event, the fire department was called to the home and he explained that ever since that night, Siddhi has been easy to startle and cry when she hears any loud sounds. Because Teacher Chen has learned about the neurobiology of stress and trauma, she wondered if loud sounds—and especially the sound of ambulance sirens—were trauma reminders for Siddhi that automatically activated her brain's survival (fight, flight, or freeze) response. Whenever Teacher Chen notices signs of stress-related behaviors in children, she uses trauma-sensitive strategies to help to calm their nervous systems and guide them back to a state of calm and self-regulation.

Teacher Chen used several trauma-sensitive strategies to help Siddhi feel safe and to stop the activation of her stress-response system:

- *Remaining calm and through co-regulation, guiding Siddhi back to regulation.* Stress *and* calmness are contagious because of our mirror neurons. By staying with Siddhi and remaining calm and using a soothing and calm voice, Teacher Chen was engaging in co-regulation, using her calm and caring presence to guide Siddhi back to a state of regulation and safety. At an unconscious level, Siddhi's brain and body were absorbing the emotional state of calm that Teacher Chen was projecting.
- *Reassuring Siddhi that she was safe.* Teacher Chen reassures Siddhi that she is safe by saying "That loud sound was an ambulance with helpers who are going take care of someone. There is nothing dangerous. You are safe. I will stay with you." When young children have trauma reminders, they are made to feel as though they are back in the initial traumatic experience. They need adults to remind them many times that they are safe and that the adults will stay with them and take care of them.
- *Using deep breathing, a somatosensory strategy to calm the stress-response system.* Teacher Chen understands that repetitive somatosensory activities are the fastest and most effective and direct way of regulating stress for children and adults (Perry, 2020). This is because they directly reach the core neural networks in the lower brain responsible for regulation and they quickly help people calm their stress and regulate their brains and bodies. When Teacher Chen encouraged Siddhi to take three deep breaths with her, she was helping Siddhi to directly reach and calm the core neural networks in her lower brain stem.

Kids as young as 3 can learn to blow soap bubbles and learn that when they slow down their breathing to 6 breaths per minute and focus on the out-breath as it flows over their upper lip, they can feel more calm and focused. (van der Kolk, 2014, p. 356)

- *Staying physically close to Siddhi as a caring and responsive adult.* By staying physically close to Siddhi and crouching down to her level, Teacher Chen was providing the most important form of support for a child impacted by trauma, relational regulation. Just being present with Siddhi; bearing witness to her stress behaviors without judgment, anger, or frustration; and instead, communicating messages of connection, empathy, and reassurance of safety is a powerful buffer for Siddhi's stress, as it helps her feel support and reduces feelings of isolation, which can be very triggering and stressful for anyone when they are frightened.
- *Offering an opportunity for voice and choice.* Because trauma reminders are associated with experiences that leave children feeling a total loss of control, creating opportunities for them to have a sense of agency and control is an important part of supporting them to strengthen resilience and to build a sense of confidence that they can cope in stressful situations. After supporting Siddhi to calm her nervous system by taking three deep breaths, Teacher Chen creates an opportunity for Siddhi to have a sense of agency in the situation by asking her which activity she would like to do next (continuing to ride on the tricycle, engaging in sensory play with the sand, which is calming for the nervous system, or listening to a storybook with the classroom aide, which would allow Siddhi to have the relational regulation of sitting close to a caregiver). Offering this chance for Siddhi to make a choice and express her opinion (voice and choice) is a small and powerful way to help her move through and metabolize the discomfort left in her body from the trauma reminder and the flood of stress chemicals in her body. By making a decision about her next activity, she is learning that she can have agency to move through the trauma reminder and that she has options for acting in moments of stress (instead of remaining stuck in a hypervigilant state), which creates the foundation for resilience and coping skills.

Recently, Teacher Chen observed Siddhi practicing some of these strategies in the dramatic play area, where she was pretending to be a firefighter and putting out fires after receiving calls from several stuffed animals that their homes and businesses are burning. Siddhi takes the phone calls and reassures the animals, "You are safe, you are going to be okay. The helpers are coming!" She then arrives and acting out the role of the firefighter, rescues the animals, puts out the fire, and then puts bandages on their injured paws. While she is putting on their bandages, she tells them, "Let's take three breaths together. You are out of danger. I will stay here with you. You are safe."

Through her imaginary play, Siddhi is communicating how young children—with the support of teachers who understand and use trauma-responsive practices—can be led to feel safe at preschool and to learn strategies that help them cope when they feel stressed or experience trauma reminders.

REFLECTION AND DISCUSSION QUESTION

- Which of the trauma-responsive strategies discussed do you use with students? Which ones do you observe your staff using?

KEY TAKEAWAYS FOR PRINCIPALS

- When principals understand what engaging and powerful learning looks like for young children in early childhood classrooms—and importantly, how it is similar to and how it differs from what they are trained to observe in classrooms with older children—they can become powerful leaders that support all children to have excellent and equitable early learning experiences.
- Powerful learning in high-quality early childhood classrooms is based on curriculum, instruction, and environments that are planned and implemented to engage children by building on their interests, providing them with opportunities for agency, movement, and learning through play.

CHAPTER 9

Assessment in Early Childhood

Assessments should be tied to children's daily activities, supported by professional development, and inclusive of families; they should be purposefully used to make sound decisions about teaching and learning, identify significant concerns that may require focused intervention for individual children, and help programs improve their educational and developmental interventions. (NAEYC, 2020, p. 31)

Assessment—the process of gathering information in order to make intentional and responsive instructional decisions—is an essential part of early childhood programs. Effective assessment in early childhood provides teachers and families with ongoing information about what children know and can do and how the learning experiences within the early learning environment are supporting them to make progress toward their individualized learning goals. Assessment in preschool is most effective when it is part of an integrated system that includes the use of both formal and informal measures to monitor children's learning and developmental progress.

Understanding the purposes of assessment, the characteristics of effective assessment with young children, and the benefits and limitations of different assessment methods and instruments is critical to ensure that assessment practices do not generate insufficient or inaccurate information that can lead to negative consequences for children, families, and early childhood teachers. Most notably, it is essential that principals be aware of an important tension related to assessment with a long history in the field of early childhood. In order for assessment results to be meaningful and valid, assessments must be conducted in a manner that is developmentally, culturally, and linguistically responsive. However, our current tools and methods fall short and are increasingly being critiqued as privileging White Eurocentric middle-class norms for development that marginalize many children, especially those who are Black, Indigenous, and People of Color (BIPOC), perpetuating cycles of oppression by positioning them through deficit.

KEY TERMS

Assessment. A systematic procedure for obtaining information from observations, interviews, portfolios, projects, and other sources, which is used to make informed judgments about learners' characteristics, understanding, and development to implement improved curriculum and teaching practices. (NAEYC, 2020, p. 35)

Authentic Assessment. Age-appropriate approaches and culturally relevant assessment in a language the child understands—for infants, toddlers, preschoolers, and children in early grades, across developmental domains and curriculum areas. (NAEYC, 2020, p. 35)

Formal and Informal Assessment. Formal assessment is cumulative and is used to measure what a student has learned. It includes standardized testing, screenings, and diagnostic evaluation. Informal assessment is ongoing and includes children's work samples and quizzes and teachers' anecdotal notes/records, observations, audio and video recordings. (NAEYC, 2020, p. 35)

Formative Assessment and Summative Assessment. Used to inform and modify real-time instruction to improve student outcomes, formative assessment refers to the teacher practice of monitoring student learning. Summative assessment takes place at the end of the instructional period to measure student learning or concept retention. (NAEYC, 2020, p. 35)

CHARACTERISTICS OF EFFECTIVE ASSESSMENT ENVIRONMENTS AND PRACTICES

Assessment with young children is different and more complex in many ways than assessment practices with older students. Without specific features in place, assessment results may not be valid, as they may be incomplete, unreliable, and/or incorrect. Effective assessments in early childhood have the characteristics discussed next.

Integrate Curriculum, Instruction, and Assessment

Effective assessment tools are part of an integrated system that is established to explicitly link curriculum, instruction, and assessment. *Assessment* does not refer only to the specific tools being used; instead, it should be recognized to be an interconnected system of decisions and activities including the selection of tool(s), the procedures in place to ensure the appropriate implementation of the assessment, as well as how assessment results are documented, analyzed, and used (Snow, 2011). In early childhood environments, this includes the use of observation, documentation, and sometimes standardized assessment tools to gather information that guides ongoing development and implementation of the curriculum and instruction and the moment-to-moment interactions teachers have with children.

Used for Only the Purposes and Demographic Groups for Which They Are Designed

It is essential that educators only use assessment tools in accordance with their intended purpose (NAEYC, 2020). Assessment in early childhood is conducted for a range of purposes, including documentation of children's learning and development, teachers' planning and design of a curriculum, instruction and the learning environment, program evaluation and quality ratings, and placement decisions. Preschool teachers most often use assessment for the first two of these purposes. It is essential that educators limit their use of assessment tools to their intended purpose. Unfortunately, there is a long history of inappropriate use of assessment tools or use of assessment instruments for one purpose when designed for another (e.g., readiness tools used for high-stakes placement decisions or formative assessment tools intended to inform teachers' instruction used for program evaluation and quality ratings) (Graue & Shepard, 1989; Meisels, 1987, 1989, 1995).

Ongoing, Responsive, and Meaningful

Authentic assessment in early childhood is curriculum-embedded. This means that teachers are observing children and documenting their developmental milestones and progress toward learning goals during their naturally occurring experiences in the classroom, including their participation in individual and collaborative play and the spontaneous conversations and interactions they have throughout the day (Meisels et al., 1995). Although, at times, teachers may set up specific activities that invite children to demonstrate particular skills, adult-structured assessment contexts should be used sparingly. To be meaningful and inform curricula and instruction, assessment should be ongoing (snapshot or single-point-in-time assessments are problematic with young children) and provide teachers with feedback they can use right away. For assessment information to effectively inform instruction, assessment results must be available to teachers immediately.

In preschool classrooms, assessment is primarily used to:

- Inform teachers' planning and implementation of curricula and instruction. By identifying what children are learning and how well they are learning about various ideas or skills, teachers use assessment data to improve their instructional practices and students' learning outcomes.

- Communicate with children's parents, families, and caregivers about their progress and experiences in the program.
- Support a process of continuous quality improvement that leads to more effective and equitable teaching, pedagogy, and early learning programs.

Assessment Is Focused on Children's Progress Toward Developmental and Learning Goals

All curricula and instruction in the early childhood classroom is guided by the specific individual and group learning goals developed for the specific group of children in the classroom (NAEYC, 2020). Learning goals are co-constructed with input from teachers, parents/families, children, and when appropriate, multidisciplinary team members (speech pathologist, physical/occupational therapist, inclusion specialist, mental health provider, etc.) and should be aligned with state early learning standards. Assessments should be strengths-based and focus on children's progress in accomplishing developmental milestones, acquiring skills and knowledge, and displaying dispositions/approaches to learning that reflect their initiative, risk taking, persistence, and other factors that create the conditions necessary for learning.

Tools and Methods Must Be Developmentally, Culturally, and Linguistically Responsive

To be meaningful, useful to teachers and families, and not cause harm, assessments in early childhood must be responsive to young children's developmental variation and the linguistic and cultural diversity in children and families entering preschool classrooms today.

Developmentally Responsive. Early childhood assessments must be developmentally responsive to the wide variation in the timelines and sequencing of young children's developmental accomplishments and learning progressions.

Culturally Responsive. Further, early childhood assessment must be responsive to children's different cultural backgrounds and experiences. This includes allowing children to show what they know and can do in multiple ways and, when using standardized instruments, ensuring that the photos and examples are meaningful and familiar to children. Being culturally responsive also means that the assessors share the racial and ethnic backgrounds of the children.

Linguistically Responsive. To be meaningful, early childhood assessments must also be linguistically responsive to the language(s) children are learning in their homes and within the preschool setting. As described in Chapter 3, learning more than one language should be recognized as an asset. Because emergent bilingual/multilingual children draw from their full linguistic repertoire when speaking, languages should not be treated as independent linguistic systems in assessment (Souto-Manning et al., 2019).

> A center's developmental profile included a section entitled "Self-Help Skills." Teachers observed and documented students' ability to feed themselves, put their belongings away, and take their jackets off. They noticed that a 3-year-old child, new to preschool, was very capable in all areas except self-feeding. In consultation with the family, the team learned that their culture did not have the same emphasis on independence. Feeding a young child was an act of love and care, so they had not yet introduced self-feeding at home.

Conducted by an Individual Who Knows the Child

It is strongly recommended that assessment with young children take place only with caregivers, teachers, and other adults familiar to the child. Otherwise, the child's stress-response systems can be easily activated into a fight, flight, or freeze survival response. When this happens, any assessment of the child's skills, knowledge, or dispositions will be significantly compromised and will likely misrepresent their actual abilities. In situations in which an unknown adult will engage in assessing young children, it is essential to include sufficient time to establish a rapport with the child before beginning. The required amount of time will vary by child; some will quickly acclimate to a new adult, whereas others will take a long period of time to feel safe and remain calm in the presence of the new adult.

Note: Reduction of the optimal time for establishing relationships with assessors often happens because teachers and staff are busy. However, the assessment data are then inaccurate, which can create negative consequences for children and their families.

Families Are Involved as Partners Throughout the Assessment Process

Families are more involved in the assessment process in early childhood than is typical with older students. Families are invited to be part of the data-collection process (sharing what they know and experience with their child), the interpretation of assessment data, as well as the development of learning goals, instructional strategies and activities teachers will use to support children in progress on their goals (Akers et al., 2015). Families are best positioned to understand children's strengths, interests, and the challenges that create barriers and prevent them from learning (e.g., sources of stress and trauma, health conditions, changes to family circumstances/life events). When families are involved in data collection, they can share their observations of how the child reacts or performs in the familiar home setting; for example, a child might be talkative at home but silent at school or exhibit extensive vocabulary in the home language but be reticent in English. Families' input when interpreting assessment data can contribute new insights that the teaching staff has not considered.

> The preschool team is concerned because after several months a child has not yet spoken in class in English or in her home language. They suspect a speech delay. When they voice concerns to the parents, the parents report that she excitedly tells them everything that happened at school in their home language each day.

> During transition times, a teacher notices that one of the children has a particularly hard time. In outside time, he runs around the playground while the others are gathering to go in. In free-choice time, he refuses to stop playing and to clean up. The teacher mentions this to his mother and asks her if she has noticed difficulty with transitions at home. She shares similar examples at home. They make plans to continue to observe and check back the following week to discuss ideas for easing him through transitions.

Developmental screening. If a screening assessment identifies a young child as having, or is at risk of having, a disability or learning/developmental need, families should receive responsive communication, including timely follow-up, evaluation, and, when appropriate, referral for specialized supports (NAEYC, 2020). Screening is used to assess whether children have specific needs that require additional evaluation and possible specialized supports and/or early intervention services. Screening is not used to diagnose or label children with deficit language.

High-stakes decisions. Any time assessment data is used for significant decisions that can profoundly impact a young child and the family (e.g., enrollment, placement), it is important that multiple sources of data be used to inform the decision. Data sources should include observations and input from teachers, family members, and specialists when appropriate. Multiple sources may include anecdotal observation notes taken over time, photos, and samples of children's creations and products, notes on checklists taken at several intervals, and notes from consultation with families.

ASSESSMENT WITH YOUNG CHILDREN IS CHALLENGING FOR A VARIETY OF REASONS

- Developmentally typical behavior and achievement of milestones is highly variable.
- Young children may not be able to demonstrate the full capacity of what they know and can do if the assessment requires skills they have not yet acquired (e.g., reading, writing, responding, holding and using pencils or markers, or recognizing symbols and thinking abstractly).
- Young children may not be able to demonstrate the full capacity of what they know and can do if the assessment is not culturally responsive or provided in their home language.
- Anxiety or activation of the stress-response system as a result of a requirement to separate from their parent or teacher, work with an unfamiliar adult, or enter an unfamiliar setting can trigger a survival reaction and greatly reduce children's ability to concentrate, speak, have focal attention, and/or self-regulate their emotions and behavior, which leads to inaccurate assessment results.

MONITORING YOUNG CHILDREN'S GROWTH AND DEVELOPMENT

Early childhood educators monitor children's growth in two main ways:

- Authentic assessment or curriculum-embedded classroom assessment
- Direct decontextualied assessment tools, sometimes referred to as formal assessments or general outcome measures (GOMs)

These two distinct assessment methods result in different types of data, and each has advantages and limitations. Curriculum-embedded approaches are the primary format used in early childhood settings because they are more comprehensive, identify multiple domains of children's development, are less disruptive, and are more likely to capture children's full range of capabilities, as teachers document children's skills within their daily activities and experiences in the classroom.

Authentic Curriculum-Embedded Assessment

Authentic assessment, also described as classroom assessment or curriculum-embedded assessment, takes place within the daily activities of the preschool classroom. It involves the collection of many different forms of assessment data, especially teachers' observations of children's play, and everyday activities and interactions in the classroom. Information is collected in many different learning contexts (individual and small- and large-group activities, circle time, book reading, outdoor play, routines, and transition times, etc.). Authentic assessment is an *ongoing process* that is informed by input from children, their parents and family members, and teachers.

Observation Is a Primary Activity in Authentic Assessment

Observation of young children—intentionally and systematically watching what children say and do in the context of daily activities and interactions— is a central technique in authentic assessment. Observation, sometimes described as "kid-watching" (Goodman, 1985) is a favored practice because it allows teachers to capture students using their skills and knowledge in real contexts as they engage in a wide range of meaningful activities. By systematically documenting what a child is doing in an everyday context and collecting ongoing observations over time, an authentic picture of growth emerges. When early childhood teachers observe children, they do the following:

Gather information. Thoughtfully watch and listen to children, noticing what they are saying and doing and how they are relating to others while striving to not bring in judgment, interpretation, evaluation, or preconceived expectations about what the children should be doing. Teachers learn to attend to a range of information that children communicate through their ways of talking and moving in the environment, use of materials, nonverbal behaviors, tone of voice, facial expressions, emotional state, and so on.

> As children play in the sand table, their teacher quietly observes their play. The youngest child in the group fills a bucket with sand and begins stirring with a stick. "Soup, who wants soup?" she asks the others at the sand table. The teacher jots down a quick anecdote about this exchange as an example of symbolic play and peer interaction.

Record information. Document what they observe using a variety of techniques and formats. These include written narrative observations (e.g., running records, anecdotal records including informal conversations with children), structured observations (time or event samples, checklists, and rating scales, formal interviews with children or family members), and electronic observations (photographs or audio or video recordings). Each observation technique is useful for different purposes, and early childhood teachers typically use a combination of different approaches.

> Often, teachers take down exact quotes from a child. Descriptive anecdotes can offer insights that are useful for building on a child's strengths, interests, and preferences. Teachers may also collect and analyze samples of the work children produce in the classroom, including drawings and paintings, photos of constructions using blocks or found materials, or arrays of math manipulatives.

During free-choice time, a teacher circulates through the classroom areas, stopping to listen and observe. As unobtrusively as possible, he snaps a quick photo of a group of children with an elaborate block building and train-track structure they have built. "Tell me about your structure," he asks and later jots down some quotes to accompany the photo.

Periodically during the year, a teacher sets up a self-portrait activity at small-group time. She invites children to use paper of various skin tones and markers to make pictures of themselves. She dates and saves these self-portraits as documentation of growth over time.

Interpret information. After observations are made and documented, teachers begin to interpret the behavior they have observed. This is a subjective process, as understanding why children display certain skills and behaviors in specific contexts is always a result of many factors (e.g., developmental capacities, cultural background, quality of the environment, neurobiology, and individual experiences, feeling of safety and/or belonging, etc.). A similar behavior can be interpreted in many different ways, even for the same child in different learning contexts. Teachers' own backgrounds and biases (e.g., social categories of identity) significantly impact what they observe and perceive in children. Therefore, it is helpful for teachers to learn to be continually working on gaining self-awareness of their own cultural perspectives and biases and to engage in reflection and conversations with colleagues and families about their observations and documentation to expand the meanings they are bringing to the observations of children.

A group of teachers is examining drawings students have made over time. They have collected samples from each child of simple crayon drawings. Laying out a series of drawings from one child, they notice the increasing control the child is demonstrating—moving from random scribbles, to spirals, to letter-like forms.

Performance Assessment

Performance assessment is a subset of authentic assessment. Performance assessment is informed by teachers' observations of children's daily activities. In the context of their classroom, children may be asked to "perform" a skill by retelling a story, reciting all the letters of the alphabet that they know, filling in rhyming patterns, or counting objects. As cautioned earlier, on-demand assessment may not be accurate because a child may not understand what is being asked, might become shy if they perceive they are being evaluated, or the way the specific task is posed may limit what they choose to share. For example, if an adult says, "Say the alphabet for me," a child may not respond if they don't know the alphabet. However, if the question was posed as, "Tell me all the letters you know," the child might share.

Portfolios

Many early childhood teachers organize the information they collect through authentic assessment into individual child portfolios. A *portfolio* is defined as a purposeful collection of children's work that illustrate children's efforts, progress, and achievements (Meisels et al., 1994). To be effective, portfolios should be integrated into the teaching, learning, and assessment process. Further, items included in a portfolio are selected because they are informative (e.g., reveal important aspects of a child's learning, thinking, or performance), easy to collect (e.g., examples of children's work that are authentically occurring in the classroom, not something contrived or created solely for the portfolio), and reflective of meaningful classroom activities (e.g., produced as a result of children's participation in meaningful classroom activities they are internally motivated to engage in) (Meisels et al., 1995).

Portfolios serve many purposes, including:

- Capturing the quality of the child's thinking, learning, and work in the classroom
- Showing the child's developmental and educational progress over time
- Involving the child in assessing their own work and achievement
- Documenting the range of classroom experiences and learning contexts available to the child
- Assisting teachers in planning curricula and instruction and arranging the environment
- Providing teachers with an opportunity to reflect on their expectations for children's learning and work in the classroom
- Providing children, teachers, families, administrators, and other decisionmakers with essential and authentic information about children's progress and classroom experiences (Meisels et al., 1994, p. 13)

POPULAR COMMERCIAL CURRICULUM-EMBEDDED ASSESSMENT SYSTEMS USED IN EARLY CHILDHOOD

Creative Curriculum Developmental Continuum. Developed to be a supplement to *The Creative Curriculum®* *Developmental Continuum for Ages 3–5* and *A Teacher's Guide to Using the Creative Curriculum® Developmental Continuum Assessment System* (Dodge et al., 2002), the Developmental Continuum was designed to support teachers in determining what individual children know and are able to do. It describes 50 skills relevant to preschool children's development.

Desired Results Developmental Profile (DRDP). The Desired Results Developmental Profile (California Department of Education, 2015) is a formative assessment instrument developed for young children and their families (early infancy to kindergarten entry). It is administered in natural settings through teacher observations, family observations, and examples of children's work. The DRDP is aligned with early learning standards in California, the Common Core State Standards, and the Head Start Child Development and Early Learning Framework. It adheres to the principles of Universal Design and includes domains that meet the federal Office of Special Education Programs (OSEP) child outcome reporting requirements for children with Individualized Family Service Plans (IFSPs) or Individual Education Plans (IEPs). The DRDP addresses cultural and linguistic responsiveness by including observation and documentation of children's behavior in both the home language and English to obtain a more accurate profile of the children's knowledge and skills across developmental domains.

HighScope Child Observation Record (COR) (HighScope, 2012). HighScope's Child Observation Record (COR Advantage) corresponds with HighScope's key developmental indicators (KDIs) (2012). COR Advantage is an observation-based assessment instrument for children from birth through kindergarten. It is designed to measure children's progress in all early childhood programs (including, but not limited to, those using the HighScope educational approach). It is divided into eight major categories with items that include eight developmental levels, ranging from zero (the simplest) to seven (the most complex). Teaching staff collect anecdotes for completing the COR during normal daily routines. The results provide detailed reports that analyze progress and are designed for various audiences, from families to government monitors.

Teaching Strategies GOLD™ Assessment System. (GOLD®). (Heroman et al., 2010). Teaching Strategies GOLD is a formative curriculum-embedded digital assessment system that has been designed and validated for use with young children ages birth to kindergarten. GOLD uses color-coded progressions to guide teachers in assessment and in individualizing instruction. GOLD is aligned to early learning standards, Common Core Standards, and the Head Start Child Development and Early Learning Framework. It addresses 10 areas of development and learning, including English language acquisition. Assessment data are stored digitally, including information collected from families. Data are summarized for multiple reporting purposes.

Work Sampling System (WSS) (Meisels et al., 1995). A comprehensive performance-based assessment system designed to be used from preschool through elementary school. The WSS is an assessment system that is responsive to classroom context. It includes three components: developmental guidelines and checklists (record children's growth in relationship to teacher expectations and national standards), portfolios (display examples of the characteristics and quality of children's work), and summary reports that replace report cards and provide performance and progress ratings for families, teachers, and administrators.

Benefits of Authentic, Curriculum-Embedded Assessment.

- They are the most common form of assessment in early childhood classrooms. Recommended by the National Association of the Education of Young Children and National Association of Early Childhood Specialists in state departments of education to guide early childhood teachers' curriculum planning and instruction.
- Provide a more comprehensive and authentic understanding of children's developmental progress and learning.
- Offer an effective and meaningful method for teachers to systematically document children's strengths and challenge areas/learning gaps and to monitor their learning over time.
- Document the specific circumstances and contexts in which a child demonstrates a specific skill, type of knowledge, or disposition as well as the level of support they need to be learning in their zone of proximal development.
- Allow teachers to be responsive to the specific interests and needs of children in the classroom.
- Can inform daily planning and implementation of developmentally, culturally, and linguistically responsive curriculum and instruction as well as interventions for children who need differentiated instruction and supports. Investment (time and money) in teacher training (e.g., observation, documentation, etc.) provides direct benefits to classroom practice (which is not true for formal assessment) (Akers et al., 2015; National Research Council of the National Academies, 2008).

Drawbacks of Authentic, Curriculum-Embedded Assessment.

- Requires substantial investment in teacher training.
- Requires clearly defined rubrics and scoring guides, which can be time-consuming to develop.

- Level of teacher burden is high. Requires significant time and effort. Teachers should be given paid time during work hours to complete the required paperwork and tasks, though often they are not.
- When teachers are actively involved with children, it can be challenging (and at times, disruptive) to stop and document significant learning moments (taking notes and photos and videos of children) (Akers et al., 2015; National Research Council of the National Academies, 2008).

Anecdotal observation is a type of qualitative data gathering strategy. As with any data gathering, there can be researcher bias. In other words, because of a teacher's investment in a child, they may interpret their behavior in a way that attributes more growth than has actually occurred. Conversely, teachers may not fully appreciate a child's expression of learning if it is culturally different than what the teacher is familiar with. This could result in a child not receiving scaffolding (or even services) at the level they actually need.

Direct Decontextualized Assessments

The second type of assessment used in early childhood are direct decontextualized instruments, also referred to as formal assessments, general outcome measures (GOMs), or decontextualized assessments (Akers et al., 2015). Direct assessments typically require an adult—sometimes someone the child knows and other times an adult unfamiliar to the child—who sits with the child and asks them to respond to specific questions, requests, and prompts (e.g., point to a picture, count these objects, hop on one foot). When the person administering the direct assessment is unfamiliar, the assumption is that this will decrease teacher bias. Direct assessments are often quantitative measures of a child's learning and growth at specific times over the course of a year or other specified time period. Examples of these assessments are readiness scales, skill inventories, and screening tools. The assessment environment (directions, presentation of materials, verbal prompts) is standardized with a goal that every child has the same testing conditions (National Research Council of the National Academies, 2008). Direct assessments are often used for large-scale research studies (e.g., Early Childhood Longitudinal Study) and program evaluations (Head Start National Reporting System). Digitally based direct assessments are not recommended for use with young children.

Benefits of Decontextualized GOM Approaches.

- Are more time efficient, as they do not require multiple observations.
- Can document patterns in a child's learning and growth over time and be compared with data from other groups of children and from other contexts.

- Standardized testing conditions can reduce teacher bias. However, the items on the assessment can still be biased and lack cultural, linguistic, or personal relevance to a specific child or group of children.
- Can help educators identify developmental delays, health issues, and/or disabilities in young children (National Research Council of the National Academies, 2008).

Drawbacks of Decontextualized GOM Assessments. Direct assessments present challenges for young children, and as a result, their validity and reliability are often questioned and critiqued (National Research Council of the National Academies, 2008; Meisels, 1989). One main problem is that children's scores on direct assessments are often highly correlated with socioeconomic status (National Research Council of the National Academies, 2008), raising equity concerns about what, specifically, they are measuring. Additional limitations of direct assessments include:

- They can be stressful for young children and if children's stress-response systems are activated, the test results are unlikely to be an accurate representation of their skills and knowledge.
- Children may struggle to remain focused and engaged. Questions and tasks that are decontextualized with no connection to children's lives may be confusing and unmotivating for children and may lead to their disengagement.
- Children may struggle to understand and/or respond to the verbal directions given by the assessor, especially if the assessment is not provided in their home language.
- Children may be unfamiliar with some of the vocabulary and use of language (e.g., "show the best answer") or may misinterpret a question or not understand what is being asked of them (if assessor uses negatives or subordinate clauses).
- Young children can be very inconsistent when adults ask them to say or do something.
- The testing context (responding directly to adults' questions) is culturally incongruent for some children and considered rude in certain cultural contexts.
- They interfere with children's meaningful learning time and teachers' instructional time.
- Most often do not provide direct benefit to classroom practice (National Research Council of the National Academies, 2008).

For all these reasons and more, the information generated by direct assessments may be inaccurate or incomplete. Further, when children do not respond to a question, adults cannot assume that this indicates that a child does not know something. When administering an assessment to a child they know, teachers sometimes find that the child does not respond or responds incorrectly to an item they are certain the child understands. Tests given in English to children who are not proficient in English will not reveal what they know and can do. Cultural and linguistic differences between children's home language and the language used in an assessment can strongly influence how children respond to a test item. Therefore, decontextualized assessments may not give useful results to plan follow-up activities or initiate referrals for services.

EXAMPLES OF DIRECT ASSESSMENTS USED IN EARLY CHILDHOOD

Screening Instruments

Ages and Stages
Denver Prescreening Developmental Questionnaire
Peabody Developmental Motor Scales
The Early Screening Inventory
DIAL (Developmental Indicators for Assessment of Learning)

Diagnostic Tests

Denver II
Dynamic Indicators of Basic Early Literacy Skills (DIBELS)
Kaufman Assessment Battery for Children
Peabody Picture Vocabulary Test
Stanford Binet Intelligence Scale
Test of Early Mathematics Ability (TEMA)
Test of Early Reading Ability (TERA)
Vineland Adaptive Behavior Scales

Readiness/Achievement Tests

Clinical Evaluation of Language Fundamentals—Preschool (CELF)
Cognitive Skills Assessment Battery
Gesell Developmental Assessment
Metropolitan Readiness Test
Peabody Individual Achievement Test—Revised (PIAT-R)
Stanford-Binet
Wechsler Preschool and Primary Scale of Intelligence
Woodcock Johnson III

ONE-TIME "SNAPSHOT" ASSESSMENTS

A snapshot assessment gives data at one point in time, and as such is an incomplete picture of a child's growth. Decisions about whether to refer a child for additional services, whether to retain or promote a child to the next level, and even how to plan a curriculum that meets a child's strengths and needs cannot be made without multiple sources of information gathered over time.

A one-time snapshot of a child entering a kindergarten classroom cannot capture all the cumulative experiences in programs, in the home, and in the community of a young child from birth to that day in kindergarten. Such assessments should not be seen as reflecting on the quality of early care and education during the prekindergarten year in isolation from demographic and opportunity/resource factors related to the home and the community, other early care and education experiences, and the resources available to support professional development and improve quality.

For example, a specific assessment may be selected because of its ease of administration but result in data too limited to inform instruction or evaluate a program's effectiveness. Likewise, an assessment may be administered to a sample of children served, rather than all children, to reduce costs or allow for more in-depth assessment, but these data cannot then be used to inform instruction for all children or for any individual child.

CONCERNS WITH STANDARDIZED TESTING IN EARLY CHILDHOOD

The use of standardized testing to assess young children is increasing in early childhood settings. Though there are some contexts in which direct standardized testing can be beneficial, there are substantial concerns with the use of testing with young children, and this testing *should never be used for high-stakes reasons,* including placement, tracking, or retention decisions. Experts warn of many reasons why standardized testing is problematic in early childhood and should be used infrequently, including:

- The validity and reliability of tests are often questionable, given the challenges young children so frequently have in testing situations (as described previously).
- Tests do not reflect decades of research describing how young children learn and how they can demonstrate what they know and can do. Their narrow focus on decontextualized skills that must be demonstrated outside an authentic context can render results that are inaccurate and/or misleading. Further, the results may not reflect children's comprehension or meaning-making processes that are central to learning.
- Tests measure a narrow range of skills and knowledge (primarily language and literacy and cognitive abilities), and they do not identify many of the central areas of focus in preschool classrooms. For example, direct assessments often do not address approaches to learning, social–emotional capacities, creativity, problem solving,

self-regulation, emergent bilingualism/multilingualism, and moral development/respect for diversity.

- Almost all tests and direct assessment instruments are culturally biased. They are overwhelmingly based on dominant, White Eurocentric middle-class perspectives and norms and are not culturally or linguistically responsive to the diversity of young children and their families. This bias has negative consequences for young children of color, as they are more easily positioned through deficit because their cultural ways of knowing, perspectives, and daily experiences are not reflected in the content or methods of communication required in most direct assessments.

- Many educators who administer direct assessments to young children are not trained in the use of standardized tests or in the interpretation of the results. This increases the risk of the test being administered inappropriately and the results misunderstood or interpreted inaccurately. This lack of understanding of standardized testing, especially the psychometric properties of specific tests, has led to the misuse of direct assessments for purposes other than what they were designed for (for example, they may be used to prevent children from starting preschool, retaining them and insisting they repeat a grade, placing them in remedial classes, or removing them from the regular classroom and placing them in a special education classroom).

- It is a well-known phenomenon that many educators feel pressure to produce high test scores among students, which leads to a narrowing of the curriculum, developmentally inappropriate learning conditions for young children, and valuable learning time being co-opted in order to "teach to the test."

REFLECTION AND DISCUSSION QUESTIONS

- The interpretations of assessment results/scores that reflect lower-than-expected or lower-than-desired learning or achievement for young children—and the actions taken in response to these products, may differ significantly across various contexts: Whereas one school/community may respond with increased intervention efforts and additional resource allocation, another school/community may respond by retaining a child, limiting the curriculum, or engaging in other punitive actions that severely limit a child's current and future learning opportunities. Sit with a team as they review assessment results for their class. How do they talk about children who are outside the median range of development for the group? What kind of supports are suggested? Do these responses increase or narrow opportunities for children?

- Review the various assessment approaches and tools used in your early childhood program to screen for early intervention. Ensure that they will yield accurate, actionable information by considering the extent to which they are developmentally responsive, culturally and linguistically appropriate, and free of bias.

EFFECTIVE AND EQUITABLE USE OF ASSESSMENT IN EARLY CHILDHOOD CLASSROOMS

- Know the purpose of the assessment and choose assessments that will yield data that address your purpose.
- Use multiple assessment tools to learn about the same aspect of development. Triangulate and confirm results using a combination of observation, checklists, and decontextualized assessments.
- Gather ongoing information on children's growth.
- Be aware of linguistic and cultural differences that may impact what a child is able or willing to share.
- Gather information about what children can do when they "stretch" in response to scaffolding from an adult or peer.
- If your school is required to collect decontextualized and/or snapshot data for district accountability purposes, know that this information has limited accuracy.
- For decisions that have a significant impact on young children, always use multiple forms of information from multiple people over time to inform the decision and never a single snapshot test score.
- Ensure that the outcomes of assessments are not used to label or blame children and families.

INVOLVING PARENTS AND FAMILIES IN ASSESSMENT

Early childhood staff involve parents and families in the assessment process in many ways. Information that teachers and other support staff gather through observations and documentation of experiences in the classroom or at school should always be combined with input from families about their child. It is the combination of these different perspectives and sources of data that provide the most accurate and complete picture of a child. Research studies highlight that parents' observations of their children are valid and reliable sources of data that should be included in early childhood assessment (National Research Council of the National Academies, 2008). There are several contexts in which teachers gather information from families that is included in the ongoing process of gathering data for assessment purposes:

- **Intake Conversations.** Teachers begin each year by gathering information from families about their child, including but not limited to, milestones in the child's growth and development and how the child responds in various settings and their interests, routines, fears, and learning preferences. Families may also share prior results of developmental screenings or evaluations or other helpful information about their child and their individual developmental trajectory and/or past learning experiences.
- **Ongoing Conversations.** Teachers should take notes about information shared in ongoing conversations with families, as this documentation provides important information about children that can be included in assessment materials.
- **Focused Conversations.** Teachers often plan for focused conversations with parents and family members to gather information about specific skills, knowledge, or dispositions that are difficult to observe in the classroom. Family members are typically asked to discuss a child's daily routines and activities so that the teacher can determine how, if at all, a child is demonstrating a skill or capacity in their home or another environment outside the classroom context.

Communication With Families of Children With Delays and/or Disabilities

Teachers and administrators will also work closely with families when assessing children who show signs of delay and/or are at risk for disabilities. Generally, after teachers collect multiple forms of data over a period of time, they arrange to meet with the child's family to share observations and invite the family to share their own perspectives, recognizing that parents and family members know the child best and have essential information to inform any understanding or interpretation of the child's capabilities.

All families want to feel reassured that educators see their children as whole human beings and genuinely like their children. They want to hear that teachers observe and appreciate their child's strengths and interests, and these observations should be the primary focus at the beginning of every parent–teacher meeting. Parents will not feel a sense of safety or belonging if teachers and/or administrators focus only on a child's vulnerabilities, challenges, or delays. This type of deficit approach is likely to create distrust, which can impede the partnership between families and schools and prevent the child from receiving the intervention support and services they need. After opening with information about a child's strengths, teachers can share their observations about the skills or behaviors that are causing some concern. Using descriptive nonjudgmental language is important, "I have observed that noise in the classroom often leads Emily to raise her voice and cover her ears and sometimes run and hide under a table where she rocks back and forth. I'm wondering if you have seen these behaviors at home and if so, how have you responded." Invite the family to share their own ideas about their child's experience and behaviors at school and listen thoughtfully without defensiveness, evaluation, or a need to "correct" their interpretation of events. Having a true partnership with families means that educators truly listen and learn from them—instead of assuming that teachers are the experts and know what is best for the child.

Many families will be thankful to have an open, caring, conversation about concerns that are raised, as they may have observed similar behaviors and had their own worries but have not known where to turn for support. Parents need to feel a sense of trust that the school is honestly interested in supporting their child and that the staff will include them as partners to identify what might be going on. With this foundation, families are more likely to participate when the school recommends that the child be evaluated or referred for additional services.

It is essential that families of young children feel reassured that no matter what support services a child may need, the child and family will not be excluded from the program if their child has a disability or special learning or developmental need. Families should never be made to feel that something is "wrong" with their child. Especially in preschool, when parents and family members are just beginning their relationship with a school/district, teachers and administrators should reinforce their shared commitment to identify the specific resources and supports best suited to an individual child's needs and family context.

Families of young children at risk for or diagnosed with disabilities may experience a range of emotions and challenges as they come to understand and accept what this means for their child and family. They may initially struggle to accept the news about their child being diagnosed with a disability, they may resist finding or accepting support and/or early intervention services, they may insist a child "will grow out of it," or they may struggle to manage the various relationships and frequency of communication with the professionals who come to their home or begin working with their child and the family. At a time that is already difficult for many families, the added demands of intervention services can be very stressful, and families need early childhood staff to have empathy and patience and to reassure the family with caring, respectful, and transparent communication that reinforces that everyone is working together in partnership on behalf of the child.

Families of children with disabilities have a primary role in making decisions about the types and extent of services they want their child to receive. By law, they must be involved in all decisions and give their consent for any special services or resources their child receives that extend beyond what other children in the classroom receive.

REFLECTION AND DISCUSSION QUESTION

- When children are being evaluated for or are receiving services related to a disability and/or special need, how do you ensure that parents and families are included as full partners in all communication, assessment, and decisionmaking?

KEY TAKEAWAYS FOR PRINCIPALS

- Although there may be unique circumstances in which standardized instruments are warranted, it is important to ensure that developmentally responsive assessment is used to support, monitor, and document children's growth. Standardized assessments should be used only on a limited basis and never as the sole data point for making high-stakes decisions.
- Principals play an important role in ensuring that communication with families about the assessment and evaluation process, and any decisions made in response to the results (e.g., further assessment, linkage with intervention services, etc.), happens in a timely manner in a format that is accessible and clear for families.
- Principals can ensure the effective and equitable use of assessment in their early childhood classrooms by:
  - » Making sure all assessment/evaluation materials for families are available in the family's home language and/or there is an interpreter available to participate in meetings.
  - » Involving someone who knows the family and shares the family's language and/or culture (e.g., community liaison or family navigator, pastor or other faith leader, elder etc.) who can help gain trust if a family is hesitant or resistant to participating and partnering in the assessment process.
  - » Reassuring families about confidentiality regarding the assessment data, explaining what data are collected, who will have access to it, how it will be used, and where it will be stored.
  - » Ensuring that *all* communication is strengths-based and emphasizes a child's strengths, interests, sources of creativity, adaptability, and resilience as well as progress and accomplishments as much as, if not more than, specific concerns. All meetings should begin and end with communication that reinforces positive and hopeful messages about the child.
  - » Supporting teachers by making sure that they have paid time during their regular workday to complete necessary paperwork and tasks associated with assessment processes.

Conclusion

> To be effective instructional leaders, elementary school principals must understand how all children in their schools learn. Teaching and learning should look different in pre-K and kindergarten than it does in 4th grade, and principals need to be able to make that distinction. (Lieberman, 2019)

Principals can profoundly impact young children's learning experiences and outcomes. They play a critical role in the quality of teachers' instruction, the climate of the learning environment for children and staff, how welcome (or not) parents and families feel to engage with the program/school, and the patterns and trajectories of student learning and outcomes at their school sites. Principals are also well positioned to be powerful bridge builders who envision and create alignment between high-quality preschool programs and early elementary grades. As attention to issues of equity is becoming more urgent across the field of early childhood education, it is important for principals to ensure that their early learning staff and programs are dedicated to disrupting harmful and biased practices. Additionally, principals must ensure that teachers and staff are working on a daily basis to support every child to feel safe, welcome, and respected so that they can build the healthy foundations in early childhood that are necessary to develop, learn, and thrive in their potential in their future years.

As readers of this book, you are already taking the most important step toward becoming an effective early learning leader—expanding your knowledge of high-quality early childhood teaching and the characteristics of early learning environments that support young children to be optimally engaged as learners in preschool settings. We recommend that you consider your learning trajectory as a marathon and not a race. Early childhood education is a complex field with policies, procedures, and practices that are dynamic and continually updated in response to expanding scientific research and data sources, the changing demographics of young children, families, and the early childhood workforce in the United States, shifting cultural and political influences, and innovative new approaches and solutions to improve the quality and delivery of services to children and families. We encourage readers to:

- *Identify one or more colleagues to collaborate with as critical friends* who can provide support, encouragement, and accountability as you learn about and practice implementing the content in this book.

- **Keep it simple.** Instead of taking on several changes all at once, begin working on one or two strategies. Becoming an effective early learning leader is long-term work. It will require principals to commit to ongoing reflection, reading, dialogue, and professional learning on topics related to early education to improve their practice one day, one interaction, one conversation, and one decision at a time.

And most important:

- **Remember to keep a focus on your "why"**—the professional values and mission driving your efforts to learn about early childhood. This will be an important guidepost in maintaining your commitment to this work.

PRINCIPALS WHO ARE EFFECTIVE EARLY LEARNING LEADERS UNDERSTAND

- How young children learn.
- What powerful learning looks and sounds like in preschool classrooms.
- The complex role of preschool teachers who guide, scaffold, and direct children's learning through play.
- That parents and families are positioned as reciprocal partners in early learning programs.
- And the importance of providing ongoing support and meaningful feedback to early childhood educators, including them as equally valued and respected professionals who are integral to the school community.
- *There has never been a more urgent and important time for the nation's principals to become effective and equitable early learning leaders. Are you ready to commit to engage in this critical learning journey?*

Conducting Effective Early Learning Walk-Through Observations

Corinne Eisenhart and Elisabeth Grinder-McLean created a tool that helps principals know what to focus on as they conduct regular walk-throughs in early childhood classrooms. The walk-through guide includes three key dimensions:

- *Focus on Learning.* Focuses in on children's actions. What are the children doing?
- *Focus on Teaching.* Guides principals' attention to the role of the teacher. What is the teacher doing?
- *Focus on Classroom Environment.* Highlights what to look for in the early learning environment.

The instrument encourages principals to look for evidence of children's active learning (diverse materials and learning activities that provide opportunities for children to explore their interests and experiment with, predict, and solve meaningful problems). It also encourages language-rich environments (teachers talking with children, not at them; a classroom alive with conversations and rich vocabulary; practice with listening skills; many reading and writing experiences including interactive read-alouds with storybooks and informational texts and discussions about books), many opportunities for interactive, purposeful play (e.g., puppetry, painting, games, building with blocks, and pretend play), and evidence of a positive caring climate (children who are joyful and feel a sense of safety as seen in their engagement, expression of joy, willingness to take risks, and progress in acquiring new skills and knowledge).

The tool is designed for principals to use during regular short visits to preschool classrooms. Though it provides guidance on many different characteristics of an effective early learning program, the tool is specifically tailored to the aspects of preschool environments that support children's language and literacy development. Principals are encouraged to use the walk-through tool for supporting conversations with teachers and cycles of continuous quality improvement, not for evaluation.

See link to the Literacy Walkthrough Template for Early Learning Classrooms (Eisenhart & Grinder-McLean, 2013) (http://www.naesp.org /sites/default/files/LiteracyWalkthroughTemplate_2.pdf).

REMEMBER TO LOOK FOR ATTENTION TO EQUITY AND DIVERSITY

It is important to note that the walk-through template does not explicitly address the important issues of diversity and equity that we have emphasized throughout this book. Therefore, we suggest that you think about this template as one resource but not as a comprehensive guide that includes everything principals should be observing when entering early childhood classrooms. Over time, you can adapt the template to include indicators that are specific to your school/community and expand the items to explicitly bring attention to various ways diversity and equity are supported in the classroom. For example, Martínez (2021) offers several questions that principals might find useful to ask as they enter and observe early childhood classrooms:

- Can children hear their first languages spoken or sung?
- Are families encouraged to support their children's development in their first language?
- Do photos of the children and families displayed in the classroom reflect their cultural backgrounds? Do they avoid stereotypical representations of food, clothing, and practices?
- Are cultural differences seen as potential resources or as challenges to overcome?
- Do classroom labels, dictations, and signs reflect the children's first languages and diverse racial/ethnic backgrounds?
- Are cultural differences discussed in a positive, respectful way?

Professional Development for Principals to Learn About High-Quality Early Childhood Education

Guiding principals to become effective leaders in early learning requires a multipronged commitment that includes both preservice (integration into credential coursework and practicum experiences) and inservice support. In what follows, we describe how one rural school district in Northern California, Eureka City School (ECS) District, has integrated several professional development opportunities that are provided annually in order to bring the attention of district leaders to early learning programs and to deepen their understanding of the various elements of high-quality preschool environments. Heather Richardson, Director of Early Childhood Education for ECS, works closely with principals in the school district and leads the planning and implementation of these events for her programs, including annual instructional school-site visits, presentation to the school board, and chats between principals and the district cabinet members.

INSTRUCTIONAL SCHOOL-SITE VISITS

Each year, school district leaders and staff tour early learning programs to observe and to provide feedback. During these visits, Heather begins the visits with a short presentation during which she shares highlights of the programs and makes recommendations to the visitors about what to look for when they enter the classrooms, typically related to district instructional standards and norms. She reinforces how children learn through play and the complex role of the teacher in a play-based classroom. She also makes visible the intentional preparation that goes into teachers' lesson-planning and the way the environment is arranged in order to:

- Facilitate engaging and relevant learning opportunities for all children (this includes providing accommodations for children with disabilities and special needs, as the ECS preschool program practices full inclusion).

- Allow for data collection for ongoing assessment in a natural and authentic way as well as to inform planning and to monitor children's progress on learning goals as they prepare them for the move into transitional kindergarten/kindergarten in the district.

After this short presentation, the group breaks into pairs or trios, and they spend time observing in classrooms. Generally, after 15 minutes, they exit the classroom they are visiting, have a short meeting to talk about what they saw, and write down a few notes. They continue with this process and visit two more classrooms. Then, the larger group reconvenes to share what they found and to provide the site administrators with feedback. At the end of the meeting, the visitors share key words that describe their experience during the visit. The site is then presented with a framed wordle to commemorate the visit. The following is a sample agenda for school-site visits:

9:30 Short presentation
10:00 Pair up and begin classroom visits of approximately 15–20 minutes each.
11:00 Group gathers to debrief and share experiences.
11:30 Closing

BOARD PRESENTATIONS

Annually, Heather Richardson has an opportunity to present to the school board during a public meeting. She has 5–10 minutes to share highlights of the early education programs. She often describes:

- Number of preschool sites, preschool children, and staff in the district.
- The reason why preschool programs emphasize social–emotional learning.
- The continuum of play-based learning (child self-determined play, adult–child collaborative play, adult-directed play) and the skills, knowledge, and dispositions children are gaining through play and their experiences in preschool.

Heather includes photographs of the children that provide explicit links between children's activities and what they are learning, as well as parent testimonials about their children's experiences in the programs (see Figure B.1).

She also makes explicit how children's participation in different learning contexts in the preschool classroom is aligned with individual learning goals across different domains (cognitive, social–emotional, and physical) and subject areas (language, literacy, mathematics, etc.) as seen in Figures B.1.5 and B.1.6.

Figure B.1. Board Presentation

Figure B.1.1: Introducing Our Youngest Learners

The District's Youngest Learners

Are interacting by exchanging toys and talking about each other's activities

Through nursery rhymes, are learning how language works and the sounds vowels and consonants make

Are beginning to recognize feelings in each other and developing a sense of empathy...and a sense of HUMOR!

Figure B.1.2: Community Values

A Community that...

Fosters relationships

Welcomes and supports all through inclusive practices

Teaches kindness and mindfulness through real, everyday experiences

Empowers students and families

Figure B.1.3: What Children Are Learning

An Environment That Supports...

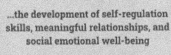

...all aspects of children's' development and creates an atmosphere of cooperation, initiative, and intellectual challenge

...the development of self-regulation skills, meaningful relationships, and social emotional well-being

...taking turns, sharing, following routines, solving problems and developing a positive self-image

Figure B.1. *(continued)*

Figure B.1.4: Parent Testimonial

Parent Comment

"Winzler Children's Center has been a true
blessing to my family and I...

...my son is learning in leaps and bounds...

...I am extremely grateful to Winzler and the
staff for the positive, healthy environment
they have provided for my son"

-Lisa Bozzoli

Figure B.1.5: Fine Motor Skills

Fine Motor Skills

Small
coordinated hand
movements

Essential for
fluent writing

Grow sustained
attention to a task

Figure B.1.6: Literacy Skills

Fountas and Pinnell Literacy

Students display
comprehension of
reading before
acquiring
decoding skills

Students
frequently engage
in reading during
play

PRINCIPAL'S "CHAT" WITH CABINET

A third format involves principals' chats with school leaders. These chats are fairly short and informal and happen once in fall and once in spring. It's an opportunity for principals to share what's going on at their site with district cabinet members. They typically last no longer than 30 minutes. Heather, as the administrator of ECS preschool programs, participates in these conversations. She is able to highlight any new projects/initiatives (participation in grant programs, inclusive practices, trauma responsiveness, etc.) in the early childhood classrooms, answer district leaders' questions (regarding staffing, programmatic operations, curriculum, etc.), advocate for the emerging needs of early childhood staff/programs (professional development topics, funding, collaboration, etc.) and reinforce the important connection between early childhood/preschool and the K–12 continuum within the district.

Resources

Child Development

Center on the Developing Child at Harvard University (https://developingchild.harvard.edu/). The Center on the Developing Child translates science related to child development into recommendations for policies and evidence-based practices. The website includes downloadable infographics, video clips, and a resource library on a range of topics, including brain architecture, toxic stress and resilience, executive function and self-regulation, and the science of adult capabilities.

Equity

Center for Equity in Early Childhood Education (CEECE) (www.ceece.org). CEECE is a nonprofit agency dedicated to improving intersectional justice and equity for young children, their families, and the early childhood workforce.

Children's Equity Project (CEP) (https://childandfamilysuccess.asu.edu/cep). The CEP works at the intersection of research, practice, and policy and focuses on pressing equity issues in early childhood, including, but not limited to, disproportionate discipline, corporal punishment, and bias; immigration and young children; language policies and supporting dual-language learners; inclusion of children with disabilities; maternal and child health disparities; and issues affecting children in tribal communities.

National Black Child Development Institute (NBCDI) (https://www.nbcdi.org/). NBCDI engages leaders, policymakers, professionals, and parents around issues that directly impact Black children and their families. NBCDI develops and delivers strengths-based, culturally relevant, evidence-based, and trauma-informed resources that respond to the unique strengths and needs of Black children around issues including early childhood education, health and wellness, literacy, and family engagement.

Gender Justice in Early Childhood (GJEC) (https://www.genderjusticeinearlychildhood.com/). This website provides free downloadable resources for early childhood professionals who are interested in creating inclusive early learning environments that support children of all genders.

UnidosUS (https://www.unidosus.org). Serves the Hispanic community through research, policy analysis, state and national advocacy efforts, and program work in communities nationwide. One area of emphasis is culturally responsive high-quality early learning programs for Latinx children and families.

Play

The American Academy of Pediatrics. The AAP has published three reports describing the importance of play for young children:

- The Power of Play: A Pediatric Role in Enhancing Development in Young Children (Yogman et al., 2018) provides information about the benefits of play, encourages pediatricians to write a prescription for play at well-child visits, and describes the importance of playful learning for the promotion of healthy child development (http://pediatrics.aappublications.org/content/142/3/e20182058).
- The Importance of Play in Promoting Healthy Child Development and Maintaining Strong Parent–Child Bond: Focus on Children in Poverty (Milteer et al. 2012) describes how children who live in poverty often face socioeconomic obstacles that impede their rights to have playtime, thus affecting their healthy social–emotional development. The report advocates recognition by parents, educators, and pediatricians of the importance of lifelong benefits that children gain from play, especially children furthest from opportunity (https://pediatrics.aappublications.org/content/129/1/e204).
- The Importance of Play in Promoting Healthy Child Development and Maintaining Strong Parent–Child Bonds (Ginsburg et al., 2007) describes why play is essential to children's development and addresses a variety of factors that have reduced play at home and in school (http://pediatrics.aappublications.org/content/129/1/e204.full).

Downloadable Briefs on Play for Early Childhood Educators and Parents/Families:

- Play: It's the Way Young Children Learn: http://earlychildhoodfunders.org/play.html
- The Power of Play for Addressing Trauma in the Early Years: http://www.earlychildhoodfunders.org/pdf/Play-and-Trauma-Brief-final-4-2020.pdf
- Additional resources, research and policy documents discussing the Value of Play for Early Learning: http://www.earlychildhoodfunders.org/pdf/playresources.pdf

Social-Emotional Learning, Toxic Stress, and Trauma

Collaborative for Social Emotional Learning (CASEL) (https://casel.org/). CASEL's mission is to help make evidence-based social–emotional learning (SEL) an integral part of education from preschool through high school. This page lists popular SEL programs for preschool (https://casel.org/guide/preschool/).

Dr. Nadine Burke Harris TEDMED 2014 Talk: How Childhood Trauma Affects Health Across a Lifetime (https://ted.com/talks/nadine_burke_harris_how_childhood_trauma_affects_health_across_a_lifetime?utm_source=tedcomshare&utm_medium=email&utm_campaign=tedspread). Pediatrician Nadine Burke Harris describes the science behind Adverse Childhood Experiences (ACEs), explaining the impact of toxic stress (abuse, neglect, and parents struggling with mental health or substance abuse issues, etc.) on brain development. This was groundbreaking talk that inspired a national conversation about the need to screen for ACEs in early childhood.

Professional Websites

Center for the Study of Child Care Employment (CSCCE) (https://cscce.berkeley.edu/). CSCCE conducts research and policy analysis about the characteristics of those who care for and educate young children and examines policy solutions aimed at improving how our nation prepares, supports, and rewards these early educators to ensure young children's optimal development. This website has many helpful downloadable reports and data displays about the early childhood workforce across the United States.

Defending the Early Years (DEY) (https://dey.org/about-us/). DEY is a nonprofit organization working for a just, equitable, and quality early childhood education for every young child. DEY advocates for active, developmentally appropriate, play-based approaches to learning. The DEY website includes research reports, policy recommendations, and resources on high-quality early childhood for educators, parents, and advocates.

Head Start Early Childhood Learning & Knowledge Center (https://eclkc.ohs.acf.hhs.gov/). This comprehensive website has information on a range of topics for early childhood professionals, including program management, child development, early childhood education, family engagement, and children's health. Though the content is specifically focused on Head Start programs, this website is widely used by early childhood professionals working in a variety of early learning contexts.

National Association for the Education of Young Children (NAEYC) (www.naeyc.org). The NAEYC is the largest professional organization in the field of early childhood. It works to promote high-quality early learning for all young children, birth through age 8, by connecting early childhood practice, policy, and research.

National Association of Elementary School Principals (NAESP) (https://www.naesp.org/prek3-leadership). NAESP developed the Pre-K–3 Leadership Academy®, a nationwide professional learning program to support principals and other school leaders with a job-embedded, sustained, and ongoing professional learning experience on effective instructional leadership practices in the early childhood, early elementary years. The yearlong learning experience results in a credential as an NAESP Pre-K-3 Leader. NAESP just published a new guide for principals titled, *Leading learning communities: A principal's guide to early learning and the early grades (pre-K–3rd grade)* (Kauerz et al., 2021).

National Indian Child Care Association (NICCA) (https://www.nicca.us/). The NICCAQ is a representative American Indian and Alaska Native organization serving the 268 Tribal Child Care Development Fund grantees that represent Tribal communities and Tribal child care and early childhood programs across the United States.

National P-3 Center (https://nationalp-3center.org/who-we-are/). The National P-3 Center provides leadership and professional learning opportunities to build shared understandings and practices for leaders in early childhood and pre-K–12 systems. The goal of the center is to improve the education continuum that children experience from birth (preschool) through 3rd grade. The center offers support and resources to guide implementation of policy and practices. They also support innovative research and P-3 evaluation projects.

References

Abel, M., Talan, T., Pollitt, K., & Bornfreund, L. (2016). *National principals' survey on early childhood instructional leadership.* McCormick Center for Early Childhood Leadership Publications. Retrieved from https://digitalcommons.nl.edu/mccormickcenter-pubs/1

Aboud, F. E. (2008). A social-cognitive developmental theory of prejudice. In S. M. Quintana & C. McKown (Eds.), *Handbook of race, racism, and the developing child* (pp. 55–71). John Wiley & Sons.

Adair, J., Phillips, L., Ritchie, J., & Sachdeva, S. (2018). Civic action and play: Examples from Maori, Aboriginal Australian and Latino communities. In J. Nicholson & D. Wisneski (Eds.), *Reconsidering the role of play in early childhood* (pp. 798–811). Taylor & Francis Press.

Akers, L., Atkins-Burnett, S., Monahan, S., Carta, J., Wasik, B. A., & Boller, K. (2015). *Issue brief: What does it mean to use ongoing assessment to individualize instruction in early childhood?* (Research Brief OPRE Report #2015-61). Mathematica Policy Research.

Americans with Disabilities Act (ADA) of 1990 (Public Law 101-336). Retrieved from https://www.govinfo.gov/content/pkg/STATUTE-104/pdf/STATUTE-104-Pg327.pdf

Arreguín-Anderson, M. G., Salinas-Gonzalez, I., & Alanis, I. (2018). Translingual play that promotes cultural connections, invention, and regulation: A LatCrit perspective. *International Multilingual Research Journal, 12,* 273–287. Retrieved from https://doi.org:10.1080/19313152.2018.1470434

Bailey, D. B., & Winton, P. J. (1987). Stability and change in parent expectations about mainstreaming. *Topics in Early Childhood Special Education, 7*(1), 73–88.

Barker, J. E., Semenov, A. D., Michaelson, L., Provan, L. S., Snyder, H. R., & Munakata, Y. (2014). Less-structured time in children's daily lives predicts self-directed executive functioning. *Frontiers in Psychology, 5,* 593.

Berk, L., & Winsler, A. (1995). *Scaffolding children's learning: Vygotsky and early childhood education.* National Association for the Education of Young Children.

Berman, R., & Abawi, Z. (2019). Thinking and doing otherwise: Reconceptualist contributions to early childhood education and care. In S. Jagger (Ed.), *Early years education and care in Canada* (pp. 165–190). Canadian Scholars, CSP Books.

Berman, R., Daniel, B. J., Butler, A., MacNevin, M., & Royer, N. (2017). Nothing or almost nothing to report: Early childhood educators and discursive constructions of colourblindness. *International Critical Childhood Policy Studies Journal, 6*(1), 52–65.

Bethell, C., Davis, M., Gombojav, N., Stumbo, S., & Powers, K. (2017). *Issue brief: A national and across state profile on adverse childhood experiences among children and possibilities to heal and thrive.* Johns Hopkins Bloomberg School of Public Health. Retrieved from https://www.greatcircle.org/images/pdfs/aces-brief-101717.pdf

Biermeier, M. A. (2015). Inspired by Reggio Emilia: Emergent curriculum in relationship-driven environments. *Young Children, 70*(5). Retrieved from https://www.naeyc.org/resources/pubs/yc/nov2015/emergent-curriculum

Bishop, R. S. (1990). Mirrors, windows, and sliding glass doors. Originally published in *Perspectives, 1*(3), ix–xi. Retrieved from https://scenicregional.org/wp-content/uploads/2017/08/Mirrors-Windows-and-Sliding-Glass-Doors.pdf

Bodrova, E., & Leong, D. (2007). *Tools of the mind: The Vygotskian approach to early childhood education.* Merrill/Prentice Hall.

Bonilla-Silva, E. (2013). *Racism without racists: Color-blind racism and the persistence of racial inequality in the United States.* Rowman & Littlefield.

Boutte, G. S., Lopez-Roberston, J., & Power-Costello, E. (2011). Moving beyond colorblindness in early childhood classrooms. *Early Childhood Education Journal, 39*(5), 335–342. Retrieved from https://doi.org:10.1007/s10643-011-0457-x

Brillante, P. (2017). Every child belongs: Welcoming a child with a disability. *Teaching Young Children, 10*(5). Retrieved from https://www.naeyc.org/resources/pubs/tyc/sep2017/every-child-belongs

Briggs-Gowan, M. J., Ford, J. D., Fraleigh, L., McCarthy, K., & Carter, A. S. (2010). Prevalence of exposure to potentially traumatic events in a healthy birth cohort of very young children in the northeastern United States. *Journal of Traumatic Stress, 23*(6), 725–733.

Brown, K., Squires, J., Connors-Tadros, L., & Horowitz, M. (2014). *What do we know about principal preparation, licensure requirements, and professional development for school leaders?* (CEELO Policy Report). New Brunswick, NJ: Center on Enhancing Early Learning Outcomes. Retrieved from http://ceelo.org/wp-content/uploads/2014/07/ceelo_policy_report_ece_principal_prep.pdf

Brown, S., & Vaughn, C. (2009). *Play: How it shapes the brain, opens the imagination, and invigorates the soul.* Penguin.

Bryant, D. J., Oo, M., & Damian, A. J. (2020). The rise of adverse childhood experiences during the COVID-19 pandemic. *Psychological Trauma: Theory, Research, Practice, and Policy, 12*(S1), S193–S194. Retrieved from https://doi.org/10.1037/tra0000711

Bunche-Smith, T. (2020). Centering the youngest Black children. In D. Jones & J. Hagopian (Eds.), *An uprising for educational justice: Black Lives Matter at school* (pp. 150–157). Haymarket Books.

Butler, J. (2019). *How safe is the schoolhouse? An analysis of state seclusion and restraint laws and Policies.* Autism National Committee. Retrieved from http://www.autcom.org/pdf/HowSafeSchoolhouse.pdf

Buysse, V., & Bailey, D. B. (1993). Behavioral and developmental outcomes in young children with disabilities in integrated and segregated settings: A review of comparative studies. *The Journal of Special Education, 26*(4), 434–461.

California Department of Education. (2015). DRDP, *Desired Results Developmental Profile (DRDP): A developmental continuum from early infancy to kindergarten entry.* Retrieved from https://www.cde.ca.gov/sp/cd/ci/documents/drdp2015preschool.pdf

California Department of Education. (2016). *The integrated nature of learning.* Sacramento, CA. Retrieved from https://www.cde.ca.gov/sp/cd/re/documents/intnatureoflearning2016.pdf

California Department of Education. (2021a). *The powerful role of play in education: Birth-8.* Retrieved from https://www.cde.ca.gov/sp/cd/re/documents/powerfulroleofplay.pdf

California Department of Education. (2021b). *Creating equitable early learning environments for young Boys of Color: Disrupting disproportionate outcomes.*

Casey, B. J., Tottenham, N., Liston, C., & Durston, S. (2005). Imaging the developing brain: What have we learned about cognitive development? *Trends in Cognitive Sciences, 9,* 104–110.

Castro, D. (2014). The development and early care and education of dual language learners: Examining the state of knowledge. *Early Childhood Research Quarterly, 29,* 693–698.

Cellano, M., Collins, M., & Hazzard, A. (n.d.) *8 tips for talking to kids about racial justice.* Retrieved from https://www.embracerace.org/resources/young-kids-racial-injustice

Center for the Study of Child Care Employment. (n.d.). *Teachers' voices: Reflections on working conditions that impact practice and program quality (SEQUAL).* Retrieved from https://cscce.berkeley.edu/topic/teacher-work-environments/sequal/teachers-voices/

Center on the Developing Child. (n.d.). *Executive function and self-regulation.* Retrieved from https://developingchild.harvard.edu/science/key-concepts/executive-function/

Center on the Social and Emotional Foundations for Early Learning (CSEFEL). (n.d.). *The Pyramid model for supporting social emotional competence in infants and young children.* Retrieved from http://csefel.vanderbilt.edu/

Cheng, X. (2015). *The politics of True Play with Cheng Xueqin.* Guest talk. Gottesman Libraries, Teachers College, Columbia University.

Cherry, M. & Harrison, V. (2019*). Hair love.* Penguin Random House.

Chien, N. C., Howes, C., Burchina, M. R., Pianta, R. C., Ritchie, S., Bryant, D. M. et al. (2010). Children's classroom engagement and school readiness gains in prekindergarten. *Child Development, 81*(5), 1534–1549. Retrieved from https://doi.org:10.1111/j.1467-8624.2010.01490.x

Clements, D., & Sarama, J. (2014). *Learning and teaching early math: The learning trajectories approach* (2nd ed.). Routledge.

Conkbayier, M. (2017). *Early childhood and neuroscience: Theory, research and implications for practice.* Bloomsbury Academic.

Copenhaver-Johnson, J. F. (2006). Talking to children about race: The importance of inviting difficult conversations. *Childhood Education, 83,* 12–22.

Corsaro, W. A. (2011). *The sociology of childhood.* Thousand Oaks, CA: Sage.

Courchesne, E., Chisum, H. J., Townsend, J., Cowles, A., Covington, J., Egaas, B., Harwood, M., Hinds, S., & Press, G. A. (2000). Normal brain development and aging: Quantitative analysis at in vivo MR imaging in healthy volunteers. *Radiology, 216,* 672–682.

Cozolino, L. (2006). *The neuroscience of human relationships: Attachment and the developing social brain.* Norton.

Craig, S. (2016). *Trauma-sensitive schools: Learning communities transforming children's lives, K–5.* Teachers College Press.

Crenshaw, K. (2011). Twenty years of critical race theory: Looking back to move forward. *Connecticut Law Review, 43*(5), 1253–1354.

Crenshaw, K. W. (1991). Mapping the margins: Intersectionality, identity politics, and violence against women of color. *Stanford Law Review, 43,* 1241–1299.

Daly, L., & Beloglovsky, M. (2014). *Loose parts: Inspiring play in young children.* Redleaf Press.

De la Peña, M. (2015). *Last stop on market street.* G.P. Putnam's Sons.

Delgado, R., & Stafancic, J. (2017). *Critical race theory: An introduction* (3rd ed.). New York University Press.

Derman-Sparks, L., Olsen-Edwards, J., & Goins, C. (2020). *Anti-bias education for young children & ourselves* (2nd ed.). National Association for the Education of Young Children.

Derman-Sparks, L., & Ramsey, P. G. (2011). *What if all the kids are white? Anti-bias multicultural education with young children and families* (2nd ed.). Teachers College Press.

DeVries, R., & Zan, B. (1994). *Moral classrooms, moral children: Creating a constructivist atmosphere in early education.* Teachers College Press.

DeVries, R., Zan, B., Hildebrandt, C., Edmiaston, R., & Sales, C. (2002). *Developing constructivist early childhood curriculum: Practical principles and activities.* Teachers College Press.

Dobbing, J., & Sands, J. (1973). Quantitative growth and development of human brain. *Archives of Disease in Childhood, 48*(10), 757–767.

Dodge, D. T., Colker, L. J., & Heroman, C. (2002). *The Creative Curriculum for preschool* (4th ed.). Teaching Strategies.

Duncan, G. J., Dowsett, C. J., Claessens, A., Magnuson, K., Huston, A. C., Klebanov, P., Pagani, L. S., Feinstein, L., Engel, M., Brooks-Gunn, J., Sexton, H., Duckworth, K., & Japel, C. (2007). School readiness and later achievement. *Developmental Psychology, 43*(6), 1428–1446. Retrieved from https://doi.org/10.1037/0012-1649.43.6.1428

Duncan, G. J., & Magnuson, K. (2011). The nature and impact of early achievement skills, attention skills, and behavior problems. In G. J. Duncan and R. Murnane (Eds.), *Whither opportunity? Rising inequality and the uncertain life changes of low-income children* (pp. 47–70). Russell Sage Press.

Dunlap, G., & Fox, L. (2015). *The Pyramid Model: PBS in early childhood programs and its relation to school-wide PBS*. Retrieved from https://challengingbehavior.cbcs.usf.edu/docs/Pyramid-Model_PBS-early-childhood-programs_School-wide-PBS.pdf

Dweck, C. (2007). *Mindset: The new psychology of success.* Ballantine Books.

Dyson, A. H. (1990). Symbol makers, symbol weavers: How children link play, pictures and print. *Young Children, 45*(2), 50–57.

Edwards, C., Gandini, L., & Forman, G. (Eds.). (1998; 2011). *The hundred languages of children: The Reggio Emilia experience in transformation* (3rd ed.). Praeger.

Ehrensaft, D. (2016). *The gender creative child: Pathways for nurturing and supporting children who live outside of gender boxes.* New York: The Experiment.

Eisenhart, C., & Grinder-McLean, E. (2013). Early learning walkthroughs. *Principal, Nov/Dec.* National Association of Elementary School Principals. Retrieved from http://www.naesp.org/sites/default/files/LiteracyWalkthroughTemplate_2.pdf

Escayg, K. A., Berman, R., & Royer, N. (2017). Canadian children and race: Toward an antiracism analysis. *Journal of Childhood Studies, 42*(2), 10–21.

Espinosa, L. M. (2015). Challenges and benefits of early bilingualism in the U.S. context. *Global Education Review, 2*(1), 40–53.

Felitti, V. J., & Anda, R. F. (2010). The relationship of adverse childhood experiences to adult health, well-being, social function, and health care. In R. Lanius, E. Vermetten, and C. Pain (Eds.), *The effects of early life trauma on health and disease: The hidden epidemic.* Cambridge University Press.

Felitti, V. J., Anda, R. F., Nordenberg, D., Williamson, D. F., Spitz, A. M., Edwards, V., Koss, M. P., & Marks, J. S. (1998). The relationship of adult health status to childhood abuse and household dysfunction. *American Journal of Preventive Medicine, 14*(4), 245–258.

Fish, L., & Zercher, C. (2017). *All about PDA: Positive descriptive acknowledgement.* CSEFEL Teaching Pyramid, WestEd Center for Child and Family Studies. Retrieved from https://www.laurafishtherapy.com/Forms/PDALFMay2017.pdf

Fisher, K. R., Hirsh-Pasek, K., Newcombe, N., & Golinkoff, R. M. (2013). Taking shape: Supporting preschoolers' acquisition of geometric knowledge through guided play. *Child Development, 84*, 1872–1878. Retrieved from https://doi.org:10.1111/cdev.12091

Fosnot, C. T., & Perry, R. S. (2005). Constructivism: A psychological theory of learning. In C. T. Fosnot (Ed.), *Constructivism: Theory, perspectives, and practice* (2nd ed.). Teachers College Press.

Fox, L., Dunlap, G., Hemmeter, L. L., Joseph, G. E. & Strain, P. S. (2003). The teaching pyramid: A model for supporting social competence and preventing challenging behavior in young children. *Young Children, 58*(4), 48–52.

Frost, J., Wortham, S., & Reifel, S. (Eds.) (2012). *Play and child development* (4th ed.). Pearson.

García, O., Flores, N., & Woodley, H. (2012). Transgressing monolingualism and bilingual dualities: Translanguaging pedagogies. In A. Yiakoumetti (Ed.), *Harnessing linguistic variation to improve education* (pp. 45–75). Peter Lang.

García, O., Kleifgen, J. A., & Falchi, L. (2008). *From English language learners to emergent bilinguals.* Campaign for Educational Equity.

García, O., & Wei, L. (2014). *Translanguaging: Language, bilingualism and education.* Palgrave Macmillan.

Gender Justice in Early Childhood. (2019). The STAR Tool to support young children's gender health. Retrieved from http://bit.ly /STARofsupportingyoungchildrensgenderdevelopment

Genishi, C., & Dyson, A. H. (2009). *Children, language, and literacy: Diverse learners in diverse times.* Teachers College Press.

Gilliam, W. (2017). *Teachers' perceptions of children's challenging behavior.* The Infant/Toddler & School-Age Child Care Institute, St. Louis, Missouri. Retrieved from https://www.occ-cmc.org/itsa-institute/pdfs/Resources/Teachers_Perception_of_Childrens_Behavior_WGilliam.pdf

Gilliam, W. S. (2005). *Prekindergartners left behind: Expulsion rates in sate prekindergarten systems.* Retrieved from https://www.fcdus.org/assets/2016/04 /ExpulsionCompleteReport.pdf

Gilliam, W. S. (2016). *Early childhood expulsions and suspensions undermine our nation's most promising agent of opportunity and social justice.* Retrieved from https://www.miamiqualitycounts.org/wp-content/uploads/2016/12/Early-Childhood-and-Suspensions-Undermine-Our-Nations-Most-Promising-Agent-of-Opportunity-and-Social-Justice.pdf

Gilliam, W. S., Maupin, A. N., Reyes, C. R., Accavitti, M., & Shic, F. (2016). *Do early educators' implicit biases regarding sex and race relate to behavior expectations and recommendations of preschool expulsions and suspensions? A research brief.* Yale Child Study Center. Retrieved from https://medicine.yale.edu /childstudy/zigler/publications/Preschool%20Implicit%20Bias%20Policy%20 Brief_final_9_26_276766_5379_v1.pdf

Ginsburg, K., Committee on Communications, and Committee on Psychosocial Aspects of Child and Family Health. (2007). The importance of play in promoting healthy child development and maintaining strong parent–child bonds. *Pediatrics, 119*(1), 182–191.

Goodman, Y. M. (1985). *Kidwatching: Observing children in the classroom.* Routledge.

Gort, M., & Pontier, R. (2012). Exploring bilingual pedagogies in dual language preschool classrooms. *Language and Education, 27,* 223–245.

Gort, M., & Sembiante, S. F. (2015). Navigating hybridized language learning spaces through translanguaging pedagogy: Dual language preschool teachers' languaging practices in support of emergent bilingual children's performance of academic discourse. *International Multilingual Research Journal, 9*(1), 7–25.

Graue, M. E., & Shepard, L. A. (1989). Predictive validity of the Gesell School Readiness Tests. *Early Childhood Research Quarterly, 4*, 303–315.

Gronlund, G., & Rendon, T. (2017). *Saving play: Addressing standards through play-based learning in preschool and kindergarten.* Redleaf Press.

Halfon, N., Shulman, E., & Hochstein, M. M. (2001). *Brain development in early childhood.* Retrieved from http://files.eric.ed.gov/fulltext/ED467320.pdf

Halpern, R. (2013). Tying early childhood education more closely to schooling: Promise, perils and practical problems. *Teachers College Record, 115*(1), 1–28.

Heckman, J. J., & Masterov, D. V. (2007). The productivity argument for investing in young children. *Review of Agricultural Economics, 29*, 446–493.

Heckman, J. J., Moon, S. H., Pinto, R., Savelyev, P. A., & Yavitz, A. (2010). The rate of return to the HighScope Perry Preschool Program. *Journal of Public Economics, 94*, 114–128.

Heroman, C., Burts, D. C., Berke, K. L., & Bickart, T. S. (2010). *Teaching Strategies GOLD® objectives for development & learning.* Washington, DC: Teaching Strategies LLC.

Hidalgo, M. A., Ehrensaft, D., Tishelman, A. C., Clark, L. F., Garofalo, R., Rosenthal, S. M., & Olson, J. (2013). The gender affirmative model: What we know and what we aim to learn. *Human Development, 56*(5), 285–290.

HighScope (2012). HighScope's Child Observation Record—COR Advantage. Retrieved from https://highscope.org/wp-content/uploads/2018/03/COR-Advantage-to-KDIs_March-2018-SS.pdf

Hirschfield, L. A. (1995). Do children have a theory of race? *Cognition, 54*, 209–252.

Hirschfeld, L. A. (2008). Children's developing conceptions of race. In S.M. Quintana & C. McKown (Eds.), *Handbook of race, racism, and the developing child* (pp. 37–54). Wiley.

Hirsh-Pasek, K., Golinkoff, R. M., Berk, L. E., & Singer, D. G. (2009). *A mandate for playful learning in the preschool: Presenting the evidence.* Oxford University Press.

Hopewell, S., & Escamilla, K. (2015). How does a holistic perspective on bi/multi-literacy help educators address the demands of Common Core State Standards for ELLs/emergent bilinguals? In G. Valdés, K. Menken, & M. Castro (Eds.), *Common Core and English language learners/emergent bilinguals: A guide for all educators* (pp. 39–40). Caslon.

Hooven, J., Runkle, K., Strouse, L., Woods, M., & Frankenberg, E. (2018). Never too early to learn: Antibias education for young children, *Phi Delta Kappan, 99*(5), 61–66.

Horn, M., & Giacobbe, M. E. (2007). *Talking, drawing, writing: Lessons for our youngest writers.* Stenhouse.

Institute of Medicine & National Research Council. (2015). *Transforming the workforce for children birth through age 8: A unifying foundation.* The National Academies Press. Retrieved from https://doi.org/10.17226/19401

Iruka, I., Curenton, S., Durden, T., & Escayg, K. A. (2020). *Don't look away: Embracing anti-bias classrooms.* Gryphon House.

Isola, R., & Cummins, J. (2019). *Transforming Sanchez School: Shared leadership, equity, and evidence.* Caslon Publishing.

Ispa-Landa, S. (2018). Persistently harsh punishments amid efforts to reform: Using tools from social psychology to counteract racial bias in school disciplinary decisions. *Educational Researcher, 47*(6), 384–390.

Iwasaki, N., Hamano, K., Okada, Y., Horigome, Y., Nakayama, J., Takeya, T., Takita, H., & Nose, T. (1997). Volumetric quantification of brain development using MRI. *Neuroradiology, 39*(12), 841–846. Retrieved from https://doi.org:10.1007/s002340050517

Jarrett, O. (2019). *A research-based case for recess: Position paper.* U.S. Play Coalition in collaboration with American Association for the Child's Right to Play (IPA/USA) and the Alliance for Childhood. Retrieved from https://usplaycoalition.org/wp-content/uploads/2019/08/Need-for-Recess-2019-FINAL-for-web.pdf

Jensen, H., Pyle, A., Zosh, J., Ebrahim, H., Scherman, A., Reunamo, J., & Hamre, B. (2019). *Play facilitation: The science behind the art of engaging young children* (white paper). The LEGO Foundation, DK.

Kagan, S., & Kauerz, K. (2012). *Early childhood systems: Transforming early learning.* Teachers College Press.

Katz, L. (1973). Perspective on early childhood education. *The Educational Forum, 27*(4), 393–398. Retrieved from https://doi.org/10.1080/00131727309339255

Katz, P. A., & Kofkin, J. A. (1997). Race, gender, and young children. In S. Luthar, J. Burack, D. Cicchetti, & J. Weisz (Eds.), *Developmental perspectives on risk and pathology* (pp. 51–74). Cambridge University Press.

Kauerz, K., Ballard, R., Soli, M., & Hagerman, S. (2021). *Leading learning communities: A principal's guide to early learning and the early grades (pre-K–3rd grade).* Alexandria, VA: National Association of Elementary School Principals.

Kauerz, K., & Coffman, J. (2013). *Framework for planning, implementing, and evaluating preK-3rd grade approaches.* Seattle, WA: College of Education, University of Washington.

Kennedy, D., Makris, N., Herbert, M., Takahashi, T., Caviness, V., Jr. (2002). Basic principles of MRI and morphometry studies of human brain development. *Developmental Science, 5,* 268–278.

Keo-Meier, C., & Ehrensaft, D. (2018). *The gender affirmative model: An interdisciplinary approach to supporting transgender and gender expansive children.* American Psychological Association.

Kidman, R., Margolis, R., Smith-Greenaway, E., & Verdery, A. M. (2021). Estimates and projections of COVID-19 and parental death in the US. *JAMA Pediatrics, 175*(7), 745–746. Retrieved from https://doi.org:10.1001/jamapediatrics.2021.0161

Kleyn, T., & Stern, N. (2018). Labels as limitations. *MinneTESOL Journal, 34,* 1–9.

Knight, S. (2009). *Forest schools and outdoor learning in the early years.* Sage.

Kohli, R., & Solórzano, D. (2012). Teachers, please learn our names!: Racial microaggressions and the K-12 classroom. *Race Ethnicity and Education, 15*(4), 441–462. Retrieved from https://doi.org/10.1080/13613324.2012.674026

Koplan, C., & Chard, A. (2014). Adverse early life experiences as a social determinant of mental health. *Psychiatric Annals, 44*(1), 39–45. doi: 10.3928/00485713-20140108-07

Ladson-Billings, G., & Tate, W. (1995). *Toward a critical race theory of education.* Teachers College Record, 97(1), 47–68.

Lam, V., Guerrero, S., Damree, N., & Enesco, I. (2011). Young children's racial awareness and affect and their perceptions about mothers' racial affect in a multiracial context. *British Journal of Developmental Psychology, 29,* 842–864. Retrieved from https://doi.org:10.1348/2044-835X.00213

Leeb, R. T., Bitsko, R. H., Radhakrishnan, L., Martinez, P., Njai, R., & Holland, K. M. (2020). Mental-health related emergency department visits among children aged < 18 years during the COVID-19 pandemic—United States. *MMWR Morbidity Mortality Weekly Report, 69,* 1675–1680. Retrieved from http://dx.doi.org/10.15585/mmwr.mm6945a3external_icon

Lenroot, R. K., & Giedd, J. N. (2006). Brain development in children and adolescents: Insights from anatomical magnetic resonance imaging. *Neuroscience and Biobehavioral Reviews, 30*(6), 718–729.

Levine, P., & Kline, M. (2007). *Trauma through a child's eyes: Awakening the ordinary miracle of healing—Infancy through adolescence.* North Atlantic Books.

Lewin-Benham, A. (2008): *Powerful children: Understanding how to teach and learn using the Reggio Approach* (Early Childhood Education Series). Teachers College Press.

Lieberman, A. (2017). *A tale of two pre-K leaders: How state policies for center directors and principals leading pre-K programs differ, and why they shouldn't.* New America Foundation. Retrieved from https://na-production.s3.amazonaws.com/documents/Tale-Two-PreK-Leaders.pdf

Lieberman, A. (2019). *Preparing principals for pre-K in Illinois: The Prairie State's story of reform and implementation.* New America Foundation. Retrieved from https://www.newamerica.org/education-policy/reports/preparing-principals-pre-k-illinois/

Liebowitz, D., & Porter, L. (2019). The effect of principal behaviors on student, teacher, and school outcomes: A systematic review and meta-analysis of the empirical literature. *Review of Educational Research, 89*(5), 785–827. Retrieved from https://doi.org/10.3102/0034654319866133

Loewenberg, A. (2015). Many new principals lack early ed knowledge. EdCentral (blog) New America Foundation. Retrieved from https://www.newamerica.org/education-policy/edcentral/elem-principals-prek/

Louv, R. (2008). *Last child in the woods: Saving our children from nature deficit disorder.* Algonquin Books.

Lubeck, S. (1994). The politics of developmentally appropriate practice: Exploring issues of culture, class and curriculum. In B. Mallory & R. New (Eds.), *Diversity and developmentally appropriate practices: Challenges for early childhood education* (pp. 17–43). Teachers College Press.

MacLachlan, C., Fleer, M. & Edwards, S. (2013). *Early childhood curriculum: Planning, assessment and implementation* (2nd ed.). Cambridge University Press.

MacNaughton, G. (2005). *Doing Foucault in early childhood studies: Applying post-structural ideas* (Contesting early childhood). Routledge.

MacNaughton, G., & Davis, K. (2009). Discourses of "race" in early childhood: From cognition to power. In G. MacNaughton & K. Davis (Eds.), *Race and early childhood education: An international approach to identity, policies and pedagogy* (pp. 17–30). Palgrave MacMillan.

Malik, R. (2017). *New data reveal 250 preschoolers are suspended or expelled every day.* Center for American Progress. Retrieved from https://www.americanprogress.org/issues/early-childhood/news/2017/11/06/442280/new-data-reveal-250-preschoolers-suspended-expelled-every-day/

Martínez, C. (2021). *Diversity in the preschool classroom: 12 considerations to avoid cultural clashes.* Teaching Strategies. Retrieved from https://teachingstrategies.com/blog/diversity-preschool-classroom-12-considerations/

McLean, C., Austin, L., Whitebook, M., & Olson, K. (2021). *Early Childhood Workforce Index—2020.* Center for the Study of Child Care Employment, University of California, Berkeley. Retrieved from https://cscce.berkeley.edu/workforce-index-2020/report-pdf/

McLean, C., Whitebook, M., & Roh, E. (2019). *From unlivable wages to just pay for early educators.* Center for the Study of Child Care Employment, University of California. Retrieved from https://cscce.berkeley.edu/from-unlivable-wages-to-just-pay-for-early-educators/

Mednick, L., & Ramsey, R. (2008). Peers, power and privilege: The social world of a second grade. *Rethinking Schools, 23,* 27–31.

Meek, S., Iruka, I. U., Allen, R., Yazzie, D., Fernandez, V., Catherine, E., McIntosh, K., Gordon, L., Gilliam, W., Hemmeter, M. L., Blevins, D., & Powell, T. (2020). *14 priorities to dismantle systemic racism in early care and education.* The Children's Equity Project. Retrieved from https://childandfamilysuccess.asu.edu/cep

Meisels, S., Jablon, J., Marsden, D., Dichtelmiller, M., Dorfman, A., & Steele, D. (1994). *The Work Sampling System: An overview* (3rd ed.). Rebus Planning Associates.

Meisels, S., Jablon, J., Marsden, D., Dichtelmiller, M., Dorfman, A., & Steele, D. (1995). *The Work Sample System: An overview* (3rd ed.). Rebus Planning Associates.

Meisels, S. J. (1987). Uses and abuses of developmental screening and school readiness testing. *Young Children, 42*(4–6), 68–73.

Meisels, S. J. (1989). High stakes testing in kindergarten. *Educational Leadership, 46,* 16–22.

Meisels, S. J. (1995). Out of the readiness maze. *Momentum, 26,* 18–22.

Mesibov, G. B., Shea, V., & Schopler, E. (2005). *The TEACCH approach to autism spectrum disorders.* Springer Science + Business Media.

Miller, E., & Almon, J. (2009). *Crisis in the kindergarten: Why children need to play in school.* Alliance for Childhood.

Milteer, R., Ginsburg, K., & the Council on Communications and Media Committee on Psychosocial Aspects of Child and Family Health and D. Mulligan. (2012). The importance of play in promoting healthy child development and maintaining strong parent–child bond: Focus on children in poverty. *Pediatrics, 129*(1), e204–e213. Retrieved from https://doi.org:10.1542/peds.2011-2953

Moll, L. C., Amanti, C., Neff, D., & Gonzalez, N. (1992). Funds of knowledge for teaching: Using a qualitative approach to connect homes and classrooms. *Theory Into Practice, 31*(2), 132–141.

National Association for Elementary School Principals (NAESP). (2014). *Leading pre-K-3 learning communities: Competencies for effective principal practice.* Retrieved from: http://www.naesp.org/sites/default/ files/leading-pre-k-3-learning-communities-executive-summary.pdf

National Association for the Education of Young Children. (2011). *Code of ethical conduct and statement of commitment.* Retrieved from https://www.naeyc.org/sites/default/files/globallyshared/downloads/PDFs/resources/position-statements/Ethics%20Position%20Statement2011_09202013update.pdf

National Association for the Education of Young Children (NAEYC). (2019). *Advancing equity in early childhood education: A position statement of the National Association for the Education of Young Children.* Retrieved from https://www.naeyc.org/sites/default/files/globally-shared/downloads/PDFs/resources/position-statements/naeycadvancingequitypositionstatement.pdf

National Association for the Education of Young Children (NAEYC). (2020). *Developmentally Appropriate Practice: A position statement of the National Association for the Education of Young Children.* Retrieved from https://www.naeyc.org/sites/default/files/globally-shared/downloads/PDFs/resources/position-statements/dap-statement_0.pdf

National Research Council of the National Academies. (2008). *Early childhood assessment: Why, what, and how.* Committee on Developmental Outcomes and Assessments for Young Children, C. E. Snow, & S. B. Van Hemel (Eds.), Board on Children, Youth, and Families, Board on Testing and Assessment, Division of Behavioral and Social Sciences and Education. The National Academies Press.

National Traumatic Stress Network. (n.d.). *What is a traumatic event?* Retrieved from https://www.nctsn.org/what-is-child-trauma/about-child-trauma

Neimi, K. (2020). *CASEL is updating the most widely recognized definition of social emotional learning. Here's why.* Retrieved from https://www.the74million.org/article/niemi-casel-is-updating-the-most-widely-recognized-definition-of-social-emotional-learning-heres-why/

Nicholson, J., Driscoll, P., Kurtz, J., Wesley, L., & Benitez, D. (2020). *Culturally responsive self-care practices for early childhood educators.* Routledge Press.

Nicholson, J., Kurtz, J., Leland, J., Wesley, L. & Nadiv, S. (2021). *Trauma-responsive practices for early childhood leaders: Creating and sustaining healing engaged organizations.* Routledge Press.

Nicholson, J., Perez, L., & Kurtz, J. (2019). *Trauma-informed practices for early childhood educators: Relationship-based approaches that support healing and build resilience in young children.* Routledge Press.

Osofsky, J., Stepka, P., & King, L. (2017). *Treating infants and young children impacted by trauma: Interventions that promote healthy development.* American Psychological Association.

Pacini-Ketchabaw, V., & Berikoff, A. (2008). The politics of difference and diversity: From young children's violence to creative power expressions. *Contemporary Issues in Early Childhood Education, 9*(3), 256–264.

Pally, R. (2000). *The mind–brain relationship.* Other Press LLC.

Parris, D., St. John, V., & Bartlett, J. (2020). *Resources to support children's well-being amid anti-Black racism, racial violence and trauma.* Child Trends. Retrieved from https://www.childtrends.org/publications/resources-to-support-childrens-emotional-well-being-amid-anti-black-racism-racial-violence-and-trauma

Pastel, E., Steele, K., Nicholson, J., Maurer, C., Hennock, J., Julian, J., Unger, T., & Flynn, N. (2019). *Supporting gender diversity in early childhood classrooms: A practical guide.* Kingsley Press.

Paus, T., Collins, D. L., Evans, A. C., Leonard, G., Pike, B., & Zijdenbos, A. (2001). Maturation of white matter in the human brain: A review of magnetic resonance studies. *Brain Research Bulletin, 54*(3), 255–266. Retrieved from https:doi.org:10.1016/S0361-9230(00)00434-2

Perea, J. (1997). The Black/White binary paradigm of race: The normal science of American racial thought. *California Law Review, 85*(5), 1213–1258. Retrieved from http://scholarship.law.berkeley.edu/californialawreview/vol85/iss5/3

Perry, B. (2001a). The neuroarcheology of childhood maltreatment: The neurodevelopmental costs of adverse childhood events. In B. Geffner (Ed.), *The cost of child maltreatment: Who pays? We all do* (pp. 15–37). Family Violence and Sexual Assault Institute.

Perry, B. (2014). The cost of caring: Understanding and preventing secondary stress when working with traumatized and maltreated children. *CTA Parent and Caregiver Education Series, 2*(7). The Child Trauma Academy Press.

Perry B. (2020). *Understanding regulation.* NN COVID Series 5. Retrieved from https://youtu.be/L3qIYGwmHYY

Perry, B., Pollard, R., Blakley, T., Baker, W., & Vigilante, D. (1995). Childhood trauma, the neurobiology of adaptation and use dependent development of the brain: How states become traits. *Infant Mental Health Journal, 16*(4), 271–291.

Perry, B., & Szalavitz, M. (2017). *The boy who was raised as a dog and other stories from a child psychiatrist's notebook. What traumatized children can teach us about loss, love and healing* (3rd ed.). Basic Books.

Perry, J. P. (2001b). *Outdoor play: Teaching strategies with young children.* Teachers College Press.

Perry, J. P. (2004). Making sense of outdoor pretend play. In D. Koralek (Ed.), *Spotlight on young children and play.* National Association for the Education of Young Children.

Perry, J. P. (2008). Children's experience of security and mastery on the playground. In E. Goodenough (Ed.), *A place for play*. National Institute for Play.

Perry, J. P. (2015). Outdoor play. In P. M. Van Hoorn, B. Nourot, K. R. Scales, & J. Alward. *Play at the Center of the Curriculum* (6th ed.). Pearson Education.

Piaget, J. (1962). *Play, dreams, and imitation in childhood*. Norton. (Original work published 1927).

Piaget, J. (1965). *The moral judgment of the child*. Free Press. (Original work published 1932).

Price, L. H., & Bradley, B. A. (2016). *Revitalizing read alouds: Interactive talk about books with young children, pre-K-2*. Teachers College Press.

Pyne, J. (2014). Gender independent kids: A paradigm shift in approaches to gender non-conforming children. *Canadian Journal of Human Sexuality, 23*(1), 1–8.

Raabe, T., & Beelmann, A. (2011). Development of ethnic, racial, and national prejudice in childhood and adolescence: A multinational meta-analysis of age differences. *Child Development, 82*, 1715–1737.

Ramani, G. B. (2012). Influence of a playful, child-directed context on preschool children's peer cooperation. *Merrill-Palmer Quarterly, 58*, 159–190.

Ramsey, P. (2015). *Teaching and learning in a diverse world: Multicultural education for young children* (Early childhood education series). Teachers College Press.

Ramsey, P., & Meyers, L. (1990). Salience of race in young children's cognitive, affective and behavioral responses to social environments. *Journal of Applied Developmental Psychology, 11*, 49–67.

Ramsey, P. G. (1991). The salience of race in young children growing up in an all-White community. *Journal of Educational Psychology, 83*, 28–34.

Reikeras, E., Moser, T., & Tonnessen, F. E. (2017). Mathematical skills and motor life skills in toddlers: Do differences in mathematical skills reflect differences in motor skills? *European Early Childhood Education Research Journal, 25*, 72–88. Retrieved from https://doi.org:10.1080/1350293X.2015.1062664

Reyes, C. R., & Gilliam, W. S. (2021). Addressing challenging behaviors in challenging environments: Findings from Ohio's early childhood mental health consultation system. *Developmental Psychopathology, 33*(2), 634–646. Retrieved from https://doi.org:10.1017/S0954579420001790

Rhoades, B. L., Warren, H. K., Domitrovich, C. E., & Greenberg, M. (2011). Examining the link between preschool social-emotional competence and first grade academic achievement: The role of attention skills. *Early Childhood Research Quarterly, 26*, 182–191.

Riley-Ayers, S., Costanza, V. J., & Center on Enhancing Early Learning Outcomes. (2014). *Professional learning academy: Supporting district implementation of early childhood policy*. Retrieved from http://ceelo.org/wp-content/uploads/2014/10/ ceelo_fast_fact_ec_academy.pdf

Rogoff, B. (2003). *The cultural nature of human development*. Oxford University Press.

Roskos, K., & Christie, J. (2007). *Play and literacy in early childhood: Research from multiple perspectives* (2nd ed.). Lawrence Erlbaum Associates.

Schachner, A., Belodoff, K., Chen, W-B., Kutaka, T., Fikes, A., Ensign, K., Chow, K., Nguyen, J., & Hardy, J. (2016). *Preventing suspensions and expulsions in early childhood settings: An administrator's guide to supporting all children's success.* Retrieved from http://preventexpulsion.org

Schön, D. (1983). *The reflective practitioner: How professionals think in action.* Basic Books.

Schore, A. N. (2003). Early relational trauma, disorganized attachment, and the development of a predisposition to violence. In M. F. Solomon & D. J. Siegel (Eds.), *Healing trauma: Attachment, mind, body, and brain* (pp. 107–167). Norton.

Shahinfar, A., Fox, N., & Leavitt, L. (2000). Preschool children's exposure to violence: Relation of behavior problems to parent and child reports. *American Journal of Orthopsychiatry, 70*(1), 115–125.

Siegel, D., & Payne Bryson, T. (2012). *Whole brain child: 12 revolutionary strategies to nurture your child's developing mind.* Bantam Books.

Simon-Cereijido, G., & Gutiérrez-Clellen, V. (2014). Bilingual education for all: Latino dual language learners with language disabilities. *International Journal of Bilingual Education and Bilingualism, 17,* 235–254.

Snow, K. (2011). *Developing Kindergarten Readiness and other large-scale assessment systems: Necessary considerations in the assessment of young children.* National Association for the Education of Young Children. Retrieved from https://nieer.org/wp-content/uploads/2012/03/Assessment_Systems.pdf

Souto-Manning, M. (2013). *Multicultural teaching in the early childhood classroom: Approaches, strategies, and tools. Preschool-2nd grade.* Teachers College Press.

Souto-Manning, M. (2018). Is play a privilege or a right? And what's our responsibility? On the role of play for equity in early childhood education. In J. Nicholson & D. Wisneski (Eds.), *Reconsidering the role of early childhood: Towards social justice and equity* (pp. 1–3). Routledge.

Souto-Manning, M., Falk, B., López, D., Cruz, L. B., Bradt, N., Cardwell, N., McGowan, N., Perez, A., Rabadi-Raol, A., & Rollins, E. (2019). A transdisciplinary approach to equitable teaching in early childhood education. *Review of Research in Education, 43,* 249–276. Retrieved from https://doi.org:103102.0091732X18821122

Souto-Manning, M., & Martell, J. (2016). *Reading, writing and talk: Inclusive teaching strategies for diverse learners, K-2.* Teachers College Press.

Souto-Manning, M., & Yoon, H. S. (2018). *Reading and rewriting worlds: Rethinking early literacies.* Routledge.

Statman-Weil, K. (2018). *Creating trauma-sensitive classrooms* (webinar). National Association for the Education of Young Children. Retrieved from https://www.youtube.com/watch?v=mjG3xNxtU1E

Steele, K., & Nicholson, J. (2019). *Radically listening to transgender and gender expansive young children: Creating epistemic justice through critical reflection and resistant imaginations.* Lexington Press.

Stein, P. T., & Kendall, J. (2004). *Psychological trauma and the developing brain. Neurologically based interventions for troubled children*. The Haworth Maltreatment and Trauma Press.

Substance Abuse and Mental Health Services Administration (SAMHSA). (2014). SAMHSA's *Concept of trauma and guidance for a trauma-informed approach*. HHS Publication No. (SMA) 14-4884. Rockville, MD: Substance Abuse and Mental Health Services Administration. Retrieved from https://ncsacw.samhsa.gov/userfiles/files/SAMHSA_Trauma.pdf

Sue, D. W., Capodilupo, C., Torino, G., Bucceri, J., Holder, A., Nadal, K., & Esquilin, M. (2007). Racial microaggressions in everyday life: Implications for clinical practice. *American Psychologist, 62*(4), 271–286. https://doi.org:10.1037/0003-066X.62.4.271

Teaching Strategies GOLD™ *Assessment System (GOLD)*. Retrieved from https://teachingstrategies.com/solutions/assess/gold/

Thomas, M. S., Crosby, S., & Vanderhaar, J. (2019). Trauma-informed practices in schools across two decades: An interdisciplinary review of research. *Review of Research in Education, 43*, 422–452.

Twardosz, S. (2012). Effects of experience on the brain: The role of neuroscience in early development and education. *Early Education and Development, 23*(1), 96–119.

Tyler, M., & Csicsko, D. L. (2005). *The skin you live in*. Chicago Children's Museum.

U.S. Administration for Children and Families (USACF). (2016). *Child maltreatment*. Retrieved from www.acf.hhs.gov/cb/resource/child-maltreatment-2016

U.S. Department of Education, Office for Civil Rights. (2016). *2013–2014 Civil rights data collection. A first look. Key data highlights on equity and opportunity gaps in our nation's public schools*. Retrieved from https://www2.ed.gov/about/offices/list/ocr/docs/2013-14-first-look.pdf

U.S. Department of Health and Human Services. (2018). *Physical activity guidelines for Americans* (2nd ed.). Washington, DC: U.S. Department of Health and Human Services. Retrieved from https://health.gov/sites/default/files/2019-09/Physical_Activity_Guidelines_2nd_edition.pdf

Valencia, R. (2010). *Dismantling contemporary deficit thinking: Educational thought and practice*. Routledge.

Van Ausdale, D., & Feagin, J. (2001). *The First R: How young children learn race and racism*. Rowman and Littlefield.

van der Kolk, B. (2014). *The body keeps the score: Brain, mind, and body in the healing of trauma*. Penguin Books.

Van Hoorn, J., Nourot, P. M., Scales, B., & Alward, K. R. (2010). *Play at the center of the curriculum* (5th ed.). Pearson.

van Oers, B. (1996). Are you sure? Stimulating mathematical thinking during young children's play. *European Early Childhood Education Research Journal, 2*, 19–33.

Vygotsky, L. (1978). *Mind in society: The development of higher psychological processes*. Harvard University Press.

Waite-Stupiansky, S. (1997). *Building understanding together: A constructivist approach to early childhood education.* Delmar.

Wertsch, J. V. (1985). From social interaction to higher psychological processes. A clarification and application of Vygotsky's theory. *Human Development, 22*(1), 1–22.

Wertsch, J. V. (1991). *Voices of the mind.* Harvard University Press.

Westmoreland, P. (2014). Racism in a Black White binary: On the reaction to Trayvon Martin's death. In K. Russell-Brown (Ed.). *UF Law Scholarship Repository.* Center for the Study of Race & Race Relations. Retrieved from https://scholarship.law.ufl.edu/cgi/viewcontent.cgi?article=1002&context=csrrr_events

Whitebook, M., King, E., Philipp, G., & Sakai, L. (2016). *Teachers' voices: Work environment conditions that impact teacher practice and program quality.* Center for the Study of Child Care Employment, University of California, Berkeley. Retrieved from https://cscce.berkeley.edu/files/2016/2016-Alameda-SEQUAL-Report-FINAL-for-Dissemination-v2.pdf

Whitebook, M., McLean, C., Austin, L. J., & Edwards, B. (2018). *Early childhood workforce index—2018.* Center for the Study of Child Care Employment, University of California. Retrieved from http://cscce.berkeley.edu/topic / early-childhood-work-force-index/2018/

Winkler, E. (2009). Children are not colorblind: How young children learn race. *PACE, 3*(3), 1–8.

Wolfberg, P. (2009). *Play and imagination in children with autism.* Teachers College Press.

Wolfe, P. (2007). *Mind, memory and learning: Translating brain research to classroom practices.* Association for Supervision and Curriculum Development.

Wood, D. J., Bruner, J., & Ross, G. (1976). The role of tutoring in problem solving. *Journal of Child Psychology and Psychiatry, 17,* 89–100.

Wood, D. J., & Middleton, D. (1975). A study of assisted problem solving. *British Journal of Psychology, 66,* 181–191.

Yogman, M., Garner, A., Hutchinson, J., Hirsh-Pasek, K., Golinkoff, R. M., and the Committee on Psychosocial Aspects of Child and Family Health, Council on Communications and Media. (2018). The power of play: A pediatric role in enhancing development in young children. *Pediatrics, 142*(2). Retrieved from http://pediatrics.aappublications.org/content/142/3/320182058

Yopp, H. K., & Stapleton, L. (2008). Conciencia fonémica en español (Phonemic awareness in Spanish). *The Reading Teacher 61*(5), 374–382.

Zosh, J., Hirsh-Pasek, K., Hopkins, E., Jensen, H., Liu, C., Neale, D., Solis, L., & Whitebread, D. (2018). Accessing the inaccessible: Redefining play as a spectrum. *Frontiers in Psychology, 9*(1124), 1–12. Retrieved from https://doi.org:10.3389/fpsyg.2018.01124

Index

About the Authors

Julie Nicholson, PhD, is professor of practice in the School of Education at Mills College, where she has been a faculty member since 2005 and directed several innovative programs including the Leadership Program in Early Childhood, a joint MBA/MA educational leadership program, and the Center for Play Research. Nicholson is also co-founder/co-director of the Center for Equity in Early Childhood Education, a non-profit organization dedicated to supporting transformative change to improve racial equity and intersectional justice for young children and families and the early childhood workforce dedicated to serving them.

Helen Maniates, PhD, is associate professor of teacher education and coordinator of the Master of Arts of Teaching Reading Program in the School of Education at the University of San Francisco. As a community-engaged scholar, her work addresses both "schooled" literacy and out-of-school literacy practices. Her research projects investigate classroom teaching at the micro level to uncover practices that extend access, increase outcomes, and operationalize social justice principles.

Serene Yee, MA, is currently an education programs consultant for the California Department of Social Services. She is an experienced public elementary school leader. She has 22 years of experience working in public education serving in various roles including vice principal for several elementary school districts and a Chinese immersion and a Chinese bilingual teacher for 8 years with the San Francisco Unified School District.

Thomas Williams Jr., PhD, currently serves as an executive strategic policy analyst in the Kentucky Department of Education Office of Special Education and Early Learning. Dr. Williams's research is focused on the home and school perception of behavior of minority males in early education. He has served as a mentor for the California Consortium for Equity in Early Childhood Education Fellowship Program, and he currently serves as a board member with the Center for Equity in Early Childhood Education.

Veronica Ufoegbune, EdD, has successfully directed many publicly funded and non-profit early learning programs, including directing UC Berkeley's child care centers. In these roles Dr. Ufoegbune has been responsible for the day-to-day oversight and leadership of the programs, ensuring compliance in the delivery of mandated services and the use of research-based emergent curriculum and comprehensive services for children and families.

Raul Erazo-Chavez, MA, is executive director of schools and programs in the Early Education Department within the San Francisco Unified School District. He is an experienced principal with expertise in the integration and alignment of early education and K–12 curricula and professional development. His passions include advocacy for parent voice, family engagement, and capacity building of principals and teachers.